Praise for *The AI-Ready CFO*

"CFOs today must evolve from scorekeeper to strategic architect, and AI is fundamentally reshaping what's possible for forward-thinking finance organizations. Glenn Hopper gives finance leaders a practical, grounded playbook for re-orchestrating teams and processes around governed, purpose-built AI to unlock faster decisions, a stronger competitive advantage, and real business impact. It is essential reading for any modern finance leader ready to drive transformation in the Finance AI era."

Scott Leshinski, President, OneStream Software

"Glenn has done the research—and the conversations—that most finance leaders don't have time for. *The AI-Ready CFO* translates that work into something practical and honest about what it actually takes to evolve the finance function in a fast-moving landscape to what businesses increasingly need. The CFO's evolution from scorekeeper to strategic operator is one of the defining questions of this era, and this book takes it seriously."

Matt Hudson, CFO, Superhuman (formerly Grammarly)

"Having interviewed and worked with hundreds of CFOs, I've seen firsthand how quickly AI is reshaping expectations for finance leaders and the challenges they and their teams face. Glenn Hopper captures this moment exceptionally well. Rather than chasing buzzwords, he focuses on the real issues CFOs care about: governance, accountability, talent, productivity, and strategic leadership. This book will help finance chiefs understand not only what AI can do, but how to lead responsibly in the age of AI."

Jack McCullough, President, The CFO Leadership Council and author of *The Rodman Paradox*

"The finance profession is at an inflection point, and the leaders who thrive will be the ones who learn to govern AI with the same rigor they bring to financial reporting. Glenn Hopper provides the frameworks and the roadmap to do exactly that, making this essential reading for any finance professional serious about what comes next."

Tom Hood, CPA, CGMA, CITP, EVP Business Engagement & Growth @ AICPA

"Glenn's latest book provides great insights and guidance of how to move fast without breaking auditability. If you are trying to understand how to set proper governance rules or identify quick wins that deliver a measurable ROI by leveraging AI tools, this book will help you do that and prepare you to become an AI-ready CFO."

Ben Chavez, Chief Financial Officer at Pair of Thieves

THE AI-READY CFO

GLENN HOPPER

THE AI-READY CFO

A STRATEGIC GUIDE TO EVALUATING AND IMPLEMENTING AI, AUTOMATION, AND ANALYTICS

WILEY

Published by John Wiley & Sons, Inc., Hoboken, New Jersey.

Library of Congress Cataloging-in-Publication Data:
Name: Hopper, Glenn author
Title: The AI-ready CFO: strategic guide to evaluating and implementing
AI, automation, and analytics / Glenn Hopper.
Other titles: Artificial intelligence-ready chief financial officer
Description: Hoboken, New Jersey: John Wiley & Sons, Inc., [2027] |
Includes bibliographical references and index.
Identifiers: LCCN 2026017999 | ISBN 9781394415885 hardback | ISBN
9781394415908 adobe pdf | ISBN 9781394415892 epub
Subjects: LCSH: Artificial intelligence–Business applications | Chief
financial officers
Classification: LCC HD45 .H635 2027
LC record available at https://lccn.loc.gov/2026017999

Cover Design: Wiley
Cover Image: PST Vector/Shutterstock
Author Photo: Courtesy of the Author

Printed and bound by CPI Group (UK) Ltd, Croydon, CR0 4YY

C9781394415885_202826

Contents

Foreword

Early in my corporate finance career at Adobe, our team spent weeks preparing strategic finance analysis, often leaving little time before deadlines to present, execute, and take action. Take a customer payback analysis project I led. The analysis itself was transformational—it reshaped how we thought about our entire product portfolio. But we spent so long preparing and wrangling the data that we infrequently took the time to perform the work. It led me to a question I couldn't shake: How many impactful business decisions were we leaving on the table simply because we never had time to get to the analysis? What if that analysis just happened automatically and clearly, so finance could spend less time running the numbers and more time acting on them? This shift has begun. And I don't say that lightly! I spent 12 years in corporate finance living in that world. But the shift I've witnessed over the past few years, building Campfire alongside finance teams navigating this transition firsthand, has convinced me that we are in the early innings of the most fundamental transformation the CFO suite has ever seen.

The finance function is moving from specialist to generalist. The newest members of your team aren't junior analysts, they're AI and AI agents. They write flux commentary by analyzing millions of rows of transactional data rather than reviewing summary tables like a human.

They refresh 13-week cash-flow forecasts by synthesizing all accounts receivable, accounts payable, seasonality patterns, and variables that were previously unachievable for any human team to process consistently. We're watching the monthly close (the smallest unit of time in accounting for as long as any of us can remember) begin to compress. It existed as a monthly cycle because it was simply too much work to close more frequently. Now, with AI enabling more real-time views of financial data, we're seeing companies move toward something closer to a continuous close.

What excites me most, though, is the shift in what a modern team looks like, how they operate, and the work that they perform. No longer manually writing flux commentary but reviewing and editing the commentary that is written by AI. Same with all other finance tasks, ranging from cashflow forecasts to bank reconciliations. The team shift is leading to the rise of the strategic accounting function. For decades, accounting has been seen as backward-looking and transactional. But when AI handles the data preparation, reconciliation, and routine analysis, accountants are freed to do what the best ones have always wanted to do: provide strategic analysis of historical data that shapes decisions. It's the natural complement to strategic finance's forward-looking work. And together, they give the CFO a complete picture that was never before possible.

But here's the uncomfortable truth: the legacy systems, processes, and ways of working that got us here are not built for this era. Legacy ERPs cannot handle the large volumes of granular data that AI craves for deeper analysis and insight. The workflows we've relied on for years were designed around human limitations: batch processing, period-end cycles, summary-level reporting. And every one of them needs to be reimagined. This is precisely the conviction that led me to start Campfire: the belief that finance infrastructure itself has to be rebuilt from the ground up for a world where AI is a first-class participant; not an afterthought bolted onto decades-old architecture.

We've seen this pattern before. When computers first entered the enterprise, Excel was invented and it changed everything. Accounting software followed. Then came the shift from on-premises to cloud. Each wave redefined the CFO's role and the tools at their disposal. AI is the next wave—and arguably the biggest—and it's on all of us as finance leaders to shepherd the CFO suite through it.

I'm frequently asked by finance peers for book recommendations on AI and finance, and for a long time my honest answer was that the space is moving so fast, there isn't one that stays current long enough to recommend. Glenn Hopper's *The AI-Ready CFO* changes that. It's the playbook I wish I'd had when I began this journey: thoughtful, practical, and grounded in the reality of what finance teams are actually facing today. Glenn doesn't just describe the future; he gives you the framework to build toward it.

I found this book to be incredibly valuable, and I hope you will too.

John Glasgow
Founder & CEO, Campfire

Acknowledgments

Whenever I start writing the acknowledgments section of my books, it turns into something that sounds like an Academy Awards acceptance speech. There are certainly numerous people to thank and acknowledge, but nobody likes reading lists. Unless it's a really funny shopping list you find in a grocery store parking lot.

So, I'll keep this moving.

When throwing out thank-yous, I always have to start with my wife, Kerith, who for more than 30 years has been the strong woman who stands behind a good man (or however that saying from the 1940s goes). But my thanks go beyond the obligatory "well of course you have to thank your spouse for their support in these kinds of things." Seriously. I wouldn't be able to pull any of this off without her undying support. She has been the steady center of gravity through three books, a consulting business, a hundred conference trips, and every late night spent arguing with a language model about discount-rate assumptions.

I also have to thank my editor, Michael Gormley, who from the very beginning of this project has helped keep me on track, on task, and on message. Frequently turning my garbled chain-of-thought ramblings into something actually digestible and helpful on the page. That is no small feat.

I want to take a moment to acknowledge my good friend, previous editor, and frequent collaborator, Andy Burt, who passed far too early last year. I remember him fondly and miss him greatly.

And I have to thank all the mentors and sponsors who've helped me along this journey since I published my first book, *Deep Finance*, back in 2021. I've had some true champions who helped position me for this opportunity, including Jack McCullough from the CFO Leadership Council, Dan Bigman of the Chief Executive Group, Ranga Bodla from NetSuite, Steve Rosvold from CFO University, and scores of others I'm sure I've overlooked in this short list. You know who you are, and I owe you.

Why This Book, and Why Now?

As I look back over my career in finance, I realize how tightly technology was always linked to the work I did. From my early days in FP&A at a large telecom company to years as a CFO in scale-up, PE-backed firms, I learned early that I had two options. I could work 100-hour weeks and sweat it out with spreadsheets, or I could lean into tech to automate reports, dig deeper into data, and turn hunches into hypotheses.

I chose the second path. And it changed how I thought about the entire function.

Telecom taught me what was possible when you had real data at scale. Millions of call records, network utilization metrics, churn signals buried in usage patterns. I started pulling in statistical methods and building models that went well beyond standard variance analysis. And when I moved into smaller PE-backed companies (regional carwash operators, legal technology firms, and everything in between), I brought that same mindset with me. The datasets were smaller, but the approach held. Build the model. Test the hypothesis. Let the numbers tell you where to look before you decide where to act. It was a data-first operating philosophy, applied to businesses that had never thought about finance that way.

I wrote my first book during COVID-19 after being genuinely amazed at the insights my team was able to achieve by applying data science to the finance function. The journalist in me (back to my first job, before business school) was compelled to share the story. That set off a mission to do my part to help transform the office of the CFO. While that transformation was bound to happen with or without me, I'm hopeful that my contributions have, in some small part, guided finance and accounting professionals along this revolutionary journey with AI and advanced analytics.

This technology is moving fast. Faster than the adoption of the personal computer, the smartphone, or broadband internet. And it's set up to be just as consequential, if not more so, in both the professional and personal realm. It's moving so quickly that as I looked at publication dates while writing *The AI-Ready CFO*, I worried the book might arrive too late. Will the bots have taken over by Fall 2026?

But as the launch date neared and the technology continued to advance, I realized something. We are still only on the front edge of this wave. And if there's anything I can do to provide some level of guidance to finance teams as we ready ourselves for this new world, now is the time.

Finally, for your reading pleasure, here's a really funny shopping list:

1. Eggs
2. Cupcake mix
3. Fermented black garlic
4. Bread
5. Industrial-strength electromagnet
6. Gooseberry preserves
7. Milk (oat is fine)
8. Faraday-cage material (check automotive aisle?)
9. Lunch meat (turkey)
10. High-capacity surge protector
11. Quail eggs (the fancy small ones)
12. EMP-shielded lunch box
13. Truffle salt
14. Butter

15. Signal-jamming device OR aluminum foil (lots of aluminum foil)
16. Dried cuttlefish snacks
17. Water (enough for six-month bunker supply)
18. Kumquats

Either someone's hosting a very eclectic dinner party or they know something about the singularity that the rest of us don't!

About the Author

Glenn Hopper is an author, speaker, and lecturer on the intersection of artificial intelligence and corporate finance. His books, *The AI-Ready CFO*, *AI Mastery for the Finance Professional*, and *Deep Finance: Corporate Finance in the Information Age*, examine how the latest wave of technology is reshaping financial processes and the operations of corporate finance departments.

Glenn's work highlights the transformative role of AI and automation in strengthening financial operations, improving accuracy, and driving data-driven decision-making. He is currently Head of AI at VAI Consulting, where he spearheads projects that deliver AI-powered solutions tailored to the finance and accounting sectors. He previously served as Head of AI R&D at Eventus Advisory Group.

His insights and expertise are regularly featured in publications such as *Fortune Magazine* and *Forbes*, and he contributes to leading content platforms, including the *AI Journal* and the Forbes Finance Council. He co-hosts Future Finance and FP&A Today, two tech-focused podcasts that spotlight leading finance professionals' success in harnessing the power of new technologies, including AI, in their day-to-day workflows. He also authors a weekly Substack newsletter, *Deep Finance Dispatch*.

Over more than two decades as a CFO in private equity-backed companies, Glenn has led initiatives in finance automation, M&A, and operational efficiency. He has a proven track record of modernizing finance departments by integrating data and automation to deliver better business intelligence, faster reporting, and improved operational performance.

In addition to his professional work, Glenn is an instructor at Duke University's Executive Education program, the Corporate Finance Institute, AICPA/CIMA, and LinkedIn Learning, where he teaches financial leaders how to leverage AI in strategic planning and makes advanced AI concepts accessible to finance professionals worldwide.

Glenn holds a Master of Liberal Arts (ALM) in Finance from Harvard University, where he also completed the Harvard Business Analytics Program. He earned his MBA from Regis University in Denver, CO.

He is an avid runner and cyclist and can frequently be found running along the Mississippi River near his home in Memphis, where he lives with his wife, Kerith, and where his grown children, Katherine, North, and Abigail, often visit.

A Personal Note on How This Book Was Made

When I wrote *Deep Finance* in 2021, I spent an entire chapter explaining what a chatbot was. Most of my readers had never actually talked to one. Alexa was a novelty, Siri was a running joke, and generative AI existed mostly as a research curiosity. I remember sitting at my desk trying to find clean metaphors for natural language processing and wondering whether any of this would land with a CFO audience.

Five years later, the idea that anyone needs an introduction to AI feels almost quaint.

Over the past three years, these tools have moved from novelty to infrastructure. More than a billion people now use some form of generative AI on a regular basis. Businesses that banned ChatGPT in 2023 are running enterprise licenses for it in 2026. AI is folded into how we plan meals, coach ourselves through workouts, draft emails, debug code, outline birthday parties, and triage our inboxes. The tools have stopped feeling like tools. They feel more like electricity. Something that hums in the background of ordinary life.

My own usage leans heavily toward work, but it shows up everywhere. I run Claude, ChatGPT, and Gemini most days, routing questions to whichever model is best at the task in front of me. I've built n8n workflows that sit between my email, my calendar, and my billing systems. Last year I rebuilt my entire company website, robocfo.ai, in Claude Code. Every line of it. The managed agents and automations running behind the scenes at G3 Consulting have quietly replaced the need for a human admin. I didn't set out to replace anyone. The math just stopped making sense the other way. That sentence would have sounded unhinged if I'd written it in 2021. In 2026 it barely raises an eyebrow.

So of course, AI was part of writing *The AI-Ready CFO*. Pretending otherwise would be absurd, and also dishonest.

Here's what AI actually did: Throughout 2025 I used OpenAI's GPT-5 and Anthropic's Claude as editorial companions. They helped me structure complex technical arguments, stress-test the logic of my frameworks, and pressure-check explanations before I handed them to readers. When a paragraph felt flabby, I'd run it through Claude and ask what a working CFO would find unclear. When I needed to map how AI governance rules had evolved from 2022 through 2025, the models helped me summarize and organize source material faster than I could have alone. They were tireless copy editors. Every sentence in this book has been read by a human, by at least one AI, and usually by me three or four times.

Here's what AI did **not** do. It didn't conduct the interviews. Every named source in this book gave me their time in a real conversation. It didn't invent the frameworks. The AI Risk Register, the Maturity Gate Process, the CFO AI Tool Map, and the build-buy-hybrid portfolio logic came from two decades of work inside real finance organizations. It didn't generate the case studies. The stories about eBay, JPMorgan Chase, Microsoft, and the rest came from published reporting, primary interviews, and investor materials, all verified by me. And it didn't write the opinions. Where I take a position, I'm the one taking it.

One thing I want to be honest about. The models I used will look primitive by the time you read these words. That is the strange part of writing a book about AI. Whatever I describe here is a photograph of a moving train. By publication, some of the tools will have new names, new capabilities, and probably new pricing. A few may not exist at all. That's fine. The frameworks are meant to outlast the current model lineup. The thinking is portable. The tools will keep changing.

Final responsibility for everything in these pages, including any mistakes, belongs to me.

Now, on to the work itself.

Introduction: The CFO's Transition from Scorekeeper to Strategic Leader

For more than a century, the role of the Chief Financial Officer (CFO) has quietly evolved alongside the modern corporation. Early finance officers were little more than senior accountants or controllers, managing accounts and ledgers. These executives had the important task of financial gatekeeping and reporting, but little else. After the 1929 stock-market crash and the Great Depression, the American Institute of Accountants and the New York Stock Exchange collaborated to create a set of standards that have become known as Generally Accepted Accounting Principles (GAAP). For publicly traded corporations, the Securities Act of 1934 and the creation of the Securities and Exchange Commission (SEC) established explicit reporting requirements.[1] The CFO was now responsible for accurate books, timely reporting, and compliance with accounting standards. Their job was to manage costs, protect the balance sheet, and ensure satisfaction among auditors, bankers, and investors. In this traditional role, the CFO was the "scorekeeper," and the job was rooted in past performance, control, and conservatism. As such, the entire finance function (though adding complexity) was still seen as a back-office necessity rather than a driver of competitive advantage.

The perception of the CFO role began to shift significantly in the late twentieth century as globalization, deregulation, and advances in technology expanded the scope of financial management. Enterprise resource planning (ERP) systems, business intelligence tools, and shared-service models extended the CFO's oversight, yet the function still largely revolved around reporting on what had already happened, not providing the insights needed to improve future decision-making. The CFO of the 1990s might have overseen accounting, treasury, mergers and acquisitions (M&A), and investor relations, but the organizational mindset remained backward-looking. Then, in 2001, the Enron scandal occurred.

Enron and Sarbanes–Oxley: Accountability as a Catalyst for Strategy

The Enron scandal exposed a fragile equilibrium: financial engineering could win accolades even as underlying risks multiplied. These risks wouldn't show up until it was too late. The 2002 Sarbanes–Oxley Act (SOX) reset the equilibrium, seeking to curb abuses and repair cracks that had emerged in modern finance. The new laws recast the CFO's role from a back-office reporter to a provider of trustworthy information and enterprise controls, with legal responsibility for them.

Two provisions in the law changed the CFO job description in practice. First, Section 302 required executive certifications, under which CFOs personally attest to the accuracy of filings and the effectiveness of disclosure controls. Second, Section 404 established internal control over financial reporting (ICFR), which compelled corporate management to design, document, and test its controls on a continuous basis. Section 404b added auditor attestation to the efficacy of the controls. These new rules and their impact on financial reporting and compliance brought the CFO to the center of financial control design, evidence gathering, and remediation as an ongoing operating discipline.

The governance infrastructure surrounding finance also deepened. Corporate boards were now expected to have independent, empowered audit committees, and the group responsible for overseeing auditors, the Public Company Accounting Oversight Board (PCAOB), lobbied for more frequent and deeper board-level interaction with the finance function. The CFO's board-level agenda expanded from sharing the "quarterly books" to explaining control processes, data quality, and (when required) remediation plans. The CFO needed to translate operational risk into quantifiable financial impact. The finance department was moving toward a forward-looking role: preventing control failures, anticipating disclosure risks, and demonstrating how process changes would sustain reporting integrity over time.

The mechanics of SOX compliance delivered important operational dividends. Implementing standardized processes, documented handoffs, role-based access, and audit trails reduced both reporting outcome variability and cycle time. Shared definitions and master data disciplines created a more reliable "single source of truth." Ultimately, this compliance-focused work became the foundation for analytics: clean data, clear ownership, repeatable workflows, and measurable performance.

This shift is the hinge between the CFO "scorekeeper" past and the digital present. The elements that make a company auditable also make it predictable. Satisfying regulatory and audit requirements has enabled predictive modeling, scenario planning, and other modern management tools, including the responsible use of AI.

The Data and Cloud Revolution: Expanding Finance's Reach

While SOX elevated the CFO's accountability, the rise of cloud computing, big data, and machine learning (ML) created an opportunity to expand the CFO's toolkit. The transformation of finance from a rearview-mirror cost function into a forward-looking engine of profit-driving decision intelligence was made possible by unprecedented access to data, scalable compute power, and algorithmic insight.

The Explosion of Enterprise Data

SOX accelerated corporate investment in structured data and disciplined processes. As businesses grew larger, more complex, and more international, they began generating and capturing exponentially more data. Beyond traditional financial data, organizations were collecting information from ERP systems, customer relationship management (CRM) platforms, human resource (HR) systems, supply-chain networks, and later "Internet of Things" (IoT) connected devices.

To explain company performance and shape investor narratives, finance now needed to integrate operational data (production volumes, logistics flows), customer data (lifetime value, churn, acquisition cost), and risk data (market exposures, credit trends). The CFO's perspective and influence expanded, as finance was tasked with unifying disparate information flows into a single coherent and auditable story.

The sheer volume of data posed new challenges. Manual processes and PC-based spreadsheets could not keep pace. Without innovation, more data meant more work and more noise, not more insight.

Cloud Computing and Elastic Scale

Enter "the Cloud." The evolution from on-premises computing to cloud-based applications transformed much of finance's operating model. Cloud-based ERP and business intelligence (BI) systems eliminated many barriers that had limited finance innovation. Instead of waiting for their IT department to provision hardware and manage upgrades or installations, CFOs could now adopt SaaS-based finance platforms that scaled elastically. In addition, smaller, mid-market companies could suddenly access tools once reserved for Fortune 500 enterprises.

The Cloud enabled near-real-time data refreshes, global consolidation, and collaboration across geographies without the once-prohibitive infrastructure investments. For the finance function, the impact was profound, spanning faster month- and quarter-end closes to automated consolidations and reconciliations. Robust, integrated dashboards became possible at scale. The evolution of cloud computing and the rise of vendors providing cloud services democratized analytics by putting key capabilities directly in the hands of finance teams.

Machine Learning Matures

With the Cloud's increase in computing power and data storage, modern ML began moving from academic research, mathematics, and statistical applications into mainstream business use. Applications of ML, particularly in fraud prevention, credit scoring, and anomaly detection, began taking hold in the 1990s, when financial institutions deployed neural networks and decision-tree models at scale. By the 2000s, these methods were widely used across finance, insurance, and telecom. By the 2010s, they had become a standard corporate capability. As algorithms improved, ML use cases broadened to include forecasting, scenario modeling, and customer-behavior prediction.

For finance professionals accustomed to static, deterministic systems (spreadsheets, ERP, robotic process automation (RPA)), access to data and algorithms began to reveal patterns previously hidden from human perception. The CFO's department was adding tools to help predict shifts in demand, quantify exposures to a myriad of risks, and run complex "what-if" scenarios in minutes instead of weeks.

Importantly, these capabilities didn't require armies of data scientists. Software vendors began embedding ML into finance applications. SaaS forecasting tools, anomaly-detection engines, and ML-assisted planning platforms gave finance leaders practical ways to experiment with advanced analytics without building models from scratch.

Lower Barriers to Entry

The impact of this technological democratization cannot be overstated. Predictive analytics at scale used to be limited to large corporations with deep IT budgets. Cloud-native vendors changed that. Mid-sized organizations gained access to ML-powered variance analysis or cash-flow forecasting as part of their standard finance stack. This meant every CFO could routinely deliver insights once considered "advanced."

When CEOs and corporate boards saw what was possible with predictive analytics and automation, they set new expectations for their CFOs. "Why are we waiting two weeks for variance explanations when other companies deliver them overnight?" was heard in boardrooms around the world.

Yes, technology changed what finance could do, but also what it was expected to do.

Strategic Consequences for CFOs

Three consequences from the convergence of regulatory, technological, and strategic change stand out:

1. **From historian to strategist.** With access to near-real-time, integrated data, CFOs were no longer just recording and reporting what already happened. They were explaining why it happened, modeling what might happen next, and proposing strategies to seize opportunities or mitigate previously unseen risks.
2. **From control to enablement.** While cloud and ML-based tools increased the importance of governance within the CFO's department, they also freed executives to spend more time enabling better decisions across the organization, not just policing the numbers.
3. **From departmental to enterprise impact.** Because CFOs could connect financial metrics to customer behavior, operational efficiency, and risk, they gained substantial influence. Finance's insights began shaping product launches, pricing decisions, and capital allocation.

In short, new technologies gave CFOs both the tools and the mandate to play offense, as well as defense.

The Bridge to Artificial Intelligence

So, finally, with all this technology and data infrastructure in place, the stage is set for the era of artificial intelligence (AI).

To review, the financial and operational controls discipline imposed by SOX created trust in reporting. The data and cloud revolutions made vast, reliable datasets and computational power available at scale. Machine learning showed that algorithms could augment human judgment. With the advent of publicly available AI and generative AI (GenAI)-powered tools, CFOs were primed with a governance mindset and the technology foundation.

The result? The modern CFO is not merely a corporate beneficiary of AI, but its natural leader. The combination of accountability and organizational access has positioned the finance department as a logical "first mover" to set the standard for responsible, strategic AI adoption across the corporation.

This book is built on this core idea. The AI-ready CFO is a finance leader who recognizes the long-term value of AI not only within the finance department but across all areas, and understands what is needed to unlock that value. The chapters in this book will help any interested finance leader gain the knowledge and skills needed to advance AI initiatives in their businesses with the confidence traditionally associated with the office of the CFO.

Note

1. "The Evolution of Accounting Standards: From GAAP to IFRS," *The University of Texas Permian Basin*, accessed August 12, 2025, https://online.utpb.edu/about-us/articles/business/the-evolution-of-accounting-standards-from-gaap-to-ifrs/

Chapter 1

The CFO's New Mandate: Leading AI and Automation

Key Takeaways

- **The evolution of CFO from custodian to architect.** The CFO is no longer just a scorekeeper of past results. With AI, finance becomes a forward-looking architect of enterprise strategy, striking a balance between accuracy and foresight. While deterministic tools confirmed what happened, the probabilistic nature of GenAI helps anticipate what might happen.
- **Where is the pressure to change coming from?** CEO, corporate board, and investor expectations have changed. Speed and clarity are more important than ever, and the CFO has a greater responsibility than ever to deliver on these expectations. Increased global complexity,

greater scrutiny from auditors and regulators, and a dearth of finance talent demand new ways to tackle finance and accounting challenges.

- **Governance as strategic asset.** GenAI's probabilistic nature demands new oversight. Outputs may be insightful but also flawed, making governance central to credibility. CFOs must ensure audit trails, explainability, and SOX/ICFR alignment, and treat governance as the foundation for adoption.
- **People before technology.** The real challenge of AI adoption is not the algorithms themselves, but rather people. Finance teams face talent shortages, rising workloads, and higher expectations. GenAI can automate routine work, but without upskilling in data literacy, prompt design, and output verification, adoption will falter. The AI-ready CFO must reorganize teams around analysis and decision support, model personal adoption of models, and champion cultural change.

The Inflection Point

On February 11, 2020, the World Health Organization gave a name to the disease that would reshape our world: COVID-19, short for the disease caused by the 2019 Novel Coronavirus. Just over a month later, by March 15, the United States had closed schools and put social distancing and mask requirements in place. Across the globe, economies came to a standstill as countries shut down, while the number of people falling ill and dying from this new virus continued to rise.[1]

The COVID-19 pandemic introduced a "never-before-seen" level of volatility in supply chains, capital markets, and customer behavior. The ever-changing situation during the pandemic demanded faster forecasts and scenario modeling to stay ahead as expectations, along with the virus, mutated almost daily. Employees were sent home, except for key personnel and first responders. Organizations that had digitized their core processes, especially in the finance function, like automated reconciliations, centralized data repositories, and embedded analytics, were better equipped to pivot and adjust in the newly mobile environment.

As the immediate effects of the pandemic waned and the turbulence subsided, the business world found itself on the other side of this inflection point. The power of the remote and hybrid organization had been unleashed, and technology innovators rushed to provide new tools that embraced this new paradigm. Among these were firms such as OpenAI, Claude, and xAI, competing to deliver GenAI products and services that could further enhance the digital-led corporation.

As companies began to adopt these powerful tools (officially or unofficially), a critical question emerged: Who should lead the charge to ensure their responsible and strategic implementation across the enterprise?

Why the CFO Is Central to AI Adoption

The spread of the unsanctioned use of AI, particularly GenAI (think employees feeding confidential data into public chatbots, or teams building unvetted forecasting models with no audit trail), throughout the business world highlighted the need for corporate leadership. Therefore, as the finance department sits at the nexus of corporate data, controls, and accountability, the CFO, not the Chief Information Officer (CIO) or Chief Transformation Officer (CTO), is often best placed to lead adoption. Consider the following advantages:

1. **Data stewardship.** Finance touches almost every transaction in the business. Whether accounts payable (AP), payroll, or revenue recognition, the data runs through finance systems. This gives the CFO both visibility and responsibility for ensuring data quality, governance, and integrity.
2. **Control environment.** CFOs are trained in compliance frameworks such as SOX and ICFR. They understand the need for evidence trails, auditability, and explainability. These are precisely the disciplines required to deploy AI responsibly and avoid the risks inherent in opaque algorithms and unreliable outputs.
3. **Enterprise visibility.** Unlike functional leaders who may focus on a single domain, the CFO has a horizontal view across operations, sales, HR, and strategy. This vantage point enables them to identify cross-functional AI use cases, such as variance analysis, scenario modeling, and demand forecasting, that cut across different silos.

In short, CFOs already possess the trust, oversight, and span of control that AI adoption requires. They are natural candidates to bring structure and governance to what might otherwise be a chaotic wave of experimentation.

From Financial Gatekeeper to Transformational Leader

Becoming a strategic leader in the age of AI requires a further shift in the CFO's mindset. Traditional finance rewarded precision and caution. AI-driven finance requires agility, experimentation, and change leadership. This change doesn't mean CFOs should abandon rigor. But it must be extended to new domains. For example, where a CFO once ensured the numbers in the financial statements sent to the board were correct, they must now also ensure that any GenAI models used for board presentations or reporting have a proper audit trail, guardrails, and reviewer sign-offs. The CFO's newly expanded AI mandate can be grouped into three dimensions:

- **Value creation.** Harnessing AI and accompanying automation to compress cycle times, reduce costs, and unlock productivity. Moving from "inbox to board book" in days instead of weeks.
- **Risk management.** Updating control frameworks to include AI usage, explainability standards, and data access, privacy, and security.
- **Change leadership.** Upskilling finance teams, building cross-functional data literacy, and reframing the CFO's office as an innovation and strategy hub, not just a reporting center.

The modern CFO needs to be as comfortable discussing data architecture as they are reviewing quarterly earnings. The goal isn't chasing technology trends, but using data and automation to enhance finance's ability to shape enterprise strategy.

Evolution Along the Continuum

Seen in its historical context, this transformation is less radical than it appears. Finance has always evolved alongside technology: from the introduction of double-entry bookkeeping in the Renaissance, to adding machines and punch cards in the early twentieth century, to spreadsheets and ERP systems in the late twentieth century. Each leap reduced the manual burden and elevated finance professionals toward higher-value analysis. AI is simply the next phase in this trajectory. The difference is the pace of change and the breadth of impact across the organization.

The "New-Age CFO," as described in my first book, *Deep Finance*, is not just a financial steward but a strategic data leader. Accuracy, compliance, and stewardship remain foundational. What's changed is that those responsibilities now coexist with an expanded mandate: harnessing technological transformation, such as AI, to create enterprise value.

As a leader of the finance department, the CFO's question isn't *should* I lead my company's AI adoption, but *how do I lead* in a way that balances innovation with governance?

The Pressure Points Driving Change

Several converging forces are pushing CFOs to take the lead on AI strategy. Each carries its own urgency, and together they create a mandate that finance leaders can't defer. Understanding where the pressure originates helps clarify why the CFO's office, and specifically the CFO's judgment, sits at the center of the response.

Board and Investor Expectations

The most immediate and substantial pressure on the CFO comes from the corporate boardroom. Boards and investors no longer view quarterly reporting as sufficient. Market volatility, geopolitical disruptions, and new competitive dynamics make lagging indicators inadequate for decision-making. They expect forward-looking insights delivered as frequently as reasonable.

In a late 2024 interview with McKinsey senior partner Lareina Lee, OpenAI's CFO, Sarah Friar, was asked: What will the finance function look like in five years? What things do you hope you'll be able to do with gen AI?

She responded, "I really hope we will move completely to the point of being the home for business insights, driving the business to go bigger and faster. Today, there's still so much in the finance department that is the look back, not the look forward. I hope in five years we'll look back at how we do things today and feel like today's methods are so outdated. I want to be able to look at my team and see that everyone is in that mode of forward-thinking and insight-driven work, and that a lot of the work we do today becomes rote work that gen AI does for us."[2]

Additionally, when a CEO and board want their CFO to explain something, they typically don't want to wait for details. The pressure isn't just speed. Depth is also critical. They don't want to know only what happened, but why it happened, and what might happen next. Board members increasingly expect scenario modeling, sensitivity analysis, and real-time KPI monitoring. This level of detail, at velocity, requires compressing the finance reporting cycle from data collection to board-ready narratives into days (and sometimes hours), not weeks. Meeting this expectation requires dynamic models and processes powered by automation, advanced analytics, ML, and now, GenAI.

> AI is actually the **number one issue** facing AICPA's corporate finance and accounting community… because boards and CEOs are asking what finance is doing with it.[3]
>
> —*Tom Hood, CPA, CGMA, CITP-EVP, Business Engagement and Growth at AICPA/CIMA*

Rising Complexity in Global Finance Operations

The second pressure point is the sheer complexity of modern business. Enterprise-scale finance operations now span multiple geographies, currencies, and regulatory regimes. Supply chains stretch across continents. Revenue is increasingly tied to intangible assets (e.g., software, IP, data) that are harder to value and monitor. Even smaller businesses face similar complexities, albeit at smaller scales.

For the finance department, this translates into constant reconciliation. Currency fluctuations, cross-border tax structures, and regional compliance obligations demand systems capable of near real-time monitoring. A transaction processed in Singapore might need to be reported in New York, taxed in Dublin, and audited in London. Multiply this by thousands of transactions, or dozens of countries, and it becomes clear that manual processes cannot keep pace.

The proliferation of enterprise-wide technology systems from ERPs, CRMs, HRIS platforms, and industry-specific tools magnifies this complexity for finance, and data collection is only one part of the challenge. These disparate datasets need to be cleaned and harmonized to ensure a single version of truth can exist across diverse sources. Without automation and AI-driven data pipelines, the risk and cost of errors increase substantially. In short, CFOs can't meet their fiduciary duties or their boards' expectations without investing in technologies that tame the chaos of ingesting, reconciling, and interpreting data at a massive scale.

Talent Constraints and Cost Pressures

The shortage of skilled finance professionals is becoming acute. A 2025 survey of senior financial executives conducted by the Controllers Council found that 43% of those polled reported either minor or significant shortages of finance talent.[4] Many CFOs struggle to find professionals capable of bridging finance expertise with analytical fluency, as this expertise is widely sought by leading data science and technology firms. Meanwhile, professionals increasingly expect modern tools and automated workflows, not endless hours of manual processes. Retention risks are real when teams feel stuck doing low-value work. In fact, the most commonly cited cause for resignation in the finance department, according to a recent Controller Council's survey, is lack of career advancement opportunities.[5]

Automation and GenAI are both a necessity and a competitive advantage in this environment. By automating repetitive processes such as journal entries, reconciliations, and variance reports, CFOs free up scarce talent to focus on higher-order analysis. More importantly, CFOs can position their organizations as forward-looking employers with strategic finance roles rather than clerical ones.

As cost pressure intensifies from external forces, including rising interest rates, inflation, geopolitical volatility, general economic uncertainty, and tighter capital markets, CFOs must guard liquidity while still funding growth initiatives. AI can offer a new lever to reduce cycle times, improve working capital management, and lower transaction costs. But like any innovation, AI tools require upfront investment and change leadership, which increases the tension on CFOs caught between near-term constraints and long-term imperatives.

Increasing Scrutiny from Regulators and Auditors

In the long list of challenges facing the CFO, regulatory and audit scrutiny has emerged as the defining pressure point in the age of AI. Regulators and auditors want answers to hard questions: How are your models validated? Can the outputs be explained and verified? Are evidence trails preserved? AI-enhanced workflows in finance impact audit and regulatory requirements in new ways.

GenAI models (as any mildly informed user of available products knows) regularly generate "hallucinations." These false facts, spit out by the platform as it tries to predict the answer a user wants, will embed inaccuracies in financial reporting if left unreviewed. In a similar vein, GenAI models need to be trained, which can introduce new biases, whether from human trainers or from bad datasets, that can distort outputs from board reports to risk assessments. These failures can have material consequences, particularly in regulated industries like banking, insurance, and healthcare.

Auditors and their overseers are already pushing for AI-specific control frameworks. The PCAOB listed AI use as one of their target priorities for audit inspections in 2025.[6] Public companies are expected by their auditors to map AI-enabled processes back to SOX and ICFR requirements. That means logging prompts, preserving outputs, and maintaining reviewer sign-offs for any AI-assisted work. (Ways to manage and address governance and controls in the use of AI CFOs will be addressed in Chapter 8.)

The added scrutiny should not stifle AI innovation. On the contrary, it will continue to ensure the trust investors, boards, and regulators have in the finance department's history of applying rigorous accounting standards.

Together, these pressures form a perfect storm. CFOs and their analyst teams can't navigate these treacherous waters by simply working harder. The only path forward is structural. The CFO's challenge, and corresponding opportunity, is to use the turbulence created by these trends as a cause to lead the corporate-wide transformation.

Why CFOs, Not CIOs, Are in the Spotlight

- Technology decisions in finance affect high-risk areas of forecasting, reporting, and compliance.

- Finance owns the data that drives enterprise value (financials, customer economics, and risk).
- Unlike CIOs, CFOs are accountable for both financial outcomes *and* governance.

Technology Decisions in Finance Carry Enterprise Risk

Let's face it, not all corporate technology choices are created equal. When a CIO selects a new document management platform or a sales team needs an email marketing platform, the potential negative implications of failure are important but manageable. However, if a CFO seeks to implement an AI-assisted forecasting, automated reconciliation, or regulatory reporting tool, the stakes will be far higher.

Finance is a function tightly bound by fiduciary responsibility. An error in payroll automation may affect employee satisfaction, but an error in financial close or SEC reporting can trigger restatements, lawsuits, or regulatory penalties. The difference is existential.

Accountability and liability are the reasons finance technology decisions are no longer just "IT projects." They're board-level considerations. Boards and investors understand that algorithmic errors erode trust; but they also realize that innovative, AI-enabled forecasting or variance analysis can change how a company allocates capital, producing better results.

The CIO isn't being sidelined in these conversations. There needs to be recognition that finance technology carries a disproportionate share of enterprise risk. Only the CFO has the context to weigh efficiency gains against compliance and regulatory requirements, and only the CFO has the legal obligation to certify the outputs of that technology.

Finance Owns the Data Most Critical for Enterprise Value

Data is yet another area of enterprise inequality. Important and valuable data may be scattered across the enterprise, but ultimately, it's financial data that defines enterprise value.

The financial statements remain the single most important measure of company performance. They capture the myriad levers that drive valuation: revenue, costs, margins, liquidity, assets, liabilities, and risk. In addition, finance increasingly is required to integrate non-financial data and information into its models and reporting. Customer lifetime value, supply-chain exposures, and environmental metrics all feed into investor narratives and capital-allocation decisions.

Finance sits at the intersection of these inputs, so it has become the natural owner of enterprise data integrity. The combination of financial, operational, customer, and risk data into a coherent story is the basis for communication with the board, investors, and regulators.

AI is only as useful as the quality of the data it trains on. Garbage in, garbage out—but on steroids! If finance owns the "golden source" of data most tied to enterprise value, it follows that finance must also lead in setting standards for its governance, integration, and accuracy. A predictive model or AI-driven financial tool built without finance's involvement risks being unmoored from the metrics that actually drive the enterprise's value.

Accountability for Both Outcomes and Governance

While CIOs are responsible for system availability, cybersecurity, and cost-effective technology operations, all of which are extremely important, they do not carry direct fiduciary consequences. CFOs have a legal responsibility to sign their names on financial statements certifying to auditors and regulators that results are true and accurate, and that corporate and financial controls are in place and effective.

The CFO, therefore, has a unique position with dual responsibilities: delivering financial outcomes while maintaining governance. They cannot delegate accountability for the integrity of financial information. Even if technology enables the production of information, the CFO remains responsible for every part of it. When GenAI or other AI tools are introduced into forecasting, close, or audit workflows, the CFO must be able to explain, document, and defend the outputs. Because the CFO is expected to ensure that governance frameworks extend beyond traditional controls to cover new technologies, they are increasingly referred to as a "chief accountability officer" for AI. This includes:

- **Audit trails.** Ensuring AI-assisted reporting preserves evidence and version control.
- **Explainability.** Demanding models that provide a rationale for outputs, not black-box predictions.

- **Oversight.** Establishing processes where human review and judgment remain central to decision-making.

The Strategic Implications

The future of AI adoption in the enterprise depends upon close CFO/CIO collaboration. The CIO remains essential for implementation, infrastructure, resource management, and cybersecurity. But the strategic choices of whether to deploy AI-based tools, how to deploy them, how to balance that innovation with controls and monitoring, and which metrics define a project's success rest with the CFO. Boards recognize this difference. Increasingly, questions about AI strategy are being asked directly to CFOs, such as:

- How will AI improve forecasting accuracy?
- What safeguards ensure compliance?
- How is financial data governed and protected?
- What ROI (return on investment) can we expect from automation investments?

In corporate boardrooms, the spotlight has shifted on AI technology. The CIO will be in the room, but the CFO needs to answer.

What Makes AI Different from Past Tech Waves

Finance has weathered multiple rounds of technology adoption, from ERP rollouts to BI platforms to RPA. Each wave reshaped parts of the workflow, and each taught hard lessons about implementation risk, change management, and ROI timelines. AI builds on all of that history, but it introduces a fundamentally different set of challenges.

ERP, BI, and RPA Set the Stage

Each of these past waves of innovation was transformative in its own way, but at their core, each was fundamentally about collection, coordination, control, and standardization.

- **ERP systems** integrated disparate financial processes into a single system of record. This gave finance leaders visibility across the enterprise and reduced the risks of fragmented reporting. The promise was accuracy and consistency.
- **BI tools** were layered on top of ERP, enabling dashboards and analysis. For the first time, finance teams could move beyond static reports to near-real-time insights. But BI was descriptive, or at most diagnostic. It only told you what had happened, and perhaps why.
- **RPA** targeted repetitive, rules-based tasks: reconciliations, data entry, and report generation. It delivered efficiency and freed up analyst time, but its scope was narrow. And it required explicit programming of every rule it needed to follow.

At their height, these technologies were vital, but they shared a common limitation. They were deterministic: given the same input, they always produced the same output. The primary risks were operational (e.g., failed integrations, bad data, or poorly designed processes), and the outputs were reliable. While this behavior is desirable in some areas, it is also limited compared to the newest incarnation of AI.

Generative and Agentic AI Systems: Moving Beyond Efficiency

The inclusion of GenAI marks a shift from deterministic to probabilistic systems. Unlike ERP, BI, or RPA, generative and agentic AI tools don't simply follow pre-programmed rules. They predict answers to questions, requests, or prompts based on probabilities generated from the data they were trained on. The quality of an AI-based tool's output depends on the quality of training data. This means they can provide data-driven insights, narratives, and even recommendations to questions, prompts, and requests that were never explicitly programmed. For finance leaders, this is both very powerful and deeply unsettling.

Readily available GenAI tools can now:

- Generate board-ready commentary from raw financials.
- Build scenario models in minutes rather than weeks.
- Surface anomalies and potential risks that might elude human analysts.

Agentic systems go even further. Agents are AI models connected to tools, data sources, and workflows that are programmed to act with prescribed and proscribed autonomy. For example, a finance department agent could be created to pull financial data, run a variance analysis, draft a management report, and circulate it for review, all with minimal human intervention.

This evolution represents a step toward true, prescriptive decision support. AI can not only help finance teams close the books faster, but also shape how executives interpret results and decide strategy. This is the categorical difference from past waves of finance technology. The potential productivity lift is enormous, but so are the risks if outputs are not properly governed.

From Rules-Based to Probabilistic: The Oversight Challenge

This probabilistic nature is what makes generative-AI-enabled systems fundamentally different. Decisions and outputs in deterministic platforms were transparent. If something went wrong, you could typically trace it back to a specific data point, formula, rule, or integration. When AI is involved, the path to the output is more opaque. The model generates an output based on reasoning derived from probability-based patterns, not step-by-step logic. The result may be accurate, incorrect, or a mix of both, depending on the AI's model and the data used to identify the patterns needed to create the output. The details on AI models and their reasoning could, and do, fill volumes of books, but for the CFO's purpose, understanding what a probabilistic tool means for finance department outputs is sufficient. The probabilistic shift, however, introduces new oversight challenges:

- **Explainability.** Can you demonstrate how an AI model arrived at a forecast or recommendation?
- **Bias.** Are outputs skewed because of gaps in the training data and/or human bias?
- **Auditability.** Can you provide an evidence trail for AI-assisted work when regulators or auditors ask?

These questions go straight to the heart of the CFO's audit-related and fiduciary responsibilities. The move from deterministic to probabilistic systems means governance must expand, not only to safeguard data integrity but also to oversee the custom instruction layers and prompts that shape outputs, and to ensure the chosen AI model is appropriate, reliable, and fit for the organization's specific needs.

The Need for New Playbooks

The adoption of AI in the finance function, particularly GenAI, requires balancing two opposing forces: innovation and control. Traditional technology playbooks for ERP and RPA implementations focused on getting systems live and ensuring output accuracy. Simple enough with these deterministic platforms. As noted earlier, the probabilistic nature of AI doesn't work well with these older technology schemes. It's not possible to set it up, connect it to data, turn it on, and monitor the output. Given the challenges of control, a blanket ban on these tools may feel like the safe route. However, the pace of evolution in AI is enabling early adopters to gain a substantial competitive advantage.

A "guardrails, not roadblocks" approach is essential to allow the finance department to evolve along with the new technology. Roadblocks, like bans on AI, are more likely to send AI use into unmonitored situations. As platforms like ChatGPT and Grok expand in personal use, employees will be increasingly less interested in leaving their newfound efficiency at the corporate front door. Using guardrails that provide clear rules, explainability standards, and oversight processes enables finance teams to leverage AI's benefits while mitigating risks as platforms and tools continue to improve. (Chapter 8 further explores the need for governance and control with AI platforms.)

Practical examples of guardrails include:

- Requiring human review and sign-off for all AI-generated reports.
- Logging prompts and outputs for audit purposes.
- Restricting sensitive data from external models by favoring private or "behind the firewall" deployments.
- Training finance teams on how AI works so they can frame tasks, spot errors, and verify results.

Guardrails are part of a governance-first posture that allows CFOs to begin to unlock AI's potential without undermining the trust of the executives they serve.

Why This Time Is Different

The differences between past and current tech waves can be summarized simply:

- ERP and RPA standardized and automated processes.
- BI provided visibility.
- Generative and agentic AI tools provide judgment-like outputs.

This last shift, from visibility to judgment, makes the current wave different. Past systems told CFOs what happened. Today's AI-based systems are on the threshold of suggesting what to do next. This leap requires CFOs to treat AI technology as an intelligent partner in the decision-making process, not just back-office infrastructure.

The Priorities for the AI-Ready CFO: The New Mandate in Practice

Knowing that AI leadership falls to the CFO is one thing. Knowing where to focus that leadership is another. The priorities below represent the operational core of the AI-ready mandate, each one grounded in the kind of measurable, auditable outcomes that finance teams are built to deliver.

Value Creation: ROI, Productivity Gains, and Agility

Boards and investors expect investments in AI and AI-based automation to deliver measurable returns. For CFOs, that means framing adoption in the language of ROI, IRR (internal rate of return), and payback periods, while also recognizing the broader strategic value that may be less measurable, such as improvements in employee satisfaction or competitive advantage.

The most immediate opportunities lie in employee productivity gains and cycle-time compression. GenAI tools can help reduce the "inbox to board book" process from weeks to days. AI-driven reconciliation processes, report drafting, and chart and table creation, for example, can free analyst time from executing lower-value tasks, enabling them to focus on forward-looking insights. This shift in focus will improve the business's overall agility, enabling faster responses to market conditions.

Value creation also comes from competitive intelligence. A finance team that can model scenarios in real time is better prepared to advise the CEO on pricing, expansion, or M&A opportunities. In volatile markets, that capability becomes a differentiator.

Some areas of value are harder to quantify, such as improved decision-making and talent retention, but they are equally important. Successful CFOs need to frame both in business terms that show AI can deliver efficiency, returns, growth, and resilience in all aspects of its value to the organization.

Risk Management: Governance, Controls, and Trust

The introduction of AI-enabled tools introduces new risks that must be managed within the CFO's traditional compliance mandate. This means aligning their use with SOX/ICFR requirements, ensuring explainability of outputs, and preserving audit trails.

Remember, AI platforms are built on probabilistic models; they can generate outputs that appear plausible but are, in fact, wrong. In finance, even a minor error can have outsized consequences. Proper governance is non-negotiable. CFOs must therefore implement new controls that extend beyond technical reliability and cover process integrity. These include:

- **SOX/ICFR alignment.** Updating control frameworks to account for AI-assisted workflows, including the logging of prompts used, preserving the outputs generated, and documenting review processes. The original compliance challenges don't go away; AI controls are just layered on top of the existing ones.
- **Explainability.** Ensuring that the AI models employed can be interrogated. Essentially asking, why did they produce a particular forecast or recommendation? Auditors and regulators are increasing their scrutiny on the use of AI in financial reporting, adding import to AI transparency.
- **Audit trails.** Requiring all systems used to record and save evidence of inputs, outputs, and human reviews. AI adoption across the enterprise will collapse under scrutiny if the AI platform cannot be effectively tracked and monitored.

The AI-ready CFO is the one who strikes a balance between being an innovator and a protector. They enable their team to benefit from the power of AI while maintaining the trust of auditors, regulators, and investors.

Change Leadership: Teams, Skills, and Adoption

Change leadership is perhaps the most challenging dimension of the new CFO mandate. Your people will be the driving force behind the transformation of the finance function, not technology. Given the paradigm shift that comes with the deployment of AI, teams will need to be reorganized, employees will need to build new skills, and a culture that embraces AI will need to be fostered in the organization.

This starts with upskilling. Thankfully, this doesn't mean all finance professionals now also need to become data scientists. However, they must understand how AI works, its limitations, and how to frame tasks for effective use. Training should focus on three practical skills: designing prompts, verifying outputs, and applying human judgment and review to the AI-generated insights.

Reorganization may also be essential. Legacy finance structures built around transactional processing and reporting must evolve toward analysis, decision support, and strategy. Individual roles may need to be redefined. There may be a need to create AI centers of excellence, or embed finance analysts in business units to manage a platform that provides real-time insights. We'll go into detail on the AI-ready organization and finance team in Chapters 10 and 11.

Finally, the CFO must serve as a role model for AI adoption. Widespread adoption can only happen when leaders demonstrate their trust in new AI tools by using them! Furthermore, showcasing quick wins and celebrating the successes from across the team will drive support for AI within the department. Resistance to change is natural, but strong leadership can turn skepticism into momentum.

Balancing Early Wins and Long-Term Roadmaps

The CFO's new mandate with AI rests on showing quick results to build confidence without undermining long-term trust. These early wins should focus on low-risk, high-visibility use cases, such as variance analysis, close commentary, or cash-flow forecasting. Such projects can demonstrate tangible benefits while keeping overall risks manageable. The quick wins will also help build internal champions: the analysts and managers who experience direct benefits of AI in their roles and become natural advocates for wider adoption.

CFOs must, however, resist any temptation to oversell early results. An AI-generated variance analysis is not the same as a full-scale forecasting overhaul. The long-term roadmap should clearly articulate how the organization will progress from pilot to enterprise-wide adoption. (Chapter 9 provides details on pilot creation and long-term planning.)

A basic phased approach might look like this:

- **Phase 1.** Quick wins in reporting and analysis.
- **Phase 2.** Broader integration into forecasting, scenario modeling, and planning.
- **Phase 3.** Cross-functional adoption, connecting finance AI systems to operations, sales, and strategy.

AI adoption is not a one-off project. The use of AI should be viewed as part of the ongoing evolution of the enterprise. Avoid the trap of inflated expectations by clearly distinguishing short-term gains from the long-term vision.

The 95% Failure Rate Everyone Quoted: What It Actually Means for CFOs

Few statistics in recent memory have been as widely cited across boardrooms and conference stages as this one: in the summer of 2025, MIT's *State of AI in Business 2025* report found that 95% of enterprise AI projects were failing to deliver a measurable impact on the enterprise profit and loss (P&L).[7]

Before you panic, understand what "failure" means here. These aren't spectacular crashes or systems breaking down. Many projects actually work fine in their pilots. The problem? They never make it to production, never scale, and never show up on the bottom line.

A Wider Pattern of Disappointment

MIT wasn't alone in documenting this mess:

- IBM Institute for Business Value (2025)—Only 25% of AI initiatives met ROI goals, and just 16% scaled across the enterprise.[8]
- S&P Global (via CIO Dive)—On average, companies abandoned ~46% of AI proofs of concept (POCs) before production.[9]
- Gartner—Forecasted that more than 40% of agentic AI projects will fail by 2027 due to unclear value and rising costs.[10]
- NTT DATA (2025)—Estimated that 70–85% of GenAI deployments miss ROI targets.[11]

Different research firms, different samples, same story: most enterprise AI projects stalled before they created value.

Why Projects Underperform

The MIT report identified workflow integration and change management as the primary weaknesses. The other research added more detail:

- Data and governance overhead consumes 30–50% of project time.
- Shadow AI is running wild. Here's the paradox: only a minority of firms purchase official licenses, but employees in more than 90% of organizations are already using AI tools informally. Your team is using ChatGPT for expense reports while you're debating your enterprise AI strategy.
- Trust issues persist. Early hallucinations or compliance missteps often cause executives to prematurely pull the plug.
- Overreach is typical. Leaders pursue autonomy and "AI CFO" concepts when focusing on narrow, well-defined tasks is more realistic.

The pattern is clear: adoption and integration are harder than the technology itself.

The Counter-Narrative (And Why It Matters)

Now, let's add some nuance.

MIT's focus on "agentic AI" was missing something important: their 95% figure likely didn't capture the productivity wins happening in the shadows, or the real gains made when leaders start small, pick the right workflows, and build adoption with governance.

Your analysts are already using ChatGPT to speed up variance analysis. Your financial planning and analysis (FP&A) team is having

Claude assist in drafting board presentations. These wins rarely show up on the balance sheet, but they're real. And when leaders move beyond ad-hoc use by selecting the right workflows, matching them with the right tools, and piloting before scale, the impact compounds into measurable time savings and fewer errors. What looks like small productivity hacks today can become durable, enterprise-level gains when structured correctly.

Wharton professor Ethan Mollick's[12] research highlights the nuances surrounding "Shadow AI." GenAI can increase productivity by around 40% for the right tasks, but actually lower performance when applied in the wrong context. Success depends less on broad adoption and more on matching the right task to the right tool.

The Framing Insight for the AI-Ready CFO

So, does the 95% failure rate prove AI is useless? Not at all. It only proves that poorly scoped projects with fuzzy ROI don't create value. Shocking, right?

The opportunity for finance leaders lies in the structured, repeatable processes you already manage. The AI tools available today won't replace your strategic judgment—nor should they. However, they can eliminate 30–40% of your routine analysis and reporting work if applied with discipline, aiding your decision-making.[13]

Notes

1. Centers for Disease Control and Prevention, "CDC Museum COVID-19 Timeline," last reviewed July 8, 2024, https://www.cdc.gov/museum/timeline/covid19.html
2. McKinsey & Company, *What an AI-powered Finance Function of the Future Looks Like*, podcast transcript, accessed November 4, 2024, https://www.mckinsey.com/capabilities/tech-and-ai/our-insights/what-an-ai-powered-finance-function-of-the-future-looks-like
3. Tom Hood (AICPA/CIMA), interviewed by Glenn Hopper, *Google Meet*, December 16, 2025.
4. Controllers Council, *Corporate Finance & Accounting Talent Study 2025* (Controllers Council, 2025), 7, https://controllerscouncil.org/wp-content/uploads/2025/08/2025-Corporate-Accounting-Finance-Talent-Study.pdf
5. Ibid., 15.

6. "PCAOB Staff Report Outlines 2025 Inspection Priorities with Focus on Driving Improvements in Audit Quality," *Public Company Accounting Oversight Board*, December 9, 2024, https://pcaobus.org/news-events/news-releases/news-release-detail/pcaob-staff-report-outlines-2025-inspection-priorities-with-focus-on-driving-improvements-in-audit-quality
7. Aditya Challapally et al., *The GenAI Divide: State of AI in Business 2025* (MIT NANDA, 2025), 3, https://www.artificialintelligence-news.com/wp-content/uploads/2025/08/ai_report_2025.pdf
8. International Business Machines Corporation, *IBM Study: CEOs Double Down on AI While Navigating Enterprise Hurdles* (International Business Machines Corporation, 2025), https://newsroom.ibm.com/2025-05-06-ibm-study-ceos-double-down-on-ai-while-navigating-enterprise-hurdles
9. Mastufa Ahmed, "AI's Big Payoff Hinges on Fixing Fragmented Data: Study," *CIO*, May 7, 2025, https://www.cio.com/article/3980164/ais-big-payoff-hinges-on-fixing-fragmented-data-study.html
10. Reinhardt Krause, "Why MIT Study on Enterprise Market Is Pressuring AI Stocks," *Investor's Business Daily*, August 20, 2025, https://www.investors.com/news/technology/artificial-intelligence-stocks-ai-stocks-mit-study/
11. Ellen Jennings-Trace, "Almost all GenAI Pilots Companies Deploy are Failing – So are they Really Worth the Hype?," *Techradar*, August 19, 2025, https://www.techradar.com/pro/almost-all-genai-pilots-companies-deploy-are-failing-are-they-really-worth-the-hype
12. Ethan Mollick, *One Useful Thing*, accessed August 1, 2025, https://www.oneusefulthing.org/
13. Glenn Hopper, "About that 95% Failure Rate... What CFOs Should Really Take from the MIT AI Report," *Deep Finance Dispatch*, August 29, 2025, https://substack.com/home/post/p-172184616

Chapter 2

What CFOs Need to Know About AI

Key Takeaways

- **AI is no longer optional for finance leaders.** This isn't another slow, multi-year tool rollout like spreadsheets, ERPs, or BI. AI is already baked into the software your team uses every day, from Excel and SAP to Teams and Zoom. If you do nothing, you're underusing platforms you already pay for, and giving competitors time to compound efficiency and insight.
- **An AI-ready CFO has three jobs:**
  - **Translator of value, not technologist.** You don't need to be a data scientist. But you do need enough AI fluency to separate real

capability from exaggerated vendor claims, manage the obvious risks, and tie adoption to business outcomes. Boards, auditors, and investors will ask the same questions: What are we using? Where is it running? What data touches it? Who approves the output?

- **Architect of a new operating rhythm.** AI pushes finance away from cycle-based reporting to continuous decision support. For example, ML can refresh forecasts as conditions change. GenAI can draft the first pass of variance narratives, disclosures, and board updates in minutes. The point isn't "faster close" for its own sake. It's earlier visibility, faster iteration, and more time spent on judgment versus assembly.
- **Guardian of controls and boundaries.** The risks are predictable: hallucinations, data leakage, weak audit trails, cost creep, bias, adoption friction, and evolving regulation. The CFO's job is to set boundaries so AI outputs are grounded in enterprise data, reviewable under SOX/ICFR expectations, and logged well enough to be explained after the fact. Don't ask whether AI can act on its own. The key question is where autonomy is acceptable without breaking trust or control.

- **Adoption is layered:**
  - **Chatbots** answer questions, but don't execute work.
  - **Copilots** draft and assist while keeping human sign-off in place (e.g., Copilot for Finance or internal tools at large banks).
  - **Agents** chain steps together across systems and workflows, with higher upside and a higher bar for auditability and compliance.
- **AI can compress cycle time and improve decisions, but only with governance, oversight, and a clear business case.** The goal is not to replace analysts. It is to elevate them, shifting effort from compiling data to advising leaders.

The bottom line—GenAI in finance isn't a bolt-on productivity feature. You can't just "sprinkle some AI" on existing processes and expect transformation. AI changes how finance produces value. CFOs who translate value clearly, enforce control standards, and adopt with discipline will build a faster, clearer decision engine. And those who wait will be explaining the gap later.

CFOs Can't Ignore AI Anymore

For most of modern corporate history, finance leaders could treat technology adoption as something that would eventually happen, on its own timeline. New tools usually arrived at the edges first. Accountants and analysts picked them up in pockets, then finance standardized them later, once the case was proven and the implementation path was clear. Spreadsheets replaced paper ledgers. ERPs replaced a patchwork of departmental systems. And BI made reporting more accessible. In each wave, there was time to watch, wait, and still keep pace.

AI is different. The "wait and see" window is basically gone, for four reasons:

1. **It's already embedded in tools you run now.** This isn't a greenfield system purchase. AI is being woven into the platforms finance already uses. If you ignore it, you are underusing software you already pay for.
2. **Your team is already using it, with or without permission.** People are using public tools to draft emails, summarize documents, and get a first pass at analysis. If that's happening without guidance, you have a data boundary problem—not just a productivity experiment.
3. **The performance gap compounds.** If one finance team uses AI to compress close, accelerate forecast refreshes, and automate routine narratives, they won't just move faster this month. They'll reinvest that capacity into deeper analysis and better decision support. Over multiple cycles, the gap becomes structural.
4. **Boards and investors are asking.** Analysts, shareholders, and sponsors want to know how management is using AI to improve performance and manage risk. A CFO who can't explain an approach will look late to the curve, even if the underlying work is solid.

Compared to earlier innovations, AI also arrived in an unusual way: it showed up everywhere all at once. Some form of AI is now inside most of the finance stack: ERP systems, planning tools, reporting suites, and the productivity layer. Excel has Copilot. Major ERP vendors have added ML to forecasting, cash visibility, and anomaly detection. Treasury and fintech platforms are building AI into forecasting and exception handling. Even collaboration tools now summarize meetings, draft follow-ups, and surface anomalies in shared work.

This is the straightforward implication for the CFO: AI is already part of the finance operating environment, whether it's formally governed or not. And if peers are using it to shorten forecast cycles, reduce invoice processing time, or improve underwriting and credit decisions, doing nothing isn't neutral. It's falling behind.

Inside Wasabi: AI, Forecasting, and the CFO's Evolving Mandate

Wasabi Technologies is a cloud object storage provider powering the AI data layer worldwide. Wasabi isn't a flashy startup; it's a global data infrastructure company. That is precisely what made this conversation critical to the book. Two reasons, actually. One, when you look closely at the companies enabling the AI transformation, the ones building the plumbing, you'll find some of the most advanced thinking on data, value, and how finance functions need to evolve. Two, Wasabi's CFO, Michael Bayer, has enabled his team to drive the use of AI at the company beyond where many enterprise-sized firms operate today.[1]

Bayer brings a rare mix of technical depth and leadership clarity. He doesn't think like a traditional finance executive, and he doesn't want to. Bayer is blunt about where things are headed: the CFO role is being redefined, and those who don't adapt will be left behind. He argues that the real value of AI isn't necessarily found in ROI spreadsheets. When AI frees smart people to reimagine how work gets done, value is created.

Marcos Bento, who leads FP&A and data initiatives at Wasabi, walked through Wasabi's AI journey from the inside. They started small, first organizing data to speed up reporting, and now run an ML model that forecasts individual customer growth with precision. The insights drive sales strategy, renewals, and product planning, and they also add value to finance by informing revenue projections. The team is building agentic tools, including a Slack integration, on top of a data lakehouse architecture that combines structured and unstructured data, all without a massive budget or an army of engineers.

- **The CFO must serve as CTO.** AI is driving business model transformation, and the CFO is best positioned to align resources with that future. Bayer argues that translating the CEO's vision into action is no longer optional for the CFO. It is their core job.
- **You don't need a massive budget to build a modern AI stack.** Wasabi's journey began with spreadsheets and a lean team, but by focusing on smart data architecture, they've built powerful forecasting and agentic tools. Bento's advice: start small, focus on business value, and evolve quickly.
- **Forget traditional ROI models; they won't get you there.** Trying to measure AI's impact with old-school metrics is like asking for the ROI of giving employees better eyesight. Instead, Wasabi focuses on unlocking time, speeding up decision-making, and enabling new ways of working.
- **Put your data team in finance, not in engineering.** Bento reports to the CFO, not the CTO, by design. When data people are embedded in finance, they stay focused on business impact, not on dashboards for their own sake.
- **Hire for curiosity and adaptability, not just skills.** Bayer's hiring rule is simple: skills can be taught, but mindset can't. He looks for people who are fearless, eager to learn, and willing to rethink how things work; because in the AI era, today's job description won't last.

We have included Bayer's and Bento's thoughts throughout the book. Their insights are timely and reflective, no matter your organization's stage of AI-readiness.

The Move to Real-Time Financial Decision Support

Finance has traditionally run on fixed cycles: monthly close, quarterly forecasts, annual planning. That cadence made sense when data moved slowly and analysis was manual. But when systems can ingest transactions, operating metrics, and external signals continuously, waiting until month-end to spot a trend is late. It's steering the ship based on last month's weather forecast.

AI supports a different rhythm. It can work alongside the monthly cycle, but it's not limited by it. ML models can pick up changes in daily sales, churn, pricing, or mix and refresh forecasts as conditions move. The practical advantage is simple: models can absorb far more data, far faster, than any team consolidating spreadsheets and exports across systems.

GenAI then handles the narrative layer. Once forecasts update, it can draft the first pass of management-ready commentary in minutes. Expense anomalies can be flagged before they land in the P&L. Instead of explaining variances weeks after the fact, finance can investigate drivers while there is still time to act.

The close still matters. But AI lets finance add a continuous layer of decision support between closes. Instead of waiting for month-end to surface issues, you can see shifts in sales, margin, or spend while they're developing and respond sooner. CFOs who leave AI on the sidelines and continue to rely only on spreadsheets may find decision support drifting to leaders who can answer questions faster, with clearer evidence.

> The CFO needs to be the chief transformation officer. [They are] the only person in the organization who understands where the business is headed and translates the CEO's vision into resource allocation.[2]
>
> —*Michael Bayer, Wasabi*

The CFO as Translator

AI is becoming unavoidable, but it isn't making life simpler. The technology is moving fast, the vendor landscape is crowded, and the failure modes are real. Models can drift, fail quietly, generate plausible-sounding errors, or expose sensitive data if they're deployed without guardrails. That's why boards and auditors are leaning in on the basics: explainability, governance, and an evidence trail you can defend.

The CFO needs to step in here as a translator. You don't need to be a data scientist. You must connect what the technology can do to the outcomes the business cares about, and you need to hold the line on control standards. The job is to cut through vendor marketing, identify where AI will actually improve performance, and make sure adoption fits your compliance and risk posture.

Take forecasting. Plenty of vendors promise "autonomous FP&A" and continuously updating models. Fine. But "autonomous" is a claim, not a specification. A CFO should turn it into due diligence:

- What data does (can) the model ingest, and from where?
- How does accuracy compare to our current baseline, by business unit and horizon?
- Can we explain the drivers, or do we just get an output?
- What's logged, what's reproducible, and what's auditable?
- Where's the human sign-off, especially when the output informs reporting or external communication?

The exact questions will vary by company size and regulatory profile, but the objective doesn't: avoid wasted spend and unmanaged risk, and convert AI adoption into measurable outcomes.

To play the translator role well, finance leaders don't need to become technologists. They do need enough working fluency to lead with clarity. At a minimum, that means:

- Recognizing AI is already embedded across the enterprise stack, whether you've formalized it or not.
- Using AI to move finance toward faster, more continuous decision support, not just faster reporting.
- Acting as the bridge between IT, vendors, and business teams, ensuring tools get adopted in ways that hold up under scrutiny.

When the CFO owns that translation layer, finance becomes a driver of strategy, not just a reporting function. When it's ignored, the center of gravity shifts to whichever team adopts AI fastest and starts answering leadership questions first.

Understanding the Technology

Finance leaders don't need an engineering-level explanation of AI. They need a working model of what the tools do, where they fit in finance workflows, and where they fail if controls aren't in place. This section covers:

- The core categories of AI that show up in finance work.
- How large language models behave in plain language.
- The predictable pitfalls that matter in a control environment.

Core Categories of AI in Finance

Most finance use cases fall into four categories: ML, GenAI, automation, and emerging agentic workflows. Each solves a different kind of problem.

Machine Learning. ML finds patterns in data and uses them to predict or classify. In finance, it shows up most often in forecasting and anomaly detection.

Forecasting models can learn from historical revenue, seasonality, external drivers, and current operating metrics to produce projections that update as conditions change. Anomaly detection models scan transactions for exceptions worth review: duplicate invoices, unexpected spend spikes, unusual revenue patterns, or outliers in collections and cash.

The practical difference from traditional methods is that these models can adapt as they ingest more data. They're built to update their parameters as the underlying relationships change.

Generative AI. GenAI produces drafts: text, summaries, explanations, and structured narratives. The most common form in the enterprise is the large language model (LLM), including systems such as OpenAI's GPT family, Anthropic's Claude, xAI's Grok, Google's Gemini, and the leading Chinese model, DeepSeek.

In finance, GenAI is most useful where language is the bottleneck. It can draft a variance explanation tied to a set of numbers, summarize a board package, prepare an investor update outline, or create a first-pass executive summary. The value is time compression, as analysts spend less time staring at a blank page and more time validating, refining, and adding judgment. Human review is still the control point.

Automation (RPA and AI-Embedded ERP Modules). RPA has been automating repetitive, rules-based work for years. AI expands what can be automated by handling messier inputs and more variable workflows.

Traditional RPA moves data between systems when the rules are stable. AI-enhanced automation can interpret unstructured inputs, like invoices in different layouts, and extract fields using language and document parsing. ERP vendors have embedded more of this directly into their platforms, for example, invoice matching and exception handling in accounts payable (AP), cash forecasting that learns from historical patterns, and reconciliation tools that flag exceptions without relying on manual sampling.

Agentic AI: The Next Evolution. Agentic AI is where GenAI stops drafting and starts running steps. Instead of generating a variance explanation and handing it back to an analyst, an agent can execute a short workflow: pull the relevant transactions from the ERP, run anomaly checks, draft the narrative, and format the output into a board-ready package.

That's possible because agents combine an LLM's text-generation capability with tools, memory, and a planning loop. The LLM provides language and interpretation. The tools provide access to systems. The planning loop ties actions together so the agent can move from a goal to a sequence of steps and produce a finished artifact.

In finance, that opens up bigger use cases. Agents can investigate variances end-to-end, run multiple forecast scenarios and summarize the differences, or automate parts of reconciliations by checking entries and flagging exceptions. The technology is still emerging, but the fact is, AI is starting to do more than assist with language. It's beginning to execute workflows.

Taken together, ML, GenAI, and automation cover most of what finance teams will deploy. ML supports prediction. GenAI accelerates drafting and explanation. Automation reduces repetitive work and connects steps across systems.

How LLMs Work

LLMs are widely adopted, and they're also the most misunderstood tool in the current AI stack for most finance leaders. CFOs don't need the math behind neural networks, but they do need a basic understanding of how an LLM behaves so expectations stay grounded.

At its core, an LLM is a prediction engine. You give it an input (a prompt), and it generates an output one token at a time based on probabilities learned during training. Tokens are fragments of words. For example, "forecasting" might be broken into "fore," "cast," and "ing." After seeing trillions of tokens in training data, the model develops a statistical sense of how language tends to fit together. Think of these as an evolution of the auto-complete function we've used for years on our mobile phones and email programs. The biggest difference is the amount of context LLMs are able to retain compared to the technology historically used for auto-complete.

So, when you ask an LLM to draft an explanation for Q2 margin variance, it isn't pulling a stored answer from a database. It's generating text in real time, choosing each next token based on the prompt, the context window, and the patterns it learned during training. The writing can sound polished, but the mechanism is still probability-driven generation, not built-in fact-checking.

How LLMs Calculate Probabilities

The most useful mental model is this: training teaches the model which token sequences are more likely than others. During training, the model is repeatedly asked to predict the next token. When it misses, its internal parameters are adjusted. After billions of iterations, those parameters act like a tuned set of weights that shape what the model considers likely.

When you enter a prompt at runtime, the model produces a probability distribution over possible next tokens. If the prompt is "the margin variance was driven by ___," it might assign 60% to "labor costs," 25% to "raw material prices," and smaller percentages to other possibilities. It then samples from that distribution to pick the next token. Settings like "temperature" affect how much randomness is introduced, which is why the same prompt can produce different outputs.

For finance leaders, the implication is important: LLMs are probabilistic. That's a different operating mode than deterministic systems, where the same inputs yield the same outputs every time.

Where Probabilities Come From: Training and Parameters

Those probability distributions come from training and from the model's parameters. LLMs are trained on massive datasets drawn from the public internet, licensed sources, and (in some cases) proprietary datasets. Through training, models learn statistical associations: which words, phrases, and structures tend to follow others. Conceptually similar multimodal models handle images, audio, and video and operate in a comparable way to text-based models.

The results of training are stored in the model's parameters, which define the probability space used to generate text. Modern models contain hundreds of billions, or even trillions, of parameters.

For example, vendors generally don't publish official parameter counts for their current frontier models, and when numbers circulate, they are typically industry estimates. So, treat the figures below as reference points, not specifications. A widely cited estimate for OpenAI's previous GPT-4 model puts it at approximately 1.76 trillion parameters. OpenAI was able to achieve this scale using a mixture-of-experts (MoE) architecture in which multiple OpenAI models (around eight) are activated selectively per request. The multimodal version GPT-4o was estimated at around 200 billion parameters.

By comparison, Anthropic's previous Claude 3.5 Sonnet was estimated to be trained with between 175 and 400 billion parameters. While xAI's Grok started at 33 billion and Grok-1 increased to 314 billion (also with an MoE architecture), followed by newer, larger versions. Later parameter counts for the latest iterations haven't been disclosed publicly.

For CFOs, the key takeaway isn't the exact parameter count. It's what the number tends to correlate with in practice: larger and more carefully trained models generally produce more coherent and contextually accurate results.

Not all models behave the same, and the differences are important. Training data choices, parameterization, and training methods are proprietary and reflect different priorities, including different embedded rules that influence how a model responds to a prompt. All of the leading frontier models approach training differently. Some emphasize scale, others emphasize safety and governance, and still others focus on efficiency.

These models evolve quickly, with meaningful capability changes arriving in short cycles. Since ChatGPT's public release in late 2022, the major platforms have moved through multiple generations, improving accuracy, multimodal features, and reasoning along the way. That cadence is why CFOs evaluating AI tools should focus less on brand names and more on specifics: which model is in production, what data boundaries and training approaches apply, how updates are managed, and what governance and change-control processes support auditability and risk management.

Why Differences in LLMs Matter

- **Scale affects capability, cost, and exposure.** Larger models often produce more coherent output and handle complex prompts better, but they can carry higher compute costs and a bigger governance burden.
- **Architecture affects performance and efficiency.** Some systems use MoE designs that activate only parts of the model for a given task. That can improve efficiency even at large scales.
- **Multimodal capability changes the use cases.** Some models can handle more than text, including images and audio. That expands what they can do in finance workflows, even when raw parameter counts aren't directly comparable.
- **Deployment model drives control posture.** Open-weight models can be hosted privately, which can improve data control and compliance options. Proprietary models are typically vendor-hosted, which shifts more of the control surface to vendor practices and contractual terms.

Big Data: The Fuel Behind AI

If LLMs are the engine, then data is the fuel. Without massive, diverse datasets, AI can't learn meaningful patterns. Training a model like GPT-5 requires analyzing trillions of tokens drawn from just as countless sources. Similarly, in finance-specific applications, the model becomes valuable only when it can be combined with a corporation's internal data, including transaction histories, forecasts, contracts, and even unstructured documents such as securities filings, proxy statements, and environmental, social, and governance (ESG) disclosures.

The promise of AI in finance is rooted in the ability to process data at a scale and speed that humans can't match. ERP and EPM (enterprise performance management) systems already generate structured data, such as ledgers and journals. Increasingly, finance teams also rely on semi-structured and unstructured data: invoices, contracts, and third-party reports. AI thrives on these varied inputs, detecting patterns and producing insights across them.

The AI-ready CFO must be asking the key questions about data governance and efficiency. More data is not always better. Poor-quality data can produce misleading results, and storing and cleaning data carries costs. The use of proprietary big datasets may also raise compliance issues: privacy regulations, data residency, and confidentiality requirements all come into play.

Predictable Pitfalls

The main risks of AI in finance aren't mysterious. They are familiar control problems in a new form and can be managed with the right design choices.

Hallucinations

GenAI can produce statements that sound confident and polished but aren't correct. In finance workflows, the response is simple: train people on appropriate use, write prompts that force specificity, require review, and keep an evidence trail. AI can draft. Finance professionals still approve.

Why do hallucinations happen? LLMs generate text by predicting likely next tokens, not by verifying against your ledger or source systems. A vague prompt like "Explain Q2 margin variance" leaves room for generic filler. A structured prompt tied to real data, such as "Explain Q2 margin variance using transaction data from cost centers 2100 and 2200, and cite sources," reduces the chance of a made-up narrative.

Two additional issues show up in practice. First, many platforms allow shared "custom instructions" that set defaults across users. That can quietly steer tone and content in ways that don't fit finance narratives. Second, unless the model is connected to your ERP, EPM, or data warehouse, it's working from general patterns rather than your specific numbers. Grounding outputs in enterprise data is what makes the draft reviewable.

Data Leakage

"Data leakage" gets discussed in ways that create more fear than clarity. Most leading providers now offer controls that let organizations limit how customer content is used, including options to opt out of training use and tighten retention. The practical question for a CFO is less "Is AI safe?" and more "What configuration are we running, and what does the contract actually say?"

Start with the basics: deployment context matters. Consumer chat products and enterprise/application programming interface (API) deployments don't behave the same way. Enterprise offerings often include explicit commitments around business data handling and provide configurable retention controls, including shorter retention windows and, in some cases, zero data retention for eligible use cases.

Next, look at security posture, not marketing language. For most finance teams, that means verifying security compliance and controls you already recognize: SOC 2 Type II reporting, encryption in transit and at rest, access controls, audit logging, and key management options where available.

Then get specific about retention and memory tradeoffs. Tighter retention policies generally reduce exposure, but they can also reduce usefulness in some workflows because the system retains less conversational context and fewer durable artifacts. Teams can still get strong results under strict retention by grounding work in approved enterprise data sources and keeping important context in controlled systems of record, rather than relying on the model to "remember" it. (Google, for example, documents how zero data retention interacts with caching behavior and performance features in its managed AI stack.)

What remains are the risks you can actually manage:

- Logging and data residency details that vary by product tier and configuration (ask for retention windows, locations, and who has access).
- User behavior, especially pasting board decks, contracts, or sensitive operating data into tools that aren't approved for that content.
- Default sharing features (team history, cross-user access) that widen exposure if they aren't configured intentionally.
- Prompt injection (where a user crafts input designed to override an AI system's built-in instructions) and other social/technical attacks that try to extract information the system should withhold.

Ultimately, while data concerns are frequently cited as reasons companies don't adopt GenAI usage, the right posture isn't panic, but it's also not blind trust. It's the same approach finance already uses for any system that touches reporting or confidential data: define approved tools and tiers, set retention and training-use settings explicitly, validate security controls, and train users on what can and can't be pasted into a prompt.

Lack of Auditability

Finance runs on traceability. If an AI tool can't show why it produced an output, and if that output can't be tied back to underlying data, it doesn't belong in a financial reporting environment. CFOs should require audit trails, logging, and override capability.

LLM behavior makes this harder than traditional systems. Excel produces the same answer from the same formula. AI outputs can vary from run to run because generation involves probabilistic sampling. Without a "reproducibility pack" that captures the input, model version, parameters, and output, an auditor can't reconstruct how a narrative or recommendation was produced.

Fine-tuning adds another layer. Vendors often adapt models using proprietary data and methods. If that process isn't documented, the logic behind outputs becomes harder to defend. In agentic workflows, variability can compound because multiple steps are chained together. If each step isn't logged, the evidence trail expected by auditors and regulators breaks.

Chat, Copilots, and Agents: Cutting Through the Noise

Finance leaders are being presented with a growing number of AI tools marketed as "agents," "copilots," or "automation." The terms are often used interchangeably, but they describe different capabilities. Understanding these distinctions helps CFOs set realistic expectations, plan for their possible use, and evaluate vendor claims across both finance and the broader enterprise.

Agents vs. Chatbots

Many products labeled as "agents" today are in fact advanced chat interfaces. They can answer questions, retrieve information, or summarize reports, but they cannot operate independently. A true agent goes further: it can plan by breaking a task into steps, use applications to complete those steps, retain memory across sessions, and pursue a goal without constant human prompts.

- **Example (Chatbot).** Wells Fargo has tested GenAI systems that read and summarize analyst reports for finance teams, saving hours of manual review but requiring humans to act on the information.[3]
- **Example (Agent).** Early pilots at Deloitte have explored agents that reconcile accounts by connecting to ERP systems, flagging mismatches, preparing draft entries, and routing them to reviewers. These are closer to true agents because they combine planning, tool use, and workflow execution.[4]

The distinction is critical: if a product only converses, it is a chatbot. If it carries out a sequence of steps toward a goal, it begins to function as an agent.

Copilots as Decision Assistants

Most AI tools in use today fall into the category of copilots. These are embedded assistants that provide drafts, insights, or explanations but leave final decisions and approvals with the user. They amplify analyst and CFO productivity while preserving human control.

- **Example.** Microsoft Copilot for Finance, announced in 2024, generates variance explanations directly in Excel, reconciles data with SAP or Dynamics 365, and drafts customer collection summaries in Outlook. The tool reduces manual effort and shortens reporting cycles, but requires human sign-off, ensuring consistency with SOX controls.
- **Example.** JPMorgan Chase's internal Copilot-style tools draft scripts for earnings calls and prepare Q&A material for investor relations, but executives still review and approve final output.

Copilots are valuable because they combine efficiency with a clear human-in-the-loop model. For CFOs, they represent a low-risk entry point into AI adoption.

Autonomous Agents in Finance Workflows

Autonomous agents are still in the early stages of adoption. Some pilot programs show agents reconciling accounts or updating forecasts with limited oversight. These systems can deliver efficiency gains but also raise compliance and auditability challenges.

- **Example.** Experimental use of generative agents at PwC UK has been reported in areas such as tax workflow automation, where the system prepares filings and reconciles documentation before human review.[5]
- **Example.** At JPMorgan, research teams have tested agents that automate portions of payment processing and fraud detection, combining multiple AI steps into end-to-end workflows.

For now, most organizations rely on hybrid models. Agents perform much of the work but route results to humans for final approval. This maintains efficiency while preserving internal control. The key question here is one of control and regulatory compliance: how much autonomy is acceptable under SOX and internal control frameworks?

Any system that influences financial reporting has to produce outputs that are explainable, verifiable, and tied back to source data. If a tool can't meet that standard, it shouldn't run without human oversight and documented controls. (Chapter 8 covers SOX/ICFR and AI alignment in detail.)

A Practical Framework for CFOs

A simple way to evaluate AI tools is to group them by capability and control posture:

- **Chatbots.** Conversational interfaces that answer questions or summarize content. Useful for knowledge retrieval and synthesis, not for executing workflows.
- **Copilots.** Embedded assistants that draft, explain, and suggest. They can speed up variance narratives, reconciliations, and board reporting, but they still depend on human review and approval.
- **Agents.** Systems that can execute multi-step workflows across tools and data sources. They can support reconciliations, forecasting, and compliance work, but they raise the bar for auditability, logging, and control design.

This framing helps finance leaders ignore labels and focus on what the tool actually does, where it touches data, and what controls are required to use it responsibly across finance and the broader enterprise.

GenAI in Finance Workflows

With a working taxonomy in place, the next step is seeing how these tools actually perform in finance workflows. The examples that follow focus on GenAI, which has the broadest near-term applicability for CFOs and their teams. These aren't hypothetical use cases. They're drawn from real finance operations.

Practical Applications

As mentioned, GenAI is already showing up in finance work, whether it is formally rolled out or adopted informally by teams looking for leverage. Traditional automation is strongest when the work is structured and repetitive. GenAI helps where the bottleneck is language and synthesis: drafting narratives, summarizing results, and turning analysis into something executives can act on. Used well, it shortens reporting cycles, improves clarity, and frees up time for higher-value work.

Variance Analysis and Board Reporting Narratives. One of the most immediate uses is turning numbers into words. Every month, analysts spend hours explaining why actuals differ from budget or forecast, then packaging those explanations into slides and narratives for leadership. GenAI can produce a first draft in minutes.

For example, a GPT-based platform connected to the general ledger can answer, "What drove the variance in SG&A this quarter?" Instead of starting with a blank slide, the analyst gets a structured draft that highlights drivers, quantifies differences, and proposes a coherent narrative. The analyst still reviews for accuracy and context, but the time spent writing and formatting drops sharply.

Drafting Disclosures, Executive Summaries, and Investor Updates. Finance communication extends well beyond internal reporting. External stakeholders expect clear, consistent updates on a tight timeline. Annual and quarterly disclosures, investor letters, and executive summaries all require careful drafting and review. GenAI can speed up that drafting by producing text that follows established structures and reflects the underlying results.

For example, an AI model can review quarterly results, identify year-over-year changes in revenue and margin, and produce a draft shareholder update. Human review is still required for tone, accuracy, and compliance, but the time from close to communication compresses. The same approach applies internally: executive summaries for leadership meetings can be drafted quickly, and finance teams can generate scenario-based talking points for strategy sessions with less churn.

Accelerating Forecast Cycles and Scenario Planning. Forecasting is another area where GenAI adds value. ML models can produce projections, and GenAI can frame and explain them. Work that used to require days of spreadsheet consolidation can be refreshed and summarized much faster.

For instance, an FP&A team can run multiple scenarios adjusting pricing assumptions, headcount growth, or capital expenditures, then ask a copilot to generate concise summaries of the impact on revenue, margin, and cash flow. Instead of walking into a meeting with static decks, finance leaders can respond to "what if" questions with updated scenarios and clear narrative framing in the moment.

The "Inbox to Board Book" Model. GenAI can also tighten the delivery paths of outputs from ad-hoc requests to structured reporting. In a traditional cycle, executives ask for data, analysts chase inputs across systems, and eventually those inputs get assembled into a presentation. It's time-consuming, inconsistent, and easy to bog down.

With GenAI, inputs from ERP, CRM, HR, and external feeds can be ingested and summarized automatically. Draft management reports or board decks can be produced in hours rather than weeks. Finance then focuses on review: validating the numbers, adding context, and tightening the story. The payoff is speed and consistency, with a process that's more repeatable and verifiable than a patchwork of manual requests.

Case Examples

The following case examples show how companies are putting GenAI to work inside their finance functions. Each illustrates a different entry point, from narrative automation to procurement to compliance, and the results they're producing.

eBay: Automating Narratives, Reconciliation, and Reporting

At eBay, CFO Brian Priest has overseen a push to embed GenAI across the finance function, treating it as more than an experimental tool.[6] AI is being used to generate product descriptions automatically from images, saving sellers time while ensuring consistency across listings, but its impact goes deeper into the finance office. GenAI now assists with financial reconciliations, combs through lengthy contracts to extract and summarize key terms, and improves procurement workflows. It also plays a role in simplifying tax compliance and sustainability reporting, two areas where the volume and complexity of required documentation can otherwise be overwhelming. For eBay, these applications show how GenAI can serve as a productivity multiplier, freeing staff from routine work while strengthening internal controls and accuracy in reporting.

JPMorgan Chase: GenAI at Enterprise Scale

JPMorgan Chase offers a view of what AI looks like when deployed at the largest scale.[7] As part of its $18 billion technology investment in 2025, the bank introduced an internal GenAI platform to support more than 200,000 employees worldwide. The system underpins the development of roughly 100 AI-powered tools, many of which touch directly on the finance function. GenAI now helps draft scripts for earnings calls, prepare Q&A materials for investor relations, and streamline client onboarding processes. It also extends into portfolio optimization, payments, and fraud detection. By centralizing AI development and pushing it across both back-office finance and customer-facing workflows, JPMorgan is demonstrating how GenAI can simultaneously enhance decision-making, accelerate reporting, and eliminate thousands of hours of low-value manual effort.

Microsoft's AI Push in Finance—Real-World Use and Strategic Vision

Microsoft's finance organization has become a key testing ground for the company's own GenAI tools.[8] As Cory Hrncirik, Microsoft's Modern

Finance Leader, shared with CFO Dive, finance professionals quickly became some of the top adopters of Copilot internally. Through the tool, routine tasks like data reconciliation—once requiring 1–2 hours per week—were reduced to just 10 minutes on average. In the treasury and financial services teams, accounts receivable reconciliation across multiple data sources saved approximately 20 minutes per account. In addition, pilot use of natural-language variance analysis in Excel offered faster, actionable insights compared to manual methods.

These developments are consistent with Microsoft's broader strategy, outlined in its February 2024 public preview announcement of Copilot for Finance. The tool is embedded into Microsoft 365 apps, including Excel, Outlook, and Teams, and connects to ERP systems like Dynamics 365 and SAP, as well as Microsoft Graph. Designed specifically to ease the burden of repetitive financial tasks, Copilot for Finance enables users to:

- Run variance analysis and reconciliation through natural-language prompts within Excel.
- Get comprehensive summaries of customer account details in Outlook.
- Convert raw data into polished visuals and reports for Teams and presentations.

Microsoft positions Copilot for Finance as a bridge between transactional grunt work and strategic value creation, helping finance teams "reclaim time" that would otherwise be spent on data entry and review. Pilot users, including internal teams, confirmed tangible returns in hours saved and efficiency gains.

Together, these insights provide both the promise and the proof. Microsoft is not only describing how AI could streamline finance, but actively proving it works within its own finance operations.

Practical Boundaries

GenAI is useful, and it has limits. Outputs still need to be verified against source data, and anything that touches disclosures or investor communication needs careful review for accuracy and compliance. The safest posture is to treat GenAI as a drafting layer, with finance owning review and approval. That means workflows where AI produces a first pass, humans validate and edit, and the final output is logged in a way that supports auditability.

The value shows up as cycle compression. Work that used to take weeks can often be produced in days, sometimes hours, without lowering the standard of review. There are additional constraints beyond accuracy.

GenAI doesn't "understand" your business in the way a finance team does. It generates language based on patterns, which can produce shallow or misleading narratives unless the output is grounded in enterprise systems and supporting evidence. It's also harder to explain than a spreadsheet model. With Excel, you can trace a formula cell by cell. With an AI-generated narrative, you need logging, inputs, and a clear record of what data was used and what assumptions were applied.

Cost is another boundary. Large models aren't free, and expenses can climb quickly if they're used indiscriminately. ROI tracking should sit alongside risk management, especially when usage scales across the organization.

Bias belongs on the list as well. Models reflect patterns in their training data and can introduce unintended skew in narratives, investor messaging, or ESG reporting.

AI adoption is also a people issue. If teams don't trust the outputs or don't understand how to review them, the time savings won't materialize.

Finally, the regulatory environment will keep evolving. Requirements around privacy, transparency, and disclosure can change, and controls that look adequate today may need to be tightened later.

These boundaries are financial, ethical, organizational, and regulatory. GenAI can accelerate reporting and analysis, but it needs governance, oversight, and clear limits.

Why This Changes Finance Work

The goal of AI in finance shouldn't be headcount replacement. Think capacity and quality. When AI can draft variance explanations, summarize scenario outputs, or produce a first-pass board update in minutes, analysts spend less time assembling and more time interpreting. CFOs get more cycles for judgment, including earlier risk detection, more scenario testing, and clearer communication to executives and boards.

Over time, that changes what finance is able to deliver. The function becomes less periodic and more continuous, with decision support happening between formal reporting cycles. Finance spends less time on manual preparation and more time on review, interpretation, and leadership.

GenAI isn't just a productivity add-on in finance. It changes how work gets produced and reviewed. CFOs who adopt it with discipline can run a tighter operation and support faster, clearer decision-making across the business.

An AI-Readiness Checklist for CFOs

Before beginning formal AI adoption, CFOs should evaluate readiness across eight dimensions: Data, People, Technology, Strategy, Change Management, Cost Discipline, Regulatory Awareness, and Vendor Transparency. The answers may not always be binary yes or no, but the process of asking the questions reveals whether conditions are favorable or whether more groundwork is required.

1. **Data foundation**
   - Is our financial and operational data clean, structured, and consistently formatted?
   - Are historical records complete enough to train or benchmark models?
   - Can we access the data easily, without relying on disconnected or manual systems?
   - Do we trust how third-party tools handle our data, including storage, privacy, and audit trails?
2. **People and skills**
   - Do finance professionals have at least basic AI literacy and training in prompt design?
   - Do we have a plan to upskill analysts and managers so AI becomes an embedded tool, not a novelty?
   - Is the team already stretched thin, and if so, have we built in capacity for adoption and experimentation?
   - Do we have internal champions who can run pilots and advocate for adoption?

3. **Technology and approach**
   - Is our ERP, EPM, and BI stack cloud-ready and capable of integrating with AI tools?
   - Have we decided whether to build in-house, buy off-the-shelf, or partner with vendors?
   - Do we have a safe pilot environment where tools can be tested without disrupting production systems?
   - Have we defined upfront how we will measure success (accuracy, time saved, cycle compression)?

4. **Strategic alignment and control**
   - Could this workflow be automated instead of hiring for it, and is there a clear ROI case?
   - Is the workflow stable and documented, or would AI simply accelerate existing disorder?
   - What is the cost of being wrong in this workflow? Is it minor and recoverable, or high-stakes and material?
   - Will the tool scale as our transaction volume or geographic footprint expands?
   - Who else depends on this process, and have we aligned expectations across the organization?
   - Can we explain in plain language how the system produces outputs, to auditors, boards, and regulators?
   - Do we have audit trails so outputs are explainable, verifiable, and tied back to source data?

5. **Change-management readiness**
   - Is our culture open to adopting AI, or is there fear and resistance among staff?
   - Do we have a communication plan to show employees how AI augments, not replaces, their work?
   - Have we identified training needs for different roles (analyst vs. manager vs. executive)?
   - Are incentives aligned so adoption improves career growth, not threatens it?

6. **Cost discipline**
   - Do we understand the compute and licensing costs associated with large models?

- Have we built a business case that ties spend directly to measurable outcomes?
- Do we have a threshold where, if ROI is not achieved, we pause or stop the project?
- Are we balancing the costs of pilots against other transformation priorities?

7. **Regulatory awareness**
   - Are we aware of emerging frameworks like the European Union's AI Act and SEC disclosure expectations?
   - Do we understand how AI adoption intersects with SOX/ICFR controls?
   - Have we documented policies for data retention, explainability, and human oversight in line with governance requirements?
   - Are we monitoring regulatory developments so today's adoption won't become tomorrow's compliance problem?
8. **Vendor transparency**
   - Do we know which underlying model powers the tool (GPT, Claude, Gemini, DeepSeek, etc.)?
   - Has the vendor disclosed what data the model was trained on and how it is updated?
   - Do we have visibility into the vendor's roadmap for governance, compliance, and reliability?
   - Does the vendor provide documentation, reproducibility packs, and audit logs for enterprise assurance?

Suggested Use of This Checklist

The checklist should not be treated as a box-ticking exercise. Use it to structure the conversation with senior management. Many CFOs find it helpful to score each question on a scale from 1 to 5. Summing the scores provides a readiness index that can be compared across projects. This makes it easier to prioritize initiatives and justify decisions.

- **Scoring.** Rate each question on a 1–5 scale (1 = not ready, 5 = fully ready).

- **Thresholds**
  - Scores below 3 in Data, Strategy, or Regulatory Awareness = not ready.
  - Scores below 3 in Change Management or People = high risk of failed adoption.
- **Output.** Build a readiness profile across the eight dimensions. This not only prioritizes projects but also creates a clear narrative for the board, CEO, and regulators about the finance function's maturity for AI adoption.

Notes

1. Michael Bayer (CFO) and Marcos Bento (FP&A Lead Analyst) (Wasabi Technologies), interviewed by Glenn Hopper, *Google Meet*, December 17, 2025.
2. Ibid.
3. Deloitte, "Autonomous Generative AI Agents Are Coming: 4 Ways to Prepare," *The Wall Street Journal*, May 29, 2025, https://deloitte.wsj.com/sustainable-business/autonomous-generative-ai-agents-are-coming-4-ways-to-prepare-c8aaf9cd
4. Rebecca Ungarino, "AI Will Affect Nearly 'Every Part' of Wells Fargo, CFO Says," *Barron's*, February 11, 2025, https://www.barrons.com/articles/wells-fargo-ai-banking-a6f84c15
5. Adam Zaki, "How PwC's Tax Team is using Agentic AI," *CFO*, June 6, 2025, https://www.cfo.com/news/how-pwcs-dom-megna-tax-team-is-using-agentic-ai-agent-os-cpa-cfo-/750062/
6. Laura Bauke and Craig Schneider, "EBay's CFO on Transforming Ecommerce with AI," *The Australian*, April 29, 2025, https://www.theaustralian.com.au/business/cfo-journal/ebays-cfo-on-transforming-ecommerce-with-ai/news-story/09b9ae5abdfda192f5694271ee5ff25b
7. Michelle Abrego, "AI is Core to JPMorgan's $18 Billion Tech Investment. Here's What its Execs Revealed about how it's Reshaping the Bank," *Business Insider*, May 24, 2025, https://www.businessinsider.com/jpmorgan-how-artificial-intelligence-transforming-workflows-efficiencies-2025-5
8. Alexei Alexis, "Inside Microsoft Finance Team's AI-driven Cost, Time Savings," *CFO Dive*, June 17, 2025, https://www.cfodive.com/news/inside-microsoft-finance-teams-ai-driven-cost-time-savings/750912/

Further Reading

1. **Hallucinations**
   - TechLife Future (May 2025)—*AI Hallucinations in Finance: Avoiding False Forecasts*. Documents how nearly 70% of AI-generated financial predictions

contained inaccuracies, demonstrating the risks of hallucination leading to false trading signals and poor decision-making (techlifefuture.com).

- BayTech Consulting—*Hidden Dangers of AI Hallucinations in Financial Services*. Explores how LLMs may invent plausible—but false—financial details like fabricated regulatory references or market data; outlines mitigations like fine-tuning and retrieval-augmented generation (RAG) (Baytech Consulting).
- Lucidworks—*Is Your AI Hallucinating? The Hidden Risks for Financial Services*. Explores how hallucinations impact trust in finance and offers approaches for accuracy and reliability (Lucidworks).
- Business Tech Magazine (Aug 2025)—*LLM Hallucinations: What Are the Implications for Financial Institutions*. Highlights the risk of hallucinated outputs in banking and compliance, using real deployments such as Google's AI tools as examples (tst.biztechmagazine.com).
- Maxim.ai—*The State of AI Hallucinations in 2025: Challenges, Solutions*. Reviews how hallucinations can erode trust, cause operational disruptions, and suggests mitigation tactics for regulated industries (Maxim AI).

2. **Prompt injection and data leakage**
   - Pangea Research Report (2025)—*Defending Against Prompt Injection*. Provides enterprise-relevant guidance, including real-world prompt injection techniques and best practices for securing AI applications against manipulation (Pangea).
   - OWASP LLM Article (2025)—*Prompt Injection—OWASP Gen AI Security Project*. Defines prompt injection vulnerabilities, including direct and indirect types, and ranks them among the top LLM security risks (OWASP Gen AI Security Project).
   - TechRadar (July 2025)—*Four-Phase Security Approach to AI Transformation*. Recommends a structured security model—covering assessment, policy, technical controls, and training—to guard against data leakage and prompt injection (TechRadar).
   - OpenAI's Defense Toolkit (Mar 2025)—*Preventing Prompt Injection in Agents*. Details tools and layers designed by OpenAI to defend against prompt injection (Markaicode).
   - ArXiv Paper (Feb 2025)—*RTBAS: Defending LLM Agents Against Prompt Injection and Privacy Leakage*. Academic work proposing system-level defenses for agent-based LLMs to preserve confidentiality and reduce injection risk (arXiv).
3. **Auditability and model risk**
   - ArXiv Paper (Mar 2025)—*Model Risk Management for Generative AI in Financial Institutions*. Examines risks like hallucinations and toxicity, and argues for enhanced model validation standards in regulated finance (arXiv).
   - Maxim.ai (May 2025)—*Evaluating AI for Finance: Is AI Credible at Assessing Investment Risk?* Compares multiple AI models in assessing investment risk,

finding considerable variance and highlighting the need for robust testing (arXiv).

4. **Multimodal and emerging risks**
    - Wall Street Journal (July 2025)—*AI Has a Safety Problem. This Is How to Manage It.* Describes a case where xAI's Grok model produced extreme content due to indirect prompt injection; recommends layered controls and prompt trust hierarchies (The Wall Street Journal).

Finance-Related AI Tools Mentioned in the Chapter

- Microsoft Copilot, https://www.microsoft.com/en-us/microsoft-copilot/organizations
- SAP ERP AI, https://www.sap.com/products/artificial-intelligence.html
- Oracle ERP AI, https://www.oracle.com/applications/fusion-ai/
- FIS Treasury AI, https://www.fisglobal.com/products/neural-treasury

Chapter 3

Modeling ROI: Payback, IRR, and Strategic Value

Key Takeaways

- **Traditional ROI models assume predictable inputs and stable outputs. AI breaks that pattern.**
  - Results vary with data quality, adoption rates, and market conditions, even after deployment.
  - Vendor claims are often marketing noise, so CFOs should validate benefits with counterfactual pilots.
  - The modeling lens has to move from "will it work?" to "what's the probability it works, when value will arrive, and how long it will last?"
- **AI returns are twofold: tangible and strategic, and CFOs need to measure both.**
  - Tangible ROI pays for the investment.

- Strategic ROI is what keeps paying back, and keeps paying back faster.
- **Tangible ROI is the quantifiable financial gain that shows up in the P&L or cash flow.**
  - Cost savings and avoidance (labor efficiency, fewer errors, cycle-time compression, reduced external spend).
  - Revenue and margin gains (pricing optimization, sales conversion lift, improved forecast-driven inventory control).
- **Strategic ROI is what makes those gains durable and compounding.**
  - Faster decision cycles.
  - Improved forecast accuracy that lowers risk premiums.
  - Knowledge capture and institutional memory.
  - Workforce leverage and talent uplift.
  - Reusable data pipelines and governance that cut the cost of future projects.
- **Strategic ROI compounds over time.**
  - This flywheel makes finance a growth engine, not just a cost center.
  - Strategic ROI doesn't show up as standalone dollars, but it raises the success rate and yield of future AI projects:
    - Capacity gains free analysts for higher-value work →
    - More capacity produces better insights →
    - Better insights accelerate decisions →
    - Faster decisions unlock earlier and larger value realization.

Framing ROI for AI Initiatives

ROI analysis is the bedrock of capital-allocation decision-making in the CFO's office. Whether evaluating a new plant, a software system, or a cost-reduction program, ROI calculations model expected costs and benefits, discount future cash flows, and compare opportunities on a relative basis. Given a few characteristics of the current state of AI, these investments demand additional scrutiny.

Traditional ROI models assume predictable inputs, stable processes, and well-understood outcomes. AI initiatives introduce uncertainty in adoption timing, output quality, and value realization. To evaluate these projects responsibly, CFOs need to go beyond expected returns and assess the timing, probability, and durability of those returns. In AI-enabled projects, ROI involves more than a calculation of predicted profit, costs, or savings. It becomes a structured judgment about where AI can deliver repeatable impact, and how much risk the organization is willing to take to capture that value. To get to the heart of ROI analysis, there are three challenges the AI-ready CFO needs to address: signal vs. noise, speed of change, and the cost of being wrong.

Signal vs. Noise

The AI market is crowded with ambitious claims. Even experienced finance leaders can struggle to separate measurable value from marketing noise. Projections of productivity gains or cost savings are often built on hypothetical assumptions or produced in controlled settings rather than verified operational data. CFOs should treat external ROI claims as unproven until validated in their own context.

That validation starts with a disciplined counterfactual baseline. The first question is simple: What would have happened if the initiative weren't implemented? Instead of relying on pre- and post-AI comparisons, which can be confounded by process redesign, data cleanup, or staffing changes, finance teams should run structured pilots or use stepped-wedge rollouts to isolate the incremental effect of AI.

Beyond isolating impact, CFOs should model portfolio dynamics rather than assume certainty for each initiative. Most organizations fund a slate of use cases where only a portion hit their projected benefits. Building success probabilities into financial models produces more realistic expected-value calculations and helps boards see why diversifying AI bets is rational rather than wasteful. This approach treats AI more like R&D, where selective failure is part of the operating model, rather than standard IT projects that usually start with an assumption of success.

Speed of Change

The second challenge is the speed of change. AI capabilities are evolving far faster than most enterprise technologies, which creates hidden risks in traditional ROI modeling. Tools that look market-leading at the start of a business case may be outperformed or commoditized before they reach scale deployment. Static ROI assumptions ignore this erosion risk and can inflate IRR calculations by projecting full benefit streams over too long a horizon. That creates both opportunity and risk. Opportunity, because fast-moving tools can deliver competitive advantage to early adopters. Risk, because sunk investments in unproven platforms can outpace their useful life.

To address this, CFOs should model time-to-value explicitly using adoption S-curves rather than linear ramps. Early-stage initiatives typically realize little value until data pipelines, skills, and process changes mature. Benefits then accelerate once adoption crosses a threshold. Shifting benefit cash flows to the right lets finance leaders stress-test how delays affect payback and IRR.

Applying benefit decay curves to account for model drift or obsolescence is equally important. If monitoring and retraining aren't funded, model accuracy will degrade as data distributions change, and projected gains will erode. Discounting future benefits, unless lifecycle management costs are built into the case, aligns ROI models with how value behaves in fast-moving AI environments.

The Cost of Being Wrong

AI projects carry asymmetric risk. A successful initiative can create compounding productivity gains, but a failed one can undermine financial integrity, internal controls, and stakeholder trust. Traditional ROI frameworks capture implementation cost and expected savings, but they rarely quantify downside exposure when outputs are wrong or controls don't hold.

CFOs should explicitly model the cost of being wrong. That means estimating potential remediation costs, reputational damage, and audit exposure if AI-generated outputs are incorrect or misused. This analysis should also account for opportunity cost: What other investments get crowded out by AI spend? A project with a nominally strong IRR can still destroy value if its risk-adjusted return is lower than alternatives like working capital reduction, core systems modernization, or accretive M&A.

Some AI initiatives, especially those focused on data infrastructure or workflow automation, also create real options. They build reusable capabilities that reduce the cost and risk of future use cases. CFOs can reflect that optionality by assigning a notional value to the strategic flexibility these investments create. Framing these initiatives as option-generating assets clarifies that their value isn't limited to near-term cost savings, it also comes from making future deployments faster and cheaper.

Altogether, a risk-adjusted view pushes AI ROI modeling beyond binary success/failure thinking. It asks, "what if this works?" "what if it doesn't?" and whether the upside justifies the capital at stake. The CFO's job is to apply the same rigor we bring to any capital investment, while adapting our models to the realities of emerging technology. The framing question, then, is not "Can this AI tool generate value?" but "Can it generate value in this workflow, with our data, and within our risk tolerance?"

The three challenges, signal vs. noise, speed of change, and cost of being wrong, set the foundation for a more nuanced and defensible approach to ROI in AI adoption. They remind CFOs that AI is a high-uncertainty, fast-moving category where the timing, probability, and durability of returns matter as much as the returns themselves. This mindset prepares the ground for evaluating hard and soft ROI in the sections that follow, where we'll introduce modeling templates and build a framework for measuring the cost of being wrong. Together, these tools equip CFOs to move past vendor promises and hype cycles, and toward disciplined decisions that balance financial return with operational safety.

Quantifying Tangible and Strategic ROI

Most new technology initiatives are treated as infrastructure projects: deterministic undertakings that either succeed or fail, and whose business cases rest almost entirely on cost avoidance or efficiency gains. AI doesn't behave this way. AI initiatives challenge how finance teams measure ROI. Outcomes remain probabilistic even after deployment because performance varies with data quality, user adoption, and changing business conditions.

This distinction shows up in the numbers. A deterministic ERP system (once implemented correctly) delivers a stable and predictable set of benefits. By contrast, an AI forecasting model might drive a 30% accuracy gain in one business unit and only 5% in another, or it may degrade over time as market dynamics change. AI ROI can't be modeled as a fixed payoff. It has to be treated as a range of probability-weighted outcomes. That makes AI investments closer to an innovation portfolio than an IT project: several use cases may stall or deliver modest gains, while a few outperform and generate returns large enough to cover the rest.

To build credible business cases, CFOs need to measure two complementary categories of value: tangible ROI and strategic ROI. Tangible ROI includes outcomes that can be quantified in financial statements within current operating models, such as direct cost reductions, avoided expenses, capacity savings, and incremental revenue or profit contribution. These benefits can be expressed in cash terms and built into capital models, but they should be probability-weighted rather than treated as guaranteed.

Strategic ROI captures broader effects that are harder to isolate immediately but compound over time: faster decision cycles, improved forecast accuracy, reduced operational risk, and reusable capabilities such as data pipelines, prompt libraries, and automation frameworks. These benefits may not land neatly in a quarterly forecast, but they expand the finance function's capacity to generate value and position the organization for future growth.

This dual lens, both tangible and strategic, enables CFOs to present AI investments as structured portfolios designed to create efficiency and profit, strengthen decision-making, and build durable capabilities.

Tangible ROI: Dollars Saved, Costs Avoided, and Revenue or Profits Generated

Tangible ROI represents the category of AI benefits that can be expressed in direct financial terms within current operating models. These are the results that flow into the P&L or cash-flow statements and can be measured against a defined baseline.

Most finance leaders focus first on cost-side benefits: automation-driven labor savings, reduced rework, cycle-time compression, and avoided vendor or system costs. These remain important. But AI can also create material impact on the revenue and margin side, and excluding those effects produces an incomplete and understated business case. Tangible ROI therefore has two components.

Cost Savings and Cost Avoidance

- Lower headcount requirements through automation and efficiency gains.

- Reduced error correction and rework costs.
- Shorter close, reconciliation, and forecast cycles that free analyst capacity for other value-creating work.
- Avoided software licensing or outsourcing expenses when AI replaces external providers.

Incremental Revenue and Profit Contribution

- Increased sales conversion or pricing precision through AI-driven customer insights.
- Higher customer retention and lifetime value from personalized outreach or churn prediction.
- Better inventory and demand forecasting that prevents stockouts and revenue loss.
- Margin expansion from more accurate cost allocations or dynamic pricing models.

Unlike deterministic IT projects, these outcomes shouldn't be modeled as guaranteed. CFOs should treat them as probability-weighted cash flows, especially on the revenue side where uncertainty is highest. That means multiplying each benefit by:

- adoption rate assumptions (e.g., 30% of eligible users by Year 1, 60% by Year 2),
- performance uplift ranges (e.g., forecast accuracy improves 5–15%), and
- gross margin conversion (translating revenue gains into contribution margin rather than top-line dollars).

For example, if an AI pricing engine is projected to increase realized prices by 2% across a $500 million revenue line, and gross margin is 40%, the model shouldn't carry $10 million in new revenue. It should carry $4 million in contribution, weighted by the probability of achieving the 2% lift and by the share of business units expected to adopt it.

This probability-weighted approach recognizes that AI outcomes vary by design and avoids overcommitting to best-case scenarios that erode credibility. It also puts cost-side and revenue-side benefits on the same analytical footing, which is essential for boards and investors who expect to see full P&L impact rather than isolated cost savings.

Tangible ROI, then, isn't a list of savings. It's a disciplined estimate of the expected-value contribution AI can make to the company's financial statements, both by lowering costs and by accelerating profitable growth.

Cost Savings and Cost Avoidance

Cost savings and cost avoidance remain core elements of tangible ROI for AI initiatives. Unlike traditional IT deployments, these gains don't show up automatically. You only capture them if teams adopt the tools, the data supports automation, and legacy steps are actually retired instead of running in parallel. The three general cost-side opportunities are as follows.

Labor Efficiency and Capacity Reallocation. AI tools can automate transactional tasks like invoice matching, journal-entry preparation, reconciliations, and variance commentary. The value isn't just headcount reduction. It's also the ability to redirect analyst hours to higher-value work.

How to Model It

1. Start with the fully loaded cost per FTE (salary + benefits + overhead).
2. Estimate the share of tasks that can be automated (e.g., 40% of AP workload) and the adoption ramp (e.g., 30% Year 1, 60% Year 2, 80% Year 3).
3. Convert hours saved into equivalent FTEs, but only count realized cost avoidance (e.g., not backfilling attrition, reducing overtime, eliminating temp support), not theoretical time savings.
4. Apply a probability factor for operational readiness (e.g., 70% if process standardization is weak).

Example. If five analysts spend 40% of their time on reconciliations at an average fully loaded cost of $120,000, that's $240,000 of addressable cost. With 70% probability of success and 60% adoption in Year 2, expected savings = $240,000 × 0.6 × 0.7 = $100,800.

Error Reduction and Rework Avoidance. AI-driven validation and anomaly detection can reduce errors that trigger manual investigation and correction, especially in high-volume processes like accounts payable or expense reporting.

How to Model It

- Use historical error rates (e.g., 2% of invoices require rework) and the average rework cost (time × hourly cost of staff involved).
- Estimate the expected error reduction from AI (based on pilot data or vendor benchmarks).
- Multiply the reduction by current rework spend and apply a probability factor for data quality and the control environment.

Example. If the finance team processes 50,000 invoices per year with a 2% error rate (1,000 errors), and each error costs $150 to resolve, that's $150,000 in rework cost. If AI is expected to cut errors by 50% with 80% probability of success, expected savings = $150,000 × 0.5 × 0.8 = $60,000 annually.

Cycle-Time Compression and Process Decommissioning. AI can shorten close and forecast cycles by automating data gathering and reconciliation, which can reduce temporary staffing and overtime and help the team finish earlier. It can also support full decommissioning of legacy manual steps or external vendor support.

How to Model It

- Quantify temporary labor or overtime spend tied to peak cycles.
- Identify which steps can be eliminated entirely, not just accelerated.
- Apply an adoption ramp and probability factor for user trust and data readiness.
- Avoid double-counting benefits that only move timing with no associated cost reduction.

Example. If financial close currently requires 600 hours of overtime at $90/hour, that's $54,000 in cost. If AI-enabled automation could eliminate 75% of that overtime with 60% adoption and 70% success probability, expected savings = $54,000 × 0.75 × 0.6 × 0.7 = $17,010.

Examples in Specific Finance Workflows

Beyond the company-level case studies above, it's useful to look at where AI creates value within specific finance workflows. The examples below break down how AI applies to individual processes, along with guidance on how to model the impact.

Accounts Payable Automation. AI-powered invoice capture and three-way matching can reduce manual entry and validation time.

How to Model It

- Start with invoice volume, time per invoice, and fully loaded labor cost.
- Estimate the percentage reduction in processing time, expected adoption ramp, and probability of successful implementation.
- Only count realized cost avoidance (e.g., avoided attrition backfill, temp labor, overtime), not theoretical time savings.

Example. A mid-market company processes 20,000 invoices per year, spending an average of 9 minutes per invoice. At $35 per labor hour, total labor cost is 20,000 × 0.15 hours × $35 = $105,000. If AI is expected to cut time by 70%, with 60% adoption in Year 2 and 80% probability of success, expected savings = $105,000 × 0.70 × 0.60 × 0.80 = $35,280 in Year 2. If headcount isn't reduced, frame this as redeployable analyst capacity rather than booking it as direct cost savings.

Audit Preparation and External Audit Fees. Automating reconciliations, policy checks, and evidence packaging can reduce external auditor billable hours.

How to Model It

- Start with annual audit fees and the portion tied to hourly billing (exclude fixed fees).
- Estimate the percentage reduction achievable and apply a readiness probability for data quality and controls.

Example. If a company spends $500,000 annually on audit fees, of which 60% is hourly ($300,000), and automation can cut those hours by 15% with 70% probability of success, expected savings = $300,000 × 0.15 × 0.70 = $31,500 annually. This can be booked as a direct cost reduction in the ROI model if the auditor scope and billing arrangements can be formally revised.

Forecasting and Planning-Cycle Compression. AI-driven data integration and forecast-model generation can shorten planning cycles by reducing manual data gathering and spreadsheet reconciliation.

How to Model It

- Calculate total hours spent per cycle × cycles per year × fully loaded cost per hour.
- Estimate percentage time reduction, adoption ramp, and probability of success.
- Classify savings as capacity gains unless headcount reductions are planned.

Example. A finance team spends 2,000 hours per quarter (8,000 annually) on forecasting at $65 per labor hour: 8,000 × $65 = $520,000. If AI tools cut this by 40%, with 50% adoption in Year 1, 75% in Year 2, and 70% probability of success, the Year 2 expected capacity savings = $520,000 × 0.40 × 0.75 × 0.70 = $109,200. Unless positions are eliminated or backfills are avoided, this value should be framed as redeployable capacity supporting higher-value analysis, rather than booked cost reduction.

Revenue/Profit-Contribution Examples

While cost savings are the most common starting point, AI can also drive measurable gains on the revenue side. The examples below show how AI contributes to pricing, demand planning, and other top-line functions where even small improvements translate into significant profit impact.

AI-Driven Pricing Optimization. AI models can analyze historical transactions, competitive benchmarks, and demand elasticity to recommend more precise pricing. Even small improvements in realized price can translate into large profit gains.

How to Model It

- Identify the revenue base affected (e.g., product line or segment).
- Estimate the expected price uplift (%) and apply it to revenue.
- Convert to contribution margin using the product line's gross margin (%).
- Weight the uplift by adoption ramp and probability of success.

Example. A $500 million product line has 40% gross margin. If AI pricing is expected to increase realized price by 2%: $500,000,000 × 0.02 =

$10,000,000 revenue gain. Convert to contribution margin: $10,000,000 × 0.40 = $4,000,000. With 50% adoption in Year 2 and a 60% probability of success, the expected Year 2 profit contribution is $4,000,000 × 0.50 × 0.60 = $1,200,000.

AI-Assisted Sales Conversion. GenAI tools can score leads, recommend next-best actions, and draft personalized outreach that boosts conversion rates without increasing sales headcount.

How to Model It

- Establish baseline leads, conversion rate, average deal size, and gross margin (%).
- Estimate the uplift in conversion and apply it to incremental deals.
- Convert to contribution margin, then weight by adoption and success probability.

Example. A sales team handles 10,000 leads annually with a 15% conversion rate and an average $20,000 deal at 50% gross margin. Baseline revenue: 10,000 × 0.15 × $20,000 = $30,000,000. If AI tools improve conversion by 3 points (to 18%): 10,000 × 0.18 × $20,000 = $36,000,000. Incremental revenue = $6,000,000. Contribution at 50% margin = $3,000,000. With a 40% adoption rate and a 70% probability of success, the expected Year 1 profit contribution is $3,000,000 × 0.40 × 0.70 = $840,000.

AI-Enhanced Demand Forecasting. ML models can improve forecast accuracy, reducing stockouts and lost sales while optimizing inventory levels.

How to Model It

- Estimate current lost sales (or back orders) from forecast error rates.
- Model the expected reduction in error and translate it into recovered revenue.
- Convert to contribution margin, then apply adoption and success probability.

Example. A retailer has $300 million in annual sales and estimates 5% lost sales from stockouts tied to forecast error ($15 million). If AI improves forecast accuracy enough to cut lost sales by 30%, the recovered revenue would be $15,000,000 × 0.30 = $4,500,000. With 35% gross margin: $4,500,000 × 0.35 = $1,575,000 profit contribution. With 50% adoption in Year 2 and 60% probability of success: $1,575,000 × 0.50 × 0.60 = $472,500 expected Year 2 profit contribution.

Why This Modeling Matters

Treating cost savings, cost avoidance, and revenue or profit as probability-weighted cash flows prevents overstated business cases built on 100% best-case assumptions and allows CFOs to integrate cost and revenue levers into one risk-adjusted capital model. Tangible ROI is not about listing theoretical efficiencies; it is about quantifying real, achievable financial impact with the same discipline applied to any other investment proposal competing for capital.

> It's not about modeling ROI perfectly at the start. Start small, show value, gain trust, and scale. The numbers will come.[1]
>
> —*Michael Bayer, Wasabi*

Strategic ROI: Building the Capacity to Realize Value

Tangible ROI shows up in the financial statements. Strategic ROI shows up in the finance function's ability to produce value at all. It may not appear as a clean dollar line in a quarterly forecast, but it will determine whether AI becomes a compounding advantage or stalls as an unrealized IT investment.

Strategic ROI represents the capabilities and operating changes created by AI adoption that increase value capture, improve resilience, and reduce execution risk. These returns show up indirectly through faster decision cycles, better forecasts, institutionalized knowledge, more leverage from the same talent base, and infrastructure that lowers the lift for future initiatives. Because strategic ROI doesn't produce discrete cash inflows, it is typically modeled as multipliers and risk adjustments. It raises the expected yield and/or reduces the volatility of future projects, which improves portfolio IRR and can reduce the risk premium applied to cash flows. There are five primary sources of strategic ROI, framed for integration into financial models.

Decision-Cycle Compression

AI can shrink the time from data analysis to decision. Tools that automate reconciliation, draft variance commentary, and refresh forecasts continuously can move decisions from a monthly cadence to weekly, or even daily. That compression saves time, but it also increases the number of decision cycles per year, which speeds value capture and reduces the time between a miss and a correction.

Where it fits in the model: Treat this as a velocity multiplier on tangible ROI. Faster cycles pull benefits forward and reduce time-to-cash, which can improve IRR even if total benefit size stays constant. Represent this by shifting benefit cash flows forward on the adoption curve and rerunning IRR/NPV.

Forecast Accuracy and Risk Anticipation

ML models can integrate hundreds of variables, detect non-linear patterns, and update forecasts as conditions change. This reduces forecast error and surfaces leading risk signals earlier. Better forecasts don't just reduce misses. They have the potential to reduce the risk premium applied to cash flows by lowering underlying business risk. When guidance is more reliable, executives can commit capital faster, and external stakeholders can apply less punitive discounting to future cash flows.

Where it fits in the model: Treat forecast accuracy as a risk adjustment on cash flows. Lower forecast error reduces return volatility, which can justify a lower discount rate (WACC) and increase NPV across initiatives.

Knowledge Capture and Organizational Memory

AI copilots can capture rationale, commentary, and decisions as work is performed, building a durable knowledge base out of what used to be siloed. This reduces turnover risk, shortens onboarding, and supports more consistent decision quality during disruption. When key staff leave, more of their judgment stays in the workflow.

Where it fits in the model. Treat this as a capability premium on adoption probability. Institutional knowledge raises the likelihood that future projects succeed and sustain benefits. In models, increase success probabilities for later-stage initiatives once knowledge assets are in place.

Workforce Leverage and Talent Uplift

AI can automate rote work and free staff to focus on analysis, decision support, and business partnering. Over time, the mix shifts: fewer transaction processors and more advisors. That leverage lets finance increase throughput without adding headcount and can improve retention by reducing burnout and expanding the scope of work.

Where it fits in the model. Treat this as a capacity multiplier on FTE productivity. Instead of assuming headcount growth to support revenue growth, hold headcount flatter while scaling output, improving operating leverage in long-range models.

Capability Building and Future Optionality

AI projects often require reusable datasets, pipelines, governance structures, and prompt libraries that lower the cost and risk of future initiatives. This creates real options: the right (but not the obligation) to pursue additional use cases faster and at lower marginal cost. These assets often outlast the initial project and become the base layer of a compounding capability stack.

Where it fits in the model. Treat these assets as option value. Assign a notional residual value or terminal cash-flow benefit to capability-building projects, similar to salvage value, or model them as lowering the cost base of future projects by a defined percentage.

Why Strategic ROI Belongs in the Model. Treating strategic ROI this way turns it from "soft benefits" into modellable drivers of speed, durability, and scalability. Strategic ROI doesn't generate standalone dollar figures, but it raises expected returns and reduces the risk profile of future initiatives. CFOs who model it explicitly can position AI investments as capability-building assets, not just cost-reduction tools, which is how boards typically evaluate durable advantage.

The Long-Term Compounding of Strategic ROI

If tangible ROI provides the cash payback, strategic ROI is the multiplier.

A finance team that saves 3,000 hours annually doesn't just reduce cost. Those hours can be reallocated to improving forecasting models, accelerating investment approvals, or deepening business partnering with commercial teams. Each of those activities can unlock additional tangible ROI, including earlier benefit realization, more accurate plans, fewer failed initiatives, and better capital-allocation decisions.

Over time, this flywheel effect compounds (Table 3.1). More capacity produces better insights. Better insights support faster decisions. Faster decisions accelerate value capture. Finance moves from a reporting

Table 3.1 The Strategic ROI Compounding Loop—with AI Tool Examples

Loop stage	Purpose in the flywheel	Example AI capabilities/tools	Strategic ROI effect
Capacity creation	Free up analyst time and reduce manual workload	• AI-enabled ERP modules (SAP Joule, Oracle Fusion AI) • RPA (UiPath, Automation Anywhere) • AP/AR automation (Tipalti, Ramp AI)	Frees finance capacity for higher-value work; lowers marginal cost of adding new projects
Insight generation	Turn raw data into faster, deeper analysis	• Predictive ML forecasting tools (Pigment AI, Anaplan PlanIQ) • Anomaly detection and variance analytics (MindBridge, BlackLine AI) • Generative analysis copilots (Microsoft Copilot for Excel/Power BI)	Improves forecast accuracy; raises decision quality and confidence

Loop stage	Purpose in the flywheel	Example AI capabilities/tools	Strategic ROI effect
Decision acceleration	Compress time from data to action	• AI planning copilots (Workday AI, Oracle Intelligent Performance Management) • Natural-language query/BI assistants (ThoughtSpot Sage, Power BI Copilot) • Scenario modeling copilots (IBM Planning Analytics with Watson)	Speeds decision cycles; shifts benefit realization earlier (boosting IRR)
Value realization	Execute faster and at higher success rates	• Autonomous reconciliation agents (BlackLine Intercompany AI, Trullion AI) • Revenue/pricing optimization AI (PROS AI, Zilliant) • AI-driven cash forecasting (Kyriba AI, Cashforce)	Increases benefit conversion rate; raises probability of success in ROI models
Capability building	Institutionalize knowledge and reusable assets	• Knowledge-capturing copilots (Notion AI, Microsoft Copilot in Teams) • AI model governance and MLOps platforms (DataRobot, Azure ML) • Prompt libraries and reusable workflow templates	Reduces risk of turnover; raises success probability and lowers cost of future projects

function to a strategic copilot of the business, influencing revenue growth, margin expansion, and risk posture. The value grows non-linearly because the same capacity supports more decisions and more initiatives over time.

In financial models, this compounding shows up as increasing returns to scale:

- rising productivity (more initiatives supported per FTE),
- reduced time-to-value (earlier benefit cash flows), and
- lower execution risk (higher success probabilities for future projects).

Think of tangible ROI as the floor of AI's value and strategic ROI as the ceiling. Tangible ROI pays for the investment. Strategic ROI is what keeps paying back at an accelerating rate. Both belong in the CFO's calculus.

Vendor ROI Inflation

Vendors tend to oversell both hard and soft ROI. They show best-case scenarios: "80% of AP tasks eliminated," "50% faster forecasting," or "60% reduction in fraud false positives." In practice, most companies capture closer to half those gains in early implementations.

Typical Overstatements

- Hard ROI is inflated by assuming headcount reductions that rarely materialize. In practice, companies redeploy staff rather than eliminate roles.
- Soft ROI is inflated by assuming instant adoption and clean data, when change management and data hygiene usually slow progress.

For CFOs, the discipline is to translate vendor promises into conservative assumptions, then test them in pilots.

Why Inflated Promises Mislead CFOs

AI ROI claims often rest on faulty assumptions:

- 100% adoption—assumes every process is replaced instantly, ignoring change resistance.
- Perfect data—assumes structured, clean data, ignoring real-world inconsistencies.

- Zero oversight—assumes outputs can be used without human review and validation.

CFOs who accept these at face value set themselves up for disappointment. The discipline is to model the range of probable outcomes, not the best case.

Advanced Considerations in AI ROI

Time-Adjusted Value Realization (Adoption Curves, Not Straight Lines)

Most ROI models assume a steady ramp of benefits, but AI value often follows an S-curve: slow early while data, skills, and workflows mature; then a step up once adoption crosses a threshold. They model time-to-value explicitly by layering adoption probability curves or scenario bands over cash flows. This produces more realistic IRR/NPV (net present value) and helps sequence initiatives to match organizational capacity. Many firms still struggle to reach scaled value, which explains early under-realization even when pilot results look strong.

Portfolio-Level ROI (Expect Some Misses, Size for the Hits)

CFOs should rarely bet on a single AI use case. Fund a portfolio where some pilots stall and a minority outperform. Treat the roadmap like an R&D or venture capital (VC) portfolio: assign success probabilities, reflect key dependencies, and compute expected value across the basket. This avoids over-crediting any one project and clarifies why a diversified slate is rational.

Attribution and Counterfactuals (Separate AI Lift from Everything Else)

AI initiatives often coincide with process redesign, data cleanup, or headcount changes, so simple before/after comparisons overstate impact. Define a counterfactual: What would performance have been without AI? Where feasible, use A/B or stepped-wedge pilots, or causal-inference techniques to isolate incremental lift. This supports ROI attribution to AI rather than to concurrent changes.

Option Value from Capabilities (Real Options, Not Only Cash This Year)

Some AI investments build reusable capabilities such as cleaner data products, connectors, or prompt libraries that reduce the cost or risk of future initiatives. Capture this by adding a real-options term to the model: the right, but not the obligation, to launch additional use cases at lower marginal cost. This frames foundational work as an asset rather than a sunk cost and aligns with finance theory on irreversible investments under uncertainty.

Capacity-Adjusted Benefits (People Constraints as a Financial Input)

Projected savings assume teams adopt the tools. In practice, adoption is constrained by skills, bandwidth, and change fatigue. Convert that constraint into numbers by applying a capacity multiplier to expected benefits and staging benefits to training milestones. In many organizations, change capacity is the gating factor for scaling value.

Opportunity Cost and Capital Discipline (What You're Not Funding)

Even strong AI IRRs need to clear the next-best alternative. Put AI proposals side-by-side with other uses of capital, including working capital reduction, core systems modernization, or accretive M&A, and make opportunity cost explicit in hurdle rates. Treat AI as one candidate in the capital-allocation queue, not a special case.

Benefit Decay and Model Obsolescence (Drift Eats ROI if Unmanaged)

AI benefits decay if models drift as data or business conditions change. Build a decay factor into benefit projections unless monitoring, retraining, and model refresh are funded. Modern machine-learning operations (MLOps) practices and vendor capabilities can detect drift, monitor skew, and trigger retraining. If those aren't in place, shorten the benefit tail in the discounted cash flow (DCF). Quantifying decay focuses investment on lifecycle management that protects ROI duration.

How to Use This Section in Your Models

- Add an adoption S-curve and capacity multiplier to time-shift benefits realistically.
- Evaluate portfolio expected ROI rather than single-case certainty.
- Require counterfactual or causal evidence before locking in enterprise-wide benefit assumptions.
- Include a real options term for capabilities that unlock future use cases.
- Deduct opportunity cost explicitly when ranking projects.
- Apply a benefit-decay schedule unless drift monitoring and retraining are funded and in place.

These adjustments don't complicate the ROI story, they make it defensible. They let a CFO explain "how big" the return is, "when it arrives," "how likely," "what else we could have done," and "how long it lasts," which is the level of rigor boards, auditors, and investors expect.

With the distinction between tangible and strategic ROI clear, the next step is to operationalize ROI modeling. We'll move from conceptual differences to practical templates for applying NPV, IRR, and payback-period analysis to AI initiatives, while incorporating the realities of fast-evolving technology discussed earlier.

Note

1. Bayer and Bento, interview, December 17, 2025.

Further Reading

Adoption S-Curves, Time-to-Value, and Scaling Challenges

- Boston Consulting Group, *AI Adoption 2024: From Pilots to Profits* (Boston, MA: Boston Consulting Group, 2024), https://www.bcg.com/publications/2024/ai-adoption-value-realization

- Deloitte, *State of Generative AI in the Enterprise: Year-end Update* (New York, NY: Deloitte Insights, 2024), https://www2.deloitte.com/insights/us/en/focus/tech-trends/2024/state-of-generative-ai.html

Counterfactuals and Impact Attribution

- Harvard Business Review, *The Right Way to Run Business Experiments*, 2023, https://hbr.org/2023/06/the-right-way-to-run-business-experiments
- Ron Kohavi, Diane Tang, and Ya Xu, *Trustworthy Online Controlled Experiments: A Practical Guide to A/B Testing* (Cambridge: Cambridge University Press, 2020).

Benefit Decay, Model Drift, and MLOps

- IBM, *Machine Learning Operations (MLOps): Managing Model Drift and Performance* (IBM Documentation, 2024), https://www.ibm.com/cloud/learn/mlops
- Google Cloud, *Monitoring Models in Production: Detecting Drift and Bias*, 2023, https://cloud.google.com/architecture/mlops-continuous-delivery-and-automation-pipelines-in-machine-learning

Opportunity Cost and Capital Allocation

- McKinsey & Company, *A CFO's Guide to Capital Allocation*, 2022, https://www.mckinsey.com/capabilities/strategy-and-corporate-finance/our-insights/a-cfos-guide-to-capital-allocation
- Richard A. Brealey, Stewart C. Myers, and Allen Franklin, *Principles of Corporate Finance*, 13th ed. (New York, NY: McGraw-Hill Education, 2020).

Real Options and Strategic Optionality

- Lenos Trigeorgis, *Real Options: Managerial Flexibility and Strategy in Resource Allocation* (Cambridge, MA: MIT Press, 1996).
- Harvard Business Review, *Real Options: When to Invest in Innovation*, 2009, https://hbr.org/2009/03/real-options-when-to-invest-in-innovation

Chapter 4

Building the Business Case: Modeling AI ROI as a Portfolio

Key Takeaways

- **AI is a portfolio, not a project.** AI should be evaluated as a portfolio of initiatives, not as a single investment with a binary outcome. Each use case carries its own cost profile, adoption curve, probability of success, and rate at which benefits erode if the system is not maintained or trusted. Some initiatives will produce steady, low-risk returns. Others will take longer, carry more uncertainty, and generate disproportionate upside. The CFO's responsibility is to make that mix explicit and to show how the portfolio, taken together, produces predictable enterprise value.

- **Model strategic ROI as modifiers, not line items.** Strategic ROI should not appear as standalone "intangible benefit" rows. Its impact is real, but it shows up by changing how the portfolio behaves over time. Faster decision cycles pull benefits forward. Better forecasts lower volatility and justify lower risk premiums. Captured knowledge and reusable workflows raise success probabilities for the next wave of initiatives and reduce marginal cost. Modeling these effects as multipliers to timing, discount rates, and probabilities allows the CFO to present AI as a governed capital platform, evaluated through portfolio allocation rather than one-off project approval.
- **Price in the downside risk.** AI introduces asymmetric downside risk that traditional ROI models often ignore. When AI-enabled workflows fail, the cost may include regulatory exposure, reputational damage, or poor capital decisions, not just lower returns. CFOs should price this explicitly by modeling the magnitude, frequency, and recoverability of potential errors as probability-weighted expected losses deducted from projected benefits. This lens also clarifies where AI fits and where it does not. High-magnitude, high-frequency processes such as external reporting are poor candidates for GenAI, while low-magnitude, high-frequency workflows such as variance analysis drafts are safer pilots.
- **Tailor the message given to each stakeholder.** CEOs care about competitive position and the cost of delay. Boards focus on fiduciary duty and capital discipline. Business unit leaders worry about disruption and accountability. Investors watch earnings volatility and disclosure reliability. The CFO keeps the underlying model consistent while adjusting the frame: measured risk-taking for the CEO, risk-adjusted returns for the board, collaborative partnership for business leaders, and controlled governance for investors.
- **ROI extends beyond the finance function.** The AI-ready CFO's role doesn't stop with proving ROI in the finance function. Once finance shows that AI initiatives can be evaluated with rigor, the CFO sets the modeling discipline for the entire organization. AI will touch every function, from sales to logistics. If each area models investments differently, the results will not be comparative. The CFO can prevent that. The CFO's capital-allocation mandate includes defining what "return" means, how risk is quantified, and which investments clear the hurdle. In the age of AI, that mandate becomes even more central.

Viewing AI as a Portfolio

AI isn't a single project with a clean deliverable. It's a portfolio of probabilistic initiatives, each with its own cost, adoption curve, probability of success, and benefit profile. A few will produce outsized gains. Others will stall or fail. The CFO has to model that variability explicitly. The executive team and board should see how the winners are expected to fund the rest, and how the capabilities built along the way reduce cost and risk in future waves.

The work highlighted in the last chapter converges at this point. Tangible ROI captures direct value through cost savings, cost avoidance, and revenue or margin gains. Strategic ROI captures how each success improves the yield of the next by accelerating cycles, improving forecast accuracy, capturing institutional knowledge, leveraging talent, and building reusable infrastructure. This chapter shows how a CFO can build a unified financial model that integrates both categories into a decision-ready portfolio view. The portfolio model does more than justify finance's AI initiatives. It sets the standard every other function will follow when proposing AI work. Establishing this discipline keeps AI inside the same capital framework the company uses for any major investment.

The ultimate output is a board-ready business case: a portfolio of use cases with risk-adjusted expected values, scenario ranges, and strategic effects that compound over time, positioned alongside other capital-allocation options. When the CFO frames AI this way, the organization can treat it as a governed investment program, not an open-ended trial.

Constructing the AI Portfolio Model: A CFO's Roadmap

An AI portfolio model is a method for organizing uncertainty so a set of probabilistic initiatives can be compared and prioritized. The goal of the model is to provide every business unit a common language for cost, benefit, risk, and timing, so proposals can be evaluated side-by-side. What follows is a basic scaffold that CFOs can use and adapt each step to their context, risk appetite, and board expectations.

Step 1: Define the Use-Case Portfolio. Break the initiative into distinct use cases, such as AI-driven pricing, FP&A forecasting automation,

AP invoice processing, or churn prediction in sales. For each use case, capture the inputs that drive the economics and the uncertainty: investment cost (including implementation and change management), expected tangible ROI, the adoption ramp over time, probability of success, and benefit decay if the model or workflow isn't maintained. This step establishes the raw building blocks. It's a use-case register, not a financial model... yet.

Step 2: Integrate Strategic ROI Multipliers. Identify which strategic effects apply and how they change future results. These shouldn't show up as separate "soft-benefit" dollar lines. They change timing and risk. Decision-cycle compression pulls benefit cash flows earlier. Improved forecast accuracy lowers volatility and can justify a lower risk premium in the discount rate. Knowledge capture increases repeatability and raises success probabilities for future waves. Workforce leverage increases throughput by freeing capacity without incremental headcount. Capability-building reduces the cost of future initiatives by reusing data pipelines, model components, and governance. Strategic effects turn the model from a list of pilots into an enterprise capability investment.

Step 3: Assemble Risk-Adjusted Portfolio Cash Flows. Convert each use case into probability-weighted, adoption-adjusted cash flows. For revenue-side gains, apply contribution margin. Discount the cash flows at a risk-adjusted hurdle rate that matches the use case's uncertainty and downside exposure, incorporating any volatility reduction where it is defensible. Then, aggregate the use cases into a combined cash-flow view that shows total cost by period, expected benefits by period, and net cash flows. Present scenario ranges, including base, downside, and upside, so the board can see the risk distribution across the portfolio.

Step 4: Position the Portfolio in the Capital Stack. Compare the portfolio's risk-adjusted IRR, payback, and NPV against other capital projects, such as ERP upgrades, M&A, or product launches. Then, make the option value explicit. Reusable infrastructure and knowledge assets can justify treating early investments more like R&D than traditional IT spend, without relaxing capital discipline. This lets the board weigh AI against other initiatives on comparable financial terms while acknowledging different risk and payoff dynamics.

Step 5: Build the Enterprise-Wide Layer. Publish the scaffold as the standard business-case structure for all departments. Require that proposed initiatives from Sales, HR, Ops, and Marketing follow the same format: cost, tangible ROI, strategic multipliers, and risk-adjusted outputs. Centralize evaluation in finance so hurdle rates, benefit classifications, and risk treatment stay consistent. This cements the CFO's role as the enterprise architect of AI capital allocation, not just the finance sponsor.

From Tool ROI to Capital Allocation

This scaffold should be viewed as a repeatable logic for evaluating a fast-moving category of investments with consistent inputs, risk treatment, and timing assumptions. It shifts the conversation from "what is the ROI of this tool?" to "how will our AI portfolio compound returns and reduce execution risk over time?" With the structure in place, business units can propose initiatives in a comparable format, and the CFO can assess them with the same capital discipline used for any major investment.

From Use Cases to Portfolio: An Illustrative Example

To see how the portfolio model works in practice, consider a hypothetical S&P 1000 enterprise. It generates roughly $8 billion in annual revenue, runs a global finance organization of 600, and operates on a mature ERP. Operational data is solid, but key finance workflows remain manual. Variance analysis, forecasting, and reconciliations consume thousands of hours each quarter. Accounts payable processes more than 300,000 invoices per year.

The board has asked the CFO to lead AI adoption across the enterprise, starting with finance as the proving ground. For the first portfolio wave, the CFO selects two initial use cases:

- Accounts payable automation, using AI-enabled invoice capture and three-way matching.
- FP&A forecasting automation, using ML models embedded in the planning platform.

These are not the only initiatives the company will pursue. They represent two categories most finance teams will face early: a transactional, efficiency-driven use case (AP) and an analytical, insight-driven use case (FP&A).

A note on scale. This example uses enterprise-level numbers to illustrate the modeling logic expected at the board level. The same framework applies in smaller organizations. The numbers will be smaller and the tooling may be simpler, but the CFO's responsibility doesn't change. Capital still needs to be allocated with discipline, risk still needs to be priced, and benefits still need to be tied to observable workflows.

Don't view this section as a template. It is only a scaffold that shows how the CFO evolves from individual use-case estimates to a combined, risk-adjusted portfolio case that can sit alongside other capital-allocation decisions. Each company will supply its own costs, benefit profiles, adoption curves, and success probabilities.

With that context in place, we can walk through how the CFO would model these two use cases as a single portfolio.

Step 1: Define the Use-Case Inputs. Start by breaking each proposed initiative into a discrete use case and documenting the core assumptions. Don't try to perfect the numbers on the first pass. The objective is to make the mechanics visible to the executive team and the board: what each use case costs, how quickly adoption ramps, how likely it is to hit expected outcomes, and how benefits hold up over time. Table 4.1 provides an illustrative input set for the two use cases in this first wave: accounts payable automation and FP&A forecasting automation.

This table doesn't produce ROI by itself. It captures the assumptions the portfolio model will run on. As the model spreads through the organization, keep it consistent. Each business unit can bring different numbers, but they should describe them in the same categories so finance can compare different use cases on an equal footing.

Capturing both tangible inputs and strategic effects at the start also signals intent. The CFO is evaluating AI as a capital investment with measurable risk, timing, and return profiles.

Step 2: Apply Strategic ROI Multipliers. Once the raw inputs are set, the next step is to apply the strategic effects that change how value shows up and how it compounds. Don't list separate "strategic-benefit" dollar lines. They change the shape of the model by pulling benefit timing

Table 4.1 Illustrative Use-Case Input Table

Attribute	AP automation	FP&A forecasting automation
Purpose	Automate invoice capture and three-way matching to reduce manual effort and errors	Deploy ML-based predictive models to improve forecast accuracy and shorten planning cycles
Initial investment cost	\$2.0M (implementation, integration, change management)	\$5.0M (platform build, data engineering, model development, training)
Annual operating cost	\$0.5M (licenses, support, maintenance)	\$1.0M (model retraining, platform licenses, support)
Addressable cost base	\$6.0M (labor + rework costs)	\$12.0M (analyst hours + planning-cycle overtime)
Expected cost savings/ avoidance	50% of addressable base at steady state	35% of addressable base at steady state
Addressable revenue impact	None (purely efficiency-driven)	\$200M revenue segment with 3% forecast error causing lost sales
Expected revenue uplift	N/A	20% reduction in forecast error → 0.5% recovered revenue
Contribution margin on revenue	N/A	40%
Adoption curve	30% Yr1 → 60% Yr2 → 80% Yr3	20% Yr1 → 50% Yr2 → 80% Yr3
Probability of success	75% (high process maturity, lower technical risk)	50% (new capability, data dependencies)
Benefit decay rate	5% annually (if maintenance lapses)	10% annually (if models not updated)
Strategic ROI attributes present	Workforce leverage, knowledge capture	Decision-cycle compression, forecast accuracy, capability-building

forward, raising success probabilities, lowering the cost of follow-on work, or increasing finance's throughput without incremental headcount. The application of strategic effects, shown in Table 4.2, converts the portfolio model from a static register of initiatives to a decision tool that reflects execution reality.

Table 4.2 Strategic ROI Multipliers Applied to Each Use Case

Strategic ROI lever	How it works	Impact on AP automation	Impact on FP&A forecasting
Decision-cycle compression	Faster cycles mean benefits start earlier and compound more quickly	Minimal impact (transactional process), leave benefit timing as-is	Major impact: pulls forecast benefits forward one planning cycle. Shift Yr2 adoption 50% → effective Yr1.5
Forecast accuracy/ risk reduction	Lower forecast error reduces outcome volatility, which can justify lowering the discount rate (risk premium)	NA	Lower discount rate from 12 to 10% in NPV model to reflect reduced forecast volatility
Knowledge capture/ organizational memory	Capturing workflows, playbooks, and prompt libraries increases future project success rates	Raises future AP-related automation project success probability from 75 to 85%	Raises success probability for future analytics projects from 50 to 65%
Workforce leverage/ talent uplift	Frees staff capacity to support more projects without additional cost	Effective capacity gain of three to five full-time equivalents, allows redeployment to variance analysis	Allows FP&A team to absorb increased forecasting frequency without headcount increase
Capability-building/ future optionality	Building reusable data pipelines, models, and governance lowers future initiative cost	Limited (AP process-specific)	Significant: reduce estimated cost of future modeling projects by 25%

How this shapes the model. AP automation remains a steady efficiency play. Benefit timing stays largely unchanged, but confidence improves and the success rate for related automation work increases modestly as processes and controls get codified.

FP&A forecasting is where the strategic effects show up more clearly. Adoption pulls forward as cycles compress, success probability improves as data and workflows stabilize, the risk premium can drop as volatility declines, and follow-on analytics work gets cheaper because core capabilities are already in place.

These strategic effects shouldn't inflate the benefit line. Expected yield and execution risk will change across the portfolio by improving timing, repeatability, and marginal cost. These effects enable the CFO to describe the program as a capability stack that compounds, not a set of disconnected tools.

Step 3: Build Risk-Adjusted Cash Flows. Now the model becomes financially operational. Convert each use case's expected savings and revenue gains into cash flows that reflect adoption and probability of success, then discount them using a risk-adjusted hurdle rate. Strategic ROI multipliers from Step 2 show up here as changes to timing, success probabilities, and discount rates. The output is an expected-value cash-flow view that can be compared across use cases and rolled into the portfolio.

Illustrative Cash Flow Build—AP Automation

Context

- Investment: \$2.0M upfront + \$0.5M/year operating
- Addressable cost base: \$6.0M
- Expected savings: 50% of base (\$3.0M steady state)
- Adoption curve: 30% Yr1 → 60% Yr2 → 80% Yr3
- Probability of success: 75% raised to 85% via knowledge capture
- Discount rate: 12% (no volatility reduction applied)

Year	Adoption (%)	Gross benefit (before risk)	Success probability	Expected benefit	OpEx	Net benefit	PV factor (12%)	PV of net benefit
1	30%	\$0.90M	85%	\$0.765M	\$0.50M	\$0.265M	0.893	\$0.24M
2	60%	\$1.80M	85%	\$1.53M	\$0.50M	\$1.03M	0.797	\$0.82M
3 (steady-state start)	80%	\$2.40M	85%	\$2.04M	\$0.50M	\$1.54M	0.712	\$1.10M

Interpretation. A low-risk, steady-return use case with modest positive NPV. It functions as a base hit in the portfolio.

Illustrative Cash Flow Build—FP&A Forecasting Automation

Context

- Upfront investment: \$5.0M
- Annual operating cost: \$1.0M
- Addressable cost base: \$12.0M (labor)
- Expected savings at steady state: 35% of base (\$4.2M)
- Revenue uplift: \$200M line × 0.5% recovered revenue = \$1.0M revenue × 40% margin = \$0.4M profit
- Adoption curve: 20% (Yr1) → 50% (Yr2) → 80% (Yr3)
- Probability of success: 65% (50% base, increased via knowledge capture)
- Discount rate: 10% (lowered from 12% via forecast accuracy)
- Decision-cycle compression: pull adoption forward by ~0.5 year by shifting 20% of Yr2 benefit into Yr1
- PV of net benefits (Yr1 − Yr3): ≈\$1.12M
- Less upfront investment: \$5.0M
- NPV (3-year view): ≈−\$3.88M
- If extended over 7 years, cumulative NPV turns positive: ≈\$2.5M

Year	Adoption (base %)	Gross benefit (before risk)	Acceleration adjustment	Success probability	Expected benefit	OpEx	Net benefit	PV factor (10%)	PV of net benefit
1	20%	\$0.92M	+\$0.46M	65%	\$0.90M	\$1.0M	−\$0.10M	0.909	−\$0.09M
2	50%	\$2.30M	−\$0.46M	65%	\$1.20M	\$1.0M	\$0.20M	0.826	\$0.17M
3 (steady-state start)	80%	\$3.68M	—	65%	\$2.39M	\$1.0M	\$1.39M	0.751	\$1.04M

Interpretation. This is a higher-risk, longer-horizon use case. Early years look unattractive on a simple payback view, but the upside is larger and the strategic effects improve timing, success probability, and the economics of follow-on analytics initiatives.

What the Cash Flow Math Shows. Risk-adjusted expected-value calculation is not the same as savings math. Timing, adoption, probability of success, and the hurdle rate do most of the work. A use case can look attractive on gross savings and still fail the investment test once you price execution risk and benefit timing. Another use case can look weak early and still earn its place because it builds capabilities that improve the yield and lower the risk of what comes next.

This prior point is the key board-level takeaway. The decision is not whether a tool pays for itself in isolation. The decision is how to allocate capital across a portfolio with different payoff profiles, different risk, and different roles in the sequence.

Step 4: Combine the Use Cases Into a Portfolio View. Once risk-adjusted cash flows are built for each use case, aggregate them into a single portfolio model. This gives the board a consolidated view of total investment, expected benefits over time, and the portfolio's overall return profile, including IRR, NPV, and payback. It also makes the risk mix visible, showing how high-certainty base hits balance higher-upside initiatives with longer ramps.

Portfolio aggregation, as seen in Table 4.3, also allows strategic effects to be reflected at the portfolio level, not just the use-case level. As the

Table 4.3 An Illustrative Portfolio Rollup

Item	AP automation	FP&A forecasting automation	Portfolio total
Upfront investment	\$2.0M	\$5.0M	\$7.0M
Annual operating cost	\$0.5M	\$1.0M	\$1.5M
Y1 risk-adjusted net benefit	\$0.27M	−\$0.10M	\$0.17M
Y2 risk-adjusted net benefit	\$1.03M	\$0.20M	\$1.23M
Y3+ risk-adjusted net benefit	\$1.54M	\$1.39M	\$2.93M
Discount rate	12%	10%	Weighted ≈ 10.7%
5-Year NPV	\$0.16M	\$2.50M	\$2.66M
Portfolio IRR	~14%	~18%	~16% blended
Strategic ROI effects	Workforce leverage, knowledge capture	Decision-cycle compression, capability-building, forecast accuracy	Combined capability lift reduces future analytics project costs by 20%, raises future success probabilities by 15%

organization builds repeatable data pipelines, operating patterns, and governance, the risk premium on later initiatives can drop and success probabilities can improve.

Interpretation

- The portfolio has a blended IRR of ~16% and a positive NPV of $2.66M at a 10.7% risk-adjusted hurdle rate.
- The AP project contributes quick, low-risk returns that help offset early losses in the FP&A project.
- The FP&A project creates reusable data infrastructure and forecast accuracy gains that lower risk and cost for future analytics initiatives, which is a strategic ROI multiplier that is not reflected in these numbers but should be highlighted in the narrative.

How This Shifts the Board Conversation. Presenting AI initiatives as a portfolio changes the question the board needs to answer. The discussion moves away from whether a single initiative pays for itself on a simple payback basis. It questions whether the company is allocating capital into a balanced set of use cases where low-risk base hits fund the learning curve and infrastructure for higher-upside capability builders, while the portfolio as a whole improves expected yield and reduces execution risk over time. Boards expect a capital-allocation case. They don't want a tool-deployment plan.

Step 5: Framing the Portfolio for the Board. With the portfolio model complete, the CFO must set the frame. The model carries the mechanics: risk-adjusted cash flows, payback timing, IRR and NPV, and the strategic multipliers that change timing, probabilities, and future cost curves. The board discussion should focus on what those mechanics mean for capital allocation and risk.

Position the AI portfolio alongside other strategic investments, such as acquisitions, ERP upgrades, or new market entries. Make the diversification explicit. Show how the program spreads risk across multiple use cases, from quick, low-risk base hits to higher-upside initiatives with longer ramps. The goal is to show how the portfolio holds together under realistic adoption and execution assumptions.

Clearly demonstrate that the model is more than a list of projects that require funding. Each successful use case should improve the economics of the next by tightening workflows, codifying patterns, and reducing the marginal cost of delivery. Adoption gets smoother, success probabilities improve, and the risk premium narrows as governance and operating discipline mature.

Do not try to persuade the board that AI is inevitable. The CFO's mandate is to show that the company is treating AI like any other investment category: priced for risk, managed through control points, and measured against competing uses of capital. When the CFO frames it this way, AI becomes a governed, compounding capital program that every function will be expected to model and manage with the same discipline.

Common ROI Modeling Mistakes in AI Initiatives

CFOs tend to miss value in AI for two reasons: they either model it like a deterministic IT project or accept optimistic assumptions that don't survive contact with adoption, data quality, and controls. The mistakes below show up repeatedly when teams try to convert pilots into board-ready business cases.

Scaling Without Decay or Required Infrastructure

Pilot results rarely replicate cleanly at scale. Adoption plateaus, exception handling grows, and model performance drifts unless it is monitored and retrained. If the model assumes pilot productivity gains roll forward without incremental integration work, logging, monitoring, retraining, and workflow redesign, the benefits will be overstated and the operating cost will be understated.

Overstating Adoption and Success Probability

The fastest way to inflate ROI is to assume immediate adoption and near-certain outcomes. In practice, adoption ramps, trust has to be earned, and edge cases surface late. Success probability should reflect data readiness, workflow maturity, and change management capacity. Vendor case studies are useful as upside scenarios. They are not a baseline.

Underestimating Total Cost of Ownership

AI initiatives carry ongoing costs. Data engineering, model maintenance, security reviews, compliance work, licensing, and change management tend to persist long after go-live. If the model includes only implementation cost and ignores the operating layer, the ROI will look cleaner than the business reality.

Using Weak Metrics or Double-Counting Benefits

AI projects often get justified with proxy metrics that do not tie to cash, margin, or risk reduction. Time saved is not value-creating unless the capacity is redeployed or cost is taken out. The same issue shows up when teams count a single benefit twice, once as cycle-time compression and again as labor savings, or once as forecast accuracy and again as revenue lift. The model needs a clear value map that prevents overlap.

Ignoring Timing and Risk Adjustment

AI value is sensitive to when benefits arrive and how reliable they are. If the model treats benefits as immediate and discounts cash flows at a generic hurdle rate, it misses the real drivers of expected value. Adoption ramps, probability-weighted outcomes, and risk-adjusted discount rates are not optional details. They are the difference between a finance-grade model and a vendor pitch.

The Cost of Being Wrong

Traditional ROI models assume underperformance shows up as lower returns. With AI, failure can create active harm, not just missed savings. A bad forecast can steer capital into the wrong place. A flawed compliance output can trigger fines, restatements, or reputational damage. Even smaller errors, such as weak variance explanations, can erode confidence in finance's work and slow adoption across the organization.

For the AI-ready CFO, this means the business case has to carry two numbers at once: expected return and expected harm. Pricing the cost of being wrong forces discipline. It helps teams choose workflows where error is containable and recoverable, and it keeps AI away from areas where mistakes destroy value or threaten the credibility of financial reporting.

Three Key Dimensions of Risk

The cost of being wrong is best evaluated through three dimensions: magnitude, frequency, and recoverability.

- **Magnitude** captures the severity of impact if the AI-enabled workflow fails. Some errors are inconvenient. Others are enterprise events. Misclassifying vendor invoices may cause payment delays measured in tens of thousands. Generating incorrect SEC disclosures can lead to restatements, regulatory action, and a loss of investor confidence measured in millions of dollars. Magnitude is the difference between a fixable miss and a balance-sheet problem.
- **Frequency** measures how often the workflow runs and how many chances the system has to be wrong. A process executed once a year carries less aggregate exposure than an output generated daily. A journal-entry workflow that runs thousands of times per quarter creates far more opportunities for defects than an annual planning model. Frequency turns a small error rate into a predictable incident over time.
- **Recoverability** measures how easily errors can be detected and reversed before they cause damage. Some outputs can be checked, corrected, and logged before they leave finance. Draft board materials are a clean example. Other outputs, such as automated submissions to regulators, are hard to unwind once filed. Low recoverability raises the cost of even small mistakes.

Together, these dimensions give CFOs a practical way to assess which workflows are suitable for AI and what control points need to be in place. They move the conversation away from generic labels like "high risk" or "low risk" and toward measurable exposure at the workflow level.

The Risk-Based AI Implementation Matrix

To operationalize this lens, map magnitude and frequency on the axes, with recoverability as an overlay (Image 4.1):

See Table 4.4 for examples.

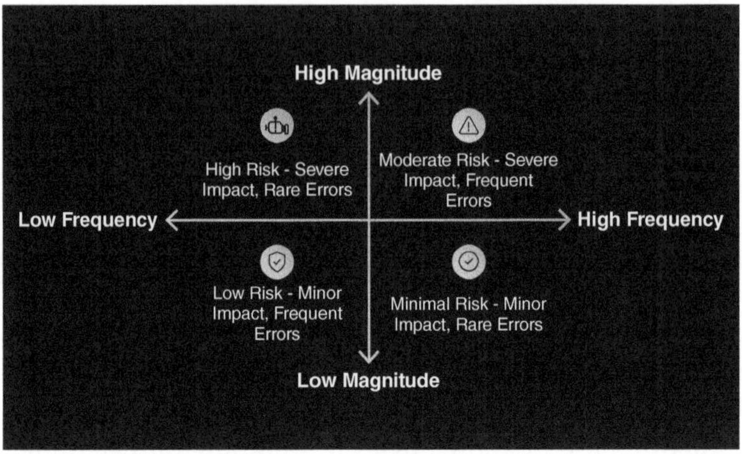

Image 4.1 Risk-Based AI Implementation Matrix

Table 4.4 Corresponding Examples in the Matrix

High Magnitude, Low Frequency These are rare but potentially catastrophic events. Think of M&A valuation models or one-time impairment analyses. Because they are infrequent, the aggregate probability of error is lower, but each error could be devastating. Manual review is essential. AI can be used as a decision-support tool not as an agent, because final judgments, the go/no-go decisions, must remain with human experts.	**High Magnitude, High Frequency** This is the danger zone. Frequent outputs with severe consequences if wrong. Examples include automated financial reporting, regulatory filings, and tax submissions. In these areas, the cost of being wrong is so high that GenAI is generally inappropriate. Only deterministic, rule-based automation with rigorous controls should be considered. Human oversight is non-negotiable.
Low Magnitude, Low Frequency Here, the stakes are minimal. For example, AI-generated first drafts of internal training materials. Even if errors occur, they are rare and consequences are minor. These are easy candidates for early adoption with minimal oversight. The flipside is the direct ROI is likely negligible and strategic ROI doesn't compound.	**Low Magnitude, High Frequency** This is the most fertile ground for AI-enabled initiatives and pilots. Daily variance analysis drafts, research summaries, or spend categorization tasks fall into this quadrant. Errors are frequent but low impact, and recoverability is high. These workflows are areas where sandboxes can be developed to build institutional comfort with AI and begin to capture the strategic ROI that can surface in future initiatives.

Risk-Stratified Use-Case Scenarios

To see how the portfolio model works in practice, consider two scenarios at different ends of the risk spectrum. A lower-risk use case shows where AI can deliver quick wins with minimal control overhead. A higher-risk scenario shows where the governance requirements increase alongside the potential impact.

Higher-Risk Scenario: Annual SEC Filing. A Fortune 500 company tested a GenAI assistant to draft sections of its 10-K. The output read well, but it included subtle factual errors. If those errors had made it into the filing, the company could have faced regulatory action and reputational damage. Magnitude was high, frequency was annual, and recoverability dropped sharply once the document was filed. The CFO stopped short of automation, kept drafting under human control, and limited AI to background research and early-stage summarization.

Lower-Risk Scenario: Monthly Variance Analysis. An FP&A team used a GenAI model to draft monthly budget-to-actual variance explanations for CFO review. Analysts checked the drafts against the general ledger and supporting schedules, corrected issues, and then routed the final version through the normal review chain. Magnitude was low, frequency was high, and recoverability was strong because outputs were easy to verify before distribution. The team saved meaningful time without introducing new exposure, which made the workflow a sensible proving ground.

What the Risk Lens Changes

Adding explicit risk weighting to ROI models will change which use cases rise to the top. Without it, the model will often push teams toward automating the biggest cost centers first. In practice, many of the most expensive workflows are also the most dangerous to automate, especially those tied to external reporting, compliance submissions, and regulated disclosures. When you price the cost of being wrong, the expected downside can overwhelm the modeled savings, even when gross benefits look attractive.

Lower-cost workflows can look less compelling on savings alone, but they are often the right starting point. They support controlled adoption, create reusable patterns, and build confidence in the controls and evidence trail, allowing the strategic benefits to start compounding.

Explicitly Connecting Risk to ROI Modeling

The cost of being wrong can't stay as a qualitative sidebar. It needs to flow through the model. One practical approach is to treat AI failure costs as probability-weighted expected losses and deduct them from the projected benefit stream, or reflect them through a higher risk premium in the discount rate (Table 4.5).

Table 4.5 Risk Factors for ROI Modeling for AI

Risk profile	Description	Typical examples	Modeling approach
High Magnitude/ High Frequency	Errors cause large losses and occur often if controls fail	Monthly-close financial reporting process, quarterly SEC filings, 8-K regulatory disclosures	• Apply explicit expected loss modeling: estimate failure cost × probability and subtract from benefit stream • Use conservative adoption curves and higher hurdle rates (WACC + 300–500 bps) • Require robust control and audit layers before deployment
High Magnitude/ Low Frequency	Rare but catastrophic errors could trigger severe compliance penalties or reputational damage; potentially existential threats	Treasury cash forecasting, tax provisioning, liquidity planning, annual reports	• Model downside scenarios explicitly (stress cases with extended delayed or negative ROI) • Include risk-adjusted contingency reserves in project costs • Require formal board sign-off and legal review before launch

Risk profile	Description	Typical examples	Modeling approach
Low Magnitude/ High Frequency	Small errors that happen often can erode efficiency or trust	Invoice coding, journal entry prep, account reconciliations	• Apply expected loss deductions but with small impact on hurdle rate • Focus on user adoption rates and monitoring costs in the model • Use shorter payback thresholds to avoid compounding minor errors
Low Magnitude/ Low Frequency	Minimal risk if errors occur and easy to recover from	Variance commentary generation, management reporting drafts	• Treat as low-risk pilots; use base hurdle rates and standard payback/IRR • Model strategic ROI multipliers more heavily (knowledge capture, capacity gains) • Can use faster adoption curves and lower success penalties

For example, a high-magnitude workflow might carry a 5% chance of a $10 million compliance error. That implies an expected loss of $500,000, which should reduce the net benefit stream or be reflected in the hurdle rate. If that adjustment drives NPV negative, the use case should not move forward under the proposed design.

This operation is consistent with how finance already prices credit and operational risk. It also forces attention to correlated risk. As AI scales, shared data sources, common prompts, and model dependencies can turn one defect into multiple failures across workflows. Folding those downside scenarios into NPV, IRR, and payback aligns AI evaluation with how boards and investors already think about risk-adjusted returns, keeping projected value tied to control, evidence, and downside containment.

The CFO's Role in Communicating AI Risk

For the AI-ready CFO, recognizing risk isn't enough. Your job is also to communicate it with precision and balance to different audiences. AI introduces new uncertainty, but the bigger failure mode is letting that uncertainty freeze the organization. If you present AI risk only as a threat, boards and CEOs will pull back. If you minimize it, you give up the credibility that makes your guidance usable.

The real skill is translating technology risk into financial risk, then tailoring the frame to the stakeholder in front of you. The CEO hears risk as competitive position and the cost of delay. The board hears fiduciary exposure. Business unit leaders hear disruption and accountability. Investors hear disclosure reliability. Each requires a different conversation, even when the underlying model stays consistent.

Framing Strategic Risk and Organizational Readiness with the CEO

Most CEOs are not focused on the mechanics of an AI rollout. They care about competitiveness, talent, and whether the company is falling behind. In that conversation, lead with the opportunity cost of delay. Slower decision cycles, lower agility, and missed margin improvement are the real threats, not isolated model errors.

The CEO needs to hear that AI investments are not a gamble. They are a controlled portfolio, structured to spread risk across use cases, learn quickly, and scale only where controls hold. The portfolio approach gives you language the CEO can use: small wins that fund the next wave, with governance that keeps speed inside a defined control envelope. Decision-cycle compression and knowledge capture should be positioned as execution advantages that improve outcomes over time, not as abstract benefits.

The message is: We will take measured risks now, with clear gates and evidence, so we do not take larger strategic risks later.

Framing Fiduciary Risk and Capital Discipline with the Board

Boards process AI risk through fiduciary duty. Their instinct is downside protection, not upside pursuit. Meet that instinct with the same discipline you would bring to treasury, M&A, or any major capital program. Show probability-weighted returns, downside scenarios, and risk-priced discount rates. Make it clear how governance prevents uncontrolled deployment, and where the model draws hard boundaries around high-stakes workflows.

Use the magnitude, frequency, and recoverability lens to segment the portfolio. That makes it obvious which workflows are candidates for early adoption and which remain under strict human control. The board should see a constrained rollout with clear control points, auditability, and stop conditions.

The message the board needs is equally direct: We have priced risk into the economics, contained exposure at the workflow level, and we will not scale beyond what controls and evidence support.

Framing Operational Risk and Accountability with Business Unit Heads

Business unit leaders care about execution and P&L accountability. Their concern is disruption. They do not want a new tool that breaks the process they own, and they do not want to be held responsible for failures they cannot control.

In these conversations, the CFO cannot sound like a gatekeeper. You need to sound like a risk partner. Finance will co-develop the business case, pressure-test assumptions, and build an adoption ramp that matches operating reality. That includes setting realistic success probabilities, defining what "good" looks like in the workflow, and agreeing on who reviews, approves, and signs off at each step.

Contain risk early by starting where consequences are manageable and recoverability is strong. Keep budgets stable by modeling ramp delays, exception handling, and failure risk, instead of pushing best-case savings into operating plans.

The message to business leaders should be practical: We will start with small, controlled steps, we will build the business case together, and finance will price the risk so you are not carrying it alone.

Framing Disclosure Risk and Confidence Signaling with Investors

Investors view AI risk through two lenses: earnings volatility and disclosure reliability. They are not looking for technical explanations. They are looking for governance signals they can trust.

The CFO should be explicit about boundaries. Material financial reporting stays under human control. Higher-risk AI pilots should be kept away from regulated outputs until accuracy, traceability, and review discipline are proven. When communicating externally, describe the control layers in plain terms. Outputs are logged. Reviews are documented. Humans approve before anything touches disclosure workflows. Fail-safes exist to stop propagation when exceptions appear.

Investors also need to see progress without recklessness. Position the company's approach as incremental and reversible, aligned to the organization's risk appetite and control maturity. That stance supports the upside case without creating a credibility gap. It signals that productivity gains are being pursued, but not at the expense of financial integrity.

The message should be simple: We are capturing the upside while protecting the business and the reliability of our numbers.

A Closing Thought

The AI-ready CFO should not minimize AI risk. Make the risk visible, measurable, and governable so the organization can move without improvising controls after the fact. That requires tailoring the message without changing the substance. The CEO hears the cost of delay. The board sees risk-adjusted returns and clear control points. Business unit leaders see partnership and shared accountability. Investors see disciplined governance and disclosure integrity.

This is how the CFO moves the organization from anxiety to execution. The next chapter closes the loop by matching the right tool to the right risk and reinforcing the principle that AI adoption should be disciplined, not reckless.

Further Reading

Portfolio Modeling and Expected Value

- McKinsey & Company, *State of AI 2024* (McKinsey Digital, 2024), https://www.mckinsey.com/capabilities/quantumblack/our-insights/the-state-of-ai-2024
- McKinsey & Company, *Unlocking Value from Technology and AI Investments*, 2023, https://www.mckinsey.com/capabilities/strategy-and-corporate-finance/our-insights/ai-and-value-creation

Common Mistakes in Modeling ROI

- James Ryseff, Brandon F. De Bruhl, and Sydne J. Newberry, "Root Causes of Failure for Artificial Intelligence Projects and How They Can Succeed," *RAND*, 2024.
- Nathan Furr and Andrew Shipilov, "Beware the AI Experimentation Trap," *Harvard Business Review*, 2025.
- "The Top 5 Mistakes Killing Machine Learning ROI," *Data Science Society News*.
- "How to Measure AI ROI and Avoid Costly Mistakes," *8allocate*, 2025.
- Aditya Challapally, Chris Pease, Ramesh Raskar, and Pradyumna Chari, "MIT's GenAI Report: The GenAI Divide: State of AI in Business 2025," *MIT/NANDA Project*, 2025.

Chapter 5

Prioritizing Use Cases and Identifying Quick Wins

Key Takeaways

- **Quick wins as the first tranche of AI investments.** Early projects must be more than "easy." They are low-risk, high-feasibility initiatives that deliver measurable ROI, build credibility with the board and CEO, and establish governance frameworks. Examples include AP invoice automation, expense audits, reporting bots, cash forecasting, and reconciliations. These wins prove that AI can work in finance without exposing the enterprise to compliance failures.
- **From gut feel to structured prioritization.** Every CFO sees dozens of possible use cases, but sequencing matters. Using an impact–feasibility matrix helps identify quick wins, strategic bets, and

non-starters. A weighted scoring rubric deepens this discipline, turning subjective debates into transparent, defensible decisions that can be shown to boards and auditors.

- **Value–risk lens for governance.** Impact and feasibility tell you what is achievable; value and risk tell you how much oversight is required. Low-risk, high-value projects can be delegated. High-value, high-risk projects demand board-level scrutiny. The CFO must communicate these distinctions clearly to the CEO, to business units, to the board, and to investors.
- **Crawl–Walk–Run as a maturity model.** AI adoption is staged, not rushed. Crawl projects demonstrate ROI and governance in safe workflows. Walk projects expand scope with integrated forecasting, anomaly detection, and reporting. Run projects deliver strategic bets like continuous close and agent-driven workflows. Not all areas move together, some may crawl while others run. The CFO sets the pace, ensuring governance maturity justifies the next allocation of capital.
- **The quick-win playbook.** Quick wins are the CFO's "starter portfolio." They deliver visible impact in months, teach governance disciplines, and free up analyst capacity for higher-value work. Use them to prove scalability at volume; use them to demonstrate value without overextending resources. Either way, they are the foundation for long-term transformation.

The bottom line—AI adoption is all about sequencing initiatives with the same rigor applied to acquisitions, or entering new markets balancing short-term credibility with long-term bets, all while ensuring strong governance.

> Accountants tend to think of data at the chart-of-accounts level… the discussion surfaced that they need it at a data element level if they're going to apply AI to it.[1]
>
> —*Tom Hood, AICPA/CIMA*

From ROI Models to Execution Discipline

In the previous chapters, we reframed how the CFO should think about ROI in the AI era: not as a deterministic IT project with simple savings math, but as a portfolio of probabilistic investments where tangible and strategic returns must both be modeled. That reframing sets the stage for the next challenge: deciding where to start.

Not all AI use cases are created equal, and not all should be pursued at once. Some are well suited to deliver early, low-risk value and credibility with stakeholders; others are more ambitious, requiring data infrastructure, governance, and board-level oversight before they can be safely deployed. As stated in earlier chapters, the CFO's responsibility is to sort these opportunities with the same capital-allocation discipline applied to other projects such as acquisitions, new market entry, or large technology transformations.

Prioritization in this context removes the emotion of enthusiasm and expectations based on vendor promises. The AI-ready CFO should be thinking about structuring a balanced portfolio of initiatives that produces near-term proof at the same time, laying the groundwork for longer-term enterprise-wide transformation. This chapter provides a roadmap for doing just that:

- How to identify and capture quick wins that show measurable value without introducing unacceptable risk.
- How to apply structured frameworks to score and prioritize use cases, moving from vendor-led selection to objective, repeatable evaluation.
- How to sequence adoption through a Crawl–Walk–Run roadmap, aligning risk appetite, data maturity, and organizational learning.
- How to distinguish between high-risk, high-value bets that warrant careful staging and safe learning pilots that accelerate capability-building.

The goal is to equip finance leaders with the tools to move from theoretical, calculated ROI to real-life execution discipline. By the end of this chapter, the AI-ready CFO will have a practical playbook for deciding what to do first, what to defer, and how to build momentum without compromising governance.

Defining Quick Wins in CFO Terms

Most CFOs can identify a dozen areas where AI might add value: accounts payable, reconciliations, forecasting, management reporting, fraud detection, and more. The temptation is to pursue many of these at once, but without clear prioritization the finance function risks spreading scarce resources too thin, piloting tools that never scale, or handing control of the agenda to vendors. The role of the CFO is not to greenlight every idea but to sequence initiatives with the discipline of a portfolio manager.

Prioritization at this stage isn't about proving that AI can generate ROI; that work should already be done. Instead, it should determine which projects come first, because the order of operations will set the tone for how the organization experiences AI. McKinsey notes that finance leaders should focus on "a very small number of use cases with meaningful impact" and fund them disproportionately rather than experimenting broadly.[2] The first deployments either establish AI as a credible source of value or as a distraction that consumes energy without delivering returns. A successful early project builds confidence with the CEO, the board, and the finance team itself, while also creating political capital to pursue more ambitious initiatives.

In this context, these are not trivial or "learning" projects. Quick wins for the CFO are low-risk, high-feasibility initiatives that demonstrate measurable benefit quickly and begin to provide a framework on how AI might be integrated safely into complex processes like regulated workflows and meet compliance requirements. They're valuable because they accomplish four things simultaneously:

- **Build credibility.** Early results reassure leadership, auditors, and staff that AI tools can work reliably in finance.
- **Demonstrate governance.** By starting with controlled processes, finance teams can refine audit trails, override mechanisms, and explainability standards before tackling higher-stakes areas. KPMG has stressed that CFOs must ring-fence high-risk workflows such as external reporting until accuracy and controls are proven.[3]
- **Preserve control.** By defining quick wins internally, CFOs prevent vendors from dictating priorities based on their sales agenda rather than the organization's strategic needs.
- **Set foundations for future projects.** Quick wins set the foundation for strategic ROI through AI-focused data cleaning and management, development of reliable process maps for AI workflow conversion, and deployment of governance structures that larger, riskier initiatives will require to succeed.

Examples of genuine quick wins in finance include AI-enabled invoice intake and matching, automated reconciliations, narrative drafting for variance explanations, and first-draft cash-flow forecasts. These are structured, repetitive, auditable workflows where errors are containable and benefits are visible to leadership. In fact, Bain Capital Ventures' 2025 research confirms that these are exactly the entry points most finance teams are pursuing today, with AP automation, expense audits, procurement, and variance commentary leading early adoption.[4]

Prioritization isn't picking "easy" projects. The CFO needs to be setting the sequence of projects in a way that reduces regulatory or compliance risks, conserves limited capacity, and establishes momentum. In practice, this means resisting the urge to pursue every possible use case and instead investing in a select few that can be executed with speed, certainty, and impact.

Quick wins form the "crawl stage" of a Crawl–Walk–Run roadmap. They provide measurable ROI in the short term, but more importantly, they prepare the finance function for larger, riskier, and more transformative initiatives. For the AI-ready CFO, they are the bridge between financial justification and sustained execution discipline.

Prioritization Framework: Impact–Feasibility Matrix

While every use case may appear attractive on paper, not every project belongs at the top of the roadmap. The real task is to establish a disciplined approach to comparing initiatives, sequencing them, and ensuring that scarce capacity is invested where it delivers maximum value with minimal risk.

The CFO's Initial Screening Lenses

Before applying any scoring model, CFOs should look at four broad factors that shape both the order of adoption and the governance required:

- **Cost.** Even with modeled ROI, projects with very high upfront investment should be deferred until the organization has proven capabilities. Given the challenges of AI in general, there is little sense in starting with the most expensive initiative.
- **Complexity.** Early projects that may work best live in those environments where processes are structured and repeatable. Invoice matching or expense auditing are strong candidates because they follow consistent rules. A process supported by clean, structured data can be automated more easily than one that depends on inconsistent spreadsheets or manual inputs. Initiatives that touch multiple systems, require deep ERP integration, or

demand extensive change management are better sequenced later, after early wins establish credibility.

- **Compliance risk.** Workflows tied directly to financial statements or regulatory filings should not be first-wave candidates. These are high-value opportunities, but they require mature controls and oversight. A useful filter is to ask: If this system made a mistake, what would be the downstream impact? Start where the impact is contained and the ability to review and override is straightforward.
- **Scale and visibility.** The best early projects are highly visible to leadership and staff, and recur frequently enough to demonstrate tangible benefits. Automating a process that occurs only once a year, even if it is costly, will not build the same organizational confidence as streamlining a monthly or daily workflow. Similarly, automating a reconciliation process that touches hundreds of accounts has more strategic weight than building a one-off model for a niche scenario. Either way, C-suite visibility into the project's success is critical for ongoing support.

These four considerations serve as entry gates; they don't eliminate projects from the roadmap, but will determine if an initiative belongs in the "crawl" stage or should be deferred to the "walk" or "run" stage.

Translating Into Impact and Feasibility

The next step is to move from these high-level filters into a structured decision model. Impact and feasibility provide the two best dimensions that capture the logic of those initial filters in more measurable terms.

Impact reflects the magnitude of the benefit if the use case is successful.

- **Labor hours saved.** For example, automating manual invoice intake in a mid-market company processing 20,000 invoices can return thousands of hours to the finance team.
- **Error reduction.** Duplicate invoices, reconciliation breaks, and manual reporting adjustments all translate into real cost and audit exposure when errors persist.
- **Decision quality.** Better forecasts and variance analysis sharpen executive choices, which can reduce the cost of capital or prevent overspending.
- **Recurrence frequency.** A process that runs daily or monthly amplifies the benefit of improvement compared to one-time or annual tasks.

Feasibility measures how easily and safely the use case can be implemented.

- **Data readiness.** If data is clean, standardized, and accessible, implementation is straightforward; fragmented or inconsistent data signals higher risk.
- **Process stability.** Routine workflows like reconciliations or invoice matching are ideal; volatile or bespoke processes like M&A modeling carry higher execution risk.
- **Integration complexity.** Use cases that slot into the ERP or reporting system with minimal disruption should come earlier in the roadmap; those requiring custom integrations belong later.
- **Compliance exposure.** The higher the regulatory stakes, the more governance is needed before automation can be trusted—for instance, SEC filings vs. internal variance commentary.

By assigning scores across these dimensions, finance leaders can move beyond intuition to a repeatable, transparent way of evaluating candidates.

Mapping Feasibility Against Impact

Plotting these scores produces a simple but powerful map (Image 5.1):

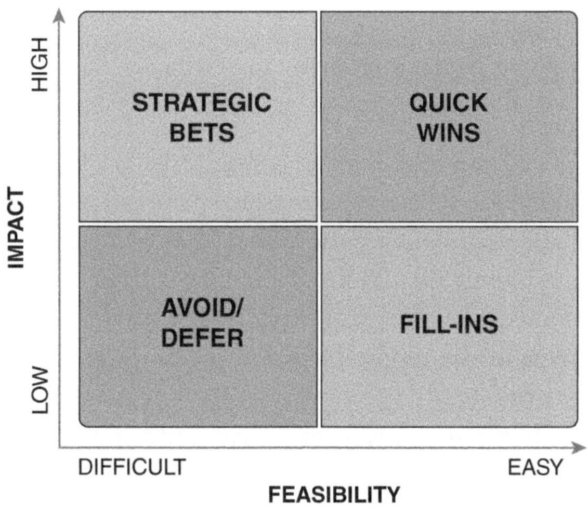

Image 5.1 AI Use-Case Feasibility Matrix

- **Quick Wins (High Impact, High Feasibility).** Start here. These projects deliver ROI quickly, build credibility, and can be executed with manageable risk.
- **Strategic Bets (High Impact, Lower Feasibility).** High-value initiatives that require more governance or integration should be staged for later, often with board oversight.
- **Fill-Ins (Low Impact, High Feasibility).** Safe, low-risk pilots that build skills and data pipelines, even if the direct financial payoff is modest.
- **Avoid/Defer (Low Impact, Low Feasibility).** Initiatives that neither deliver value nor can be implemented easily should be excluded.

This matrix provides a first filter to eliminate hype-driven projects and focus resources on initiatives that are both valuable and achievable.

While the impact–feasibility matrix provides CFOs with a simple way to visualize where each use case belongs, it remains a directional tool. To transition from high-level categorization to actual sequencing, finance leaders require a more granular approach for comparing initiatives on consistent terms. That is where a weighted prioritization rubric becomes indispensable. By assigning scores and weights to each dimension (from hours saved to compliance exposure), the rubric transforms qualitative judgments into quantitative rankings. This enables CFOs to document decisions, defend them to the board, and ensure that resources are allocated to initiatives with the optimal balance of value and feasibility.

Using the Weighted Scoring Rubric

The spreadsheet rubric (Table 5.1) adds rigor by quantifying both impact and feasibility. Each use case is rated numerically on the defined criteria, with weights applied to reflect organizational priorities. For example, if error reduction and compliance carry more weight in a regulated industry, they may count more heavily than hours saved. This approach allows CFOs to:

- **Rank projects objectively.** Preventing bias or vendor pressure from dictating priorities.
- **Document decisions.** Creating a clear audit trail for why some initiatives move forward and others are staged.
- **Sequence intelligently.** Even expensive, high-value projects can be placed in the roadmap, but in the "walk" or "run" stages rather than the "crawl."

Table 5.1 AI Use-Case Prioritization Rubric

			Project 1	Project 2	Project 3	Project 4	Project 5
Category	**Criterion**	**Weight (x)**	**Score**	**Score**	**Score**	**Score**	**Score**
Impact	Hours saved/cycle time	2					
	Error reduction/control quality	1.5					
	Decision impact/ stakeholder value	1.5					
	Frequency/recurrence	1					
Feasibility	Data availability and quality	2					
	Process stability and clarity	1					
	Integration complexity	0.5					
	Compliance risk	0.5					
	Prioritization score		0	0	0	0	0

How to Use This Sheet

1. Rate each criterion 1–5 based on your team's consensus.
2. The sheet multiplies the score by the weight and sums weighted scores to get a total out of 100.
3. Plot the use case on the prioritization matrix using its impact total vs. feasibility total.

Score	Meaning
1	Very low—minimal benefit or very challenging to achieve
2	Low—some benefit or notable challenges exist
3	Moderate—clear benefit, moderate effort or complexity
4	High—strong benefit, relatively straightforward to achieve
5	Very high—transformative benefit, very easy to implement

Impact

Criterion	Definition
Hours saved/cycle time	The potential of the AI solution to reduce manual work or shorten key process cycles (e.g., month-end close, forecast updates).
Error reduction/control quality	The extent to which the AI solution will reduce mistakes, improve data accuracy, and strengthen internal controls.
Decision impact/ stakeholder value	How much the AI output will improve the quality, speed, or confidence of decisions made by management, stakeholders, or clients.
Frequency/recurrence	How often the process occurs in a given period; high-frequency processes create more cumulative value from automation.

Feasibility

Criterion	Definition
Data availability and quality	Whether the necessary data is accessible, clean, and complete enough for the AI to work effectively.
Process stability and clarity	How well the process is documented, standardized, and consistently followed; unstable or ambiguous processes are harder to automate.
Integration complexity	The level of difficulty in connecting the AI to existing systems, tools, and workflows. Lower complexity = easier to pilot.

Criterion	Definition
Compliance risk	The likelihood that the AI could cause compliance, audit, or regulatory issues (SOX/ICFR, PII, etc.) if not properly controlled. Lower risk = higher feasibility.

Sample Use Cases

To see how the rubric works in practice, consider two potential AI initiatives that both show attractive ROI.

1. **Accounts payable invoice automation.** Automating invoice capture and three-way match to reduce manual entry time and error rates.
2. **AI-enhanced tax provisioning.** Using ML to improve accuracy and speed in quarterly and year-end tax provision calculations.

Both initiatives may return positive NPV in the ROI model, but the sequencing decision depends on how they score across the rubric's impact and feasibility dimensions.

Use Case 1: Accounts Payable Invoice Automation

Accounts payable is one of the most common starting points for AI in finance. The process is high-volume, rule-driven, and generates enough structured data to train models quickly. Here's how the scoring rubric applies to this use case.

Impact

- Hours saved/cycle time: 5 × 2.0 = 10.0
- Error reduction/control quality: 4 × 1.5 = 6.0
- Decision impact/stakeholder value: 3 × 1.5 = 4.5
- Frequency/recurrence: 5 × 1.0 = 5.0

Impact subtotal = 25.5 (out of max 30.0)

Feasibility

- Data availability and quality: 4 × 2.0 = 8.0
- Process stability and clarity: 5 × 1.0 = 5.0

- Integration complexity: 3 × 0.5 = 1.5
- Compliance risk: 4 × 0.5 = 2.0

Feasibility subtotal = 16.5 (out of max 20.0)
Position on matrix: High Impact, High Feasibility → **Quick Win**

Use Case 2: AI-Enhanced Tax Provisioning

Impact

- Hours saved/cycle time: 3 × 2.0 = 6.0
- Error reduction/control quality: 5 × 1.5 = 7.5
- Decision impact/stakeholder value: 5 × 1.5 = 7.5
- Frequency/recurrence: 2 × 1.0 = 2.0

Impact subtotal = 23.0

Feasibility

- Data availability and quality: 2 × 2.0 = 4.0
- Process stability and clarity: 2 × 1.0 = 2.0
- Integration complexity: 2 × 0.5 = 1.0
- Compliance risk: 1 × 0.5 = 0.5

Feasibility subtotal = 7.5
Position on matrix: High Impact, Low Feasibility → **Strategic Bet**

Result

While both projects have attractive ROI as modeled in Chapter 3, the rubric clarifies sequencing. Invoice automation should be prioritized as a crawl-stage quick win, while tax provisioning belongs in the run-stage roadmap once data quality and governance controls are mature.

The scoring system removes subjectivity. Instead of debating which project "feels" more valuable, the CFO can show the board a transparent comparison with weighted totals tied to finance-relevant criteria.

Additionally, every organization will have its own understanding of the potential benefits and challenges of any particular project, and will bring that knowledge to the rubric, creating a bespoke analysis as opposed to applying a one-size-fits-all approach to determining priority.

ROI tells you whether an AI initiative has value. The prioritization framework tells you when to pursue it. By applying the initial screening lenses, translating them into impact and feasibility scores, and using the matrix to guide sequencing, CFOs can ensure that early investments build credibility and capability while laying the groundwork for more complex, higher-stakes projects down the line.

Distinguishing Value and Risk

The value–risk lens is the final analysis of the individual AI project and tells the CFO how much oversight is required as initiatives move forward. Even high-value projects may not be worth the effort if their risk exposure outweighs their benefit at an early stage. Conversely, modest projects with minimal risk can play an important role in building organizational confidence.

How This Differs from Impact–Feasibility

At first glance, the value–risk matrix (Image 5.2) may appear similar to the impact–feasibility framework, but the distinction is important.

- **Impact–feasibility** focuses on achievability and efficiency, which projects can deliver measurable benefit and be implemented quickly.
- **Value–risk** shifts to governance and capital protection, which projects require board-level scrutiny and which can be delegated to operating teams.

A simple two-axis view helps translate potential opportunities into portfolio language that boards and CEOs readily understand:

- **High Value, Low Risk.** These projects should be pursued aggressively. They are the closest equivalent to financial "arbitrage"—opportunities to capture clear returns with limited downside. Many early automation use cases fall here.
- **High Value, High Risk.** These projects warrant serious board oversight. The CFO may stage them later in the roadmap, or ensure they're paired with rigorous controls. AI-driven tax provisioning or external financial disclosures fit this category.

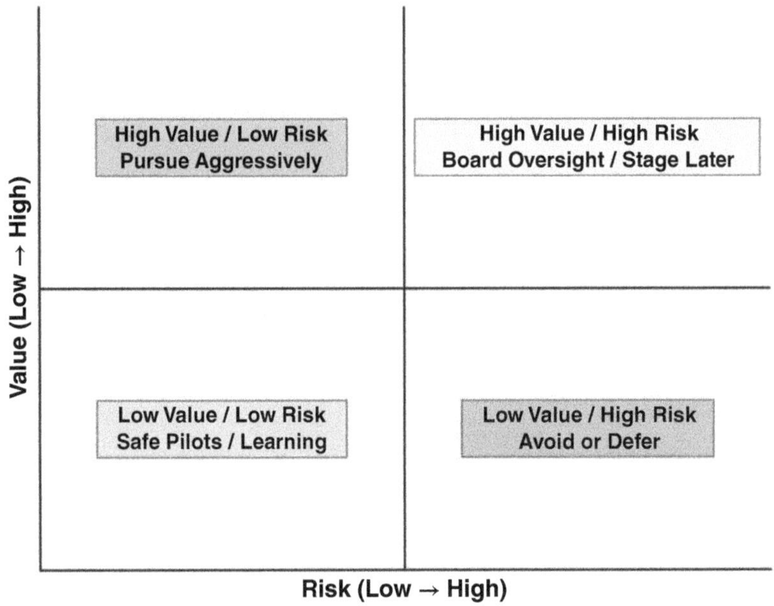

Image 5.2 The Value–Risk Matrix

- **Low Value, Low Risk.** These can serve as safe training grounds. While they don't transform the P&L, they allow finance teams to test controls and workflows with minimal exposure.
- **Low Value, High Risk.** These should be avoided or deferred. The potential payoff doesn't justify the exposure, and pursuing them early can undermine credibility.

This distinction gives the AI-ready CFO a way to speak the language of both operations and oversight. One framework helps sort projects into a logical sequence; the other helps justify the governance model around each project. The purpose of this mapping is not to exclude high-risk opportunities forever, but to sequence them properly.

Communicating Value and Risk

By making the trade-offs visible, a CFO can set expectations with their executive team and board. The matrix shows why a finance function might begin with invoice automation rather than jumping directly into

AI-driven forecasting, even if the latter promises greater long-term value. It provides a simple, yet disciplined, way to communicate priorities and ensure that adoption progresses in a controlled, strategic manner.

Corporate boards and investors also expect the CFO to ensure that AI initiatives don't jeopardize reporting integrity or compliance obligations. By classifying use cases through a value–risk lens, CFOs can explain the risk-adjusted rationale behind the sequencing:

- **To the CEO**—which projects strengthen decision-making with minimal downside.
- **To business units**—which initiatives can be tested in their workflows without triggering compliance concerns.
- **To the board**—which projects require oversight because the downside is material.
- **To investors**—which projects enhance financial discipline while preserving controls.

The Crawl–Walk–Run Roadmap

Once use cases are prioritized by feasibility and impact, then mapped according to value and risk, the next step is staged implementation. If this process works effectively, you'll avoid the mistake many organizations make by trying to jump from manual processes directly into ambitious, fully autonomous systems. The step-by-step approach of identifying the right initiatives and their proper place in an implementation sequence naturally leads to developing a custom-designed maturity model within a Crawl–Walk–Run framework. Following this simple approach, every organization can establish its own capital-allocation logic, governance requirements, and strategic value for each stage, based on its current comfort level with AI and aligned with the priorities and values established during the planning process.

AI implementation should be managed as a portfolio from the beginning. Not all initiatives progress at the same rate, nor should they. While some areas may remain in the crawl phase for an extended period, others may mature rapidly and be ready to implement run-level initiatives sooner. The interconnectivity and relationships between different departments—including IT, compliance, and operations—will likely be deciding factors in reaching the run stage. An AI-ready CFO must follow a planned path and allocate capital across a mix of initiatives, balancing quick wins that build credibility with more ambitious, high-value investments. At the same time, ensuring governance keeps pace as required by each stage.

Crawl: Building Credibility and Control

In the crawl stage, the CFO directs investment toward low-risk, high-feasibility initiatives that can be delivered quickly and measured accurately. As previously described, these projects are organized, rules-based workflows, such as invoice matching, expense audits, or initial variance explanations. These projects are not meant to transform the finance department or corporate strategy, but serve a crucial role to:

- Deliver early, measurable ROI that builds credibility with the rest of the leadership team and the board.
- Establish the review and override mechanisms that will become the foundation of governance as the initiatives take on greater significance.
- Begin to free up resource capacity that can be redeployed to more strategic uses.

At this first stage, the AI-ready CFO needs to demonstrate financial discipline by showing value quickly, but testing that value in areas where, if problems arise, it cannot materially harm the organization. Evolving out of the crawl stage will take time. The organization's comfort with AI technology, adaptability to change, and overall risk tolerance will serve as the guide for understanding when a crawl is ready to turn into a walk.

Walk: Expanding Scope with Governance Discipline

During the walk stage, once credibility is established, the CFO can begin introducing more interconnected and judgment-driven projects. These might include cash-flow forecasting, financial reporting narratives, or anomaly detection. While these projects offer greater economic benefits, they also come with increased governance requirements, as they intersect with accounting, compliance, and regulatory concerns. The key at this stage is the critical "human-in-the-loop" review. AI can draft, but finance professionals review, validate, and add context.

In the walk phase, the CFO must ensure:

- Audit trails have been standardized and are both reliable and explainable.
- The developed methods of control can scale across ERP and BI systems.
- The finance team builds the organizational strength to handle greater complexity without losing control.

Proving that AI-enabled processes can successfully operate at scale within the finance function, while ensuring that governance and oversight keep pace, is the essence of the walk stage.

Run: Deploying Strategic Bets

The run stage is when the finance function pursues its most ambitious goals. These could include rolling forecasts, continuous close, and autonomous, agent-driven workflows. The rewards are greater. With faster cycle times and near real-time reporting, finance is elevated to a true strategic partner of the CEO and board. However, the risks are also higher. Without the governance foundations established during the crawl and walk phases, the chances of material accounting, regulatory, and financial compliance failures or misstatements rise significantly. These initiatives might require direct board-level oversight, substantial capital investments, and coordination with IT, operations, and risk management. Success relies as much on culture and accountability as on algorithms.

Maturity Model, Not a Timeline

Crawl–Walk–Run is not a rigid (or even linear) calendar. Some initiatives, or entire organizations, may remain in crawl for extended time periods, while others may move quickly into the walk phase. What matters more is that each stage prepares the ground for the next. The urge to accelerate prematurely must be avoided. As CFO, you set the pace. You decide to advance only when governance maturity and organizational confidence justify the next allocation of capital. The AI-ready CFO must ensure that AI adoption is sustainable and aligned with the enterprise's tolerance for risk, delivering demonstrable value, financial discipline, and superior governance.

The Quick-Win Playbook

Before committing to large-scale AI programs, most CFOs find it useful to identify a set of early wins that can build organizational confidence and demonstrate measurable ROI. The playbook that follows outlines how to scope, prioritize, and sequence those initial investments.

Framing the First Tranche of AI Investments

Quick wins are going to be the first tranche of your AI portfolio, designed to demonstrate ROI, test governance, and build organizational confidence.

> Speed is God. Best ideas win. And if we're not making mistakes, we're not trying hard enough.[5]
>
> —*Michael Bayer, Wasabi*

For enterprises, these wins validate scale and readiness for bigger bets. For mid-market firms, they provide proof points that resources are well spent and that finance can deliver value without excessive complexity.

For enterprises, they demonstrate scalability and risk controls at volume. For mid-market firms, they deliver tangible efficiency without requiring major infrastructure overhauls. In both cases, they allow the CFO to present early results in hard ROI and in organizational learning to the CEO and board within extremely short timeframes.

1. **Invoice and Document Automation (AP + Beyond)**
   - **What it is.** Automating invoice intake, purchase order matching, approval routing, and document processing with OCR + NLP. AI extracts vendor names, payment terms, and amounts from unstructured files (PDFs, receipts, contracts) and matches them against purchase orders and the general ledger.
   - **Value delivered**
     - Substantially reduce cost per invoice, accelerate cycle times, and improve days payable outstanding (DPO).
     - Eliminate manual entry and errors, free staff to redeploy capacity toward higher-value work.

- **Governance test.** Establishes auditability, ensuring each extracted field is verified against system-of-record data. Introduces review/override controls for approvals.
- **Foundation for later.** Builds organizational confidence in AI handling structured + unstructured data, preparing the ground for reconciliation automation and close acceleration.

2. **Expense Audit Automation**
   - **What it is.** AI reviews expense claims for duplicates, policy breaches, and anomalies.
   - **Value delivered**
     - Cuts external audit adjustments, reduces fraud exposure, and improves compliance culture.
     - Demonstrates quick efficiency wins without needing deep technical integration.
   - **Governance test.** Validates explainability; every flagged item is documented with a reason code, strengthening trust in AI decisions.
   - **Foundation for later.** Extends anomaly detection capability into higher-stakes workflows like revenue assurance or treasury operations.

3. **Narrative and Reporting Bots (FP&A and Board)**
   - **What it is.** GenAI copilots draft explanations for budget variances and first-pass narratives for board and management reporting.
   - **Value delivered**
     - Cuts reporting cycle times by days or weeks, delivers consistency across business units, and supports quarterly earnings preparation.
     - Frees analysts from drafting, allowing them to partner more closely with business units on decision support.
   - **Governance test.** Tests human-in-the-loop workflows, where AI generates and finance validates, logging every change for audit purposes.
   - **Foundation for later.** Establishes narrative automation capabilities that can scale to investor relations updates, board packs, and integrated scenario planning.

4. **Cash Flow Forecasting**
   - **What it is.** ML models forecast short-term liquidity by analyzing historical collections, payroll schedules, and payment cycles.

- **Value delivered**
  - Improves accuracy and timeliness of forecasts, lowering perceived risk and cost of capital.
  - Prevents cash crunches and supports better working capital management.
  - Results visible in as little as a quarter, making it one of the most compelling CFO-ready quick wins.
- **Governance test.** Reinforces the discipline of logging assumptions, reconciling AI outputs with analyst judgment, and version-controlling forecast iterations.
- **Foundation for later.** Creates the foundation for rolling forecasts and continuous planning.

5. **Account Reconciliation Automation**
   - **What it is.** AI automates reconciliations between accounts and systems, surfacing exceptions for review.
   - **Value delivered**
     - Reduces audit fees, speeds monthly and quarterly close, and strengthens controls.
     - Relieves overextended staff and improves confidence in reported numbers.
   - **Governance test.** Codifies escalation rules, which exceptions trigger review, which trigger hard stops, teaching finance how to apply AI within Sarbanes–Oxley or equivalent frameworks.
   - **Foundation for later.** Positions the organization for continuous close initiatives, enabling near real-time reporting.

Bringing It All Together: CFO Value from Quick Wins

Each of these five plays offers tangible ROI (cost and cycle-time savings) while also serving as strategic pilots for governance, auditability, and cultural readiness.

- Enterprises can show that AI can scale without sacrificing controls.
- Mid-market firms can demonstrate that limited resources can still produce measurable impact.

Quick wins build the foundation for walk-stage projects, such as cash forecasting and board-level reporting, and ultimately for run-stage initiatives, including continuous-close or autonomous-agent workflows. Quick wins are the CFO's way of gaining organizational credibility and leadership buy-in while testing the systems, controls, and cultural adoption needed for broader AI transformation.

Notes

1. Hood, interview, December 17, 2025.
2. Ankur Agrawal, Ben Ellencweig, Rohit Sood, and Michele Tam, "Gen AI: A guide for CFOs," *McKinsey and Company*, November 15, 2023, https://www.mckinsey.com/capabilities/strategy-and-corporate-finance/our-insights/gen-ai-a-guide-for-cfos?
3. KPMG, *AI in Finance: US Report* (KPMG, 2024), 24–26, https://kpmg.com/kpmg-us/content/dam/kpmg/pdf/2024/audit/ai-in-finance-us-report-dec-2024.pdf
4. Abby Meyers and Nicole Falasco, "AI and the Office of the CFO in 2025: AI Spend to Increase Across Strategic and Administrative Activities," *BCV*, February 18, 2025, https://baincapitalventures.com/insight/ai-and-the-office-of-the-cfo-in-2025/
5. Bayer and Bento, interview, December 17, 2025.

Further Reading

- Boston Consulting Group, *Unlocking Potential from AI and GenAI. Executive Perspectives (Finance)*, October 2024, https://www.bcg.com/assets/2024/executive-perspectives-unlocking-impact-from-ai-finance-24oct.pdf. Crisp framing on where value shows up in finance, sequencing work, and operating-model implications; includes "how to get started" guidance CFOs can adapt.
- Deloitte, "The Path to GenAI Adoption in Finance," *Deloitte United States, CFO Insights*, accessed October 2025, https://www.deloitte.com/us/en/programs/chief-financial-officer/articles/the-path-to-genai-adoption-in-finance.html. Emphasizes picking a few use cases first, data readiness, and governance; maps well to a Crawl–Walk–Run rollout.
- Deloitte, "Advancing the Finance Function with Artificial Intelligence," *Deloitte Global*, accessed October 2025, https://www.deloitte.com/global/en/alliances/workday/analysis/advancing-the-finance-function-with-artificial-intelligence.html. Useful for capability/skills shifts and the implications for prioritization.

- Deloitte, "FinanceAI™: Harness the Power of Modern Finance," *Deloitte United States*, accessed October 2025, https://www.deloitte.com/us/en/services/consulting/services/ai-in-finance.html. Verticalized examples of high-impact finance use cases; helpful menu when you need concrete "starter" workflows (AP automation, close/recon, narrative drafting).

Chapter 6

The Landscape of AI Tools for the CFO's Team

Key Takeaways

- **Tool selection is value modeling in practice.** Every tool decision should trace back to measurable outcomes, both tangible ROI and strategic positioning. If you can't quantify what a tool delivers, you're not ready to buy it.
- **Governance maturity sets the pace, not vendor urgency.** The right tool adopted before your organization can govern it responsibly creates more risk than value. Let your control framework dictate the timeline.
- **Architecture should match the value horizon.** Start with embedded efficiency tools that prove returns quickly, then scale toward agent-driven intelligence as confidence and capability grow. This

progression positions the CFO as the architect of AI-enabled financial performance.

The Expanding AI Universe in the CFO's Domain

In the previous chapters, we established the financial logic for AI: how to assess its value, estimate its returns, and select use cases based on impact and feasibility. Now, the focus shifts from why to what, from measuring potential to exploring the growing landscape of AI tools that can realize that potential.

This is no longer a theoretical idea. AI is already integrated throughout the financial ecosystem. It can be found in the spreadsheets analysts use, in the ERP modules that handle payables and receivables, in treasury forecasting tools, and in reporting systems that produce board-ready reports. AI tools are not simply an add-on; they are increasingly woven into the fabric of finance.

That reality presents both opportunities and challenges. A decade ago, finance transformation mostly followed a straightforward approach: consolidate systems, standardize data, automate processes, and centralize reporting. The AI technology landscape is now much more fragmented and evolves at a faster pace.

AI capabilities are appearing everywhere:

- **Within enterprise platforms** such as embedded copilots and analytics engines.
- **In standalone, finance-specific solutions** targeting cash, forecasting, and close automation.
- **In foundational model ecosystems** where LLMs and agentic frameworks support a new generation of intelligent applications.

The result is a universe of tech options that expands in all directions at once, and understanding it doesn't mean tracking every product on the market. The AI-ready CFO needs to develop a framework for evaluation, identifying which categories of tools can improve performance and control, and which ones add unnecessary complexity or risk.

This chapter provides the framework. It outlines the main categories of AI tools relevant to the CFO's organization, from accounting to procurement, treasury to HR. It explains how these tools vary in maturity, integration, and strategic importance, and how they align with the ROI and prioritization models discussed earlier. It also highlights the tradeoffs the CFO must consider: speed vs. control, embedded convenience vs. standalone differentiation, and innovation vs. governance readiness.

The aim is not to build a product catalog, but to develop a clear understanding of the AI ecosystem shaping the finance function today. Every AI project, whether a quick win in accounts payable or a long-term investment in predictive analytics, relies on this ecosystem. Understanding its details will help the CFO make informed decisions, allocate resources wisely, and collaborate with the CIO and Chief Information Security Officer (CISO) on where technology intersects with control.

> The things that work for ERP adoption are the things that work for AI adoption. If you shortcut it, you're going to get crappy results.[1]
>
> —*Ranga Bodla, OracleNetsuite*

The following sections unpack that universe:

- First, by defining the three layers of the AI stack that currently shape the finance toolset: platform, application, and interface.
- Second, by mapping the category of tools across each function of the CFO's domain.
- Third, by framing how to match these tools to the organization's ROI goals and readiness level.

This chapter connects financial case-building with execution strategy. It makes sure that when the CFO shifts from ROI to procurement, they do so clear about which tools to choose and why each one fits into the bigger picture of value creation.

The Three Layers of AI in the Finance Stack

AI isn't just a single technology. It consists of multiple interconnected layers, each playing a different role in transforming data into insights and actions. Understanding this layered structure is crucial. It shapes how AI capabilities are integrated into the organization, how they interact with existing systems, and where risks and rewards are concentrated.

The AI stack (Table 6.1) can be thought of in three layers: platform, application, and interface. Each represents a different level of abstraction, from the foundational models that power AI, to the applications and systems that operationalize it in the enterprise, to the interfaces that make it usable.

How the Layers Interact

Each layer serves a distinct purpose, but none operates in isolation. A finance team drafting a board report with Microsoft's Copilot (interface) relies on embedded AI in Excel and Power BI (application), which in turn depend on foundation models like GPT or Claude (platform). Together, these layers form a vertical chain of value creation from model intelligence to business insight.

Recognizing this structure informs how AI decisions are made. It defines *who* to involve, *what* to measure, and *how* to control for risk.

- **At the platform layer.** The CFO works closely with the CIO, CISO, and General Counsel to assess enterprise exposure, contractual obligations, and data usage boundaries. The goal is assurance, knowing that every model behind a financial output can be explained and audited.
- **At the application layer.** The CFO acts as a portfolio manager, balancing quick wins (e.g., invoice automation) with strategic bets (e.g., continuous forecasting). This is the layer where ROI modeling, prioritization, and capital allocation converge.
- **At the interface layer.** The CFO becomes a change leader, ensuring the finance team (and other departments) use AI responsibly and effectively. Adoption, training, and internal communication become as important as the tools themselves.

Why Layer Awareness Matters

Understanding these layers allows the CFO to:

Table 6.1 The AI Technology Stack

Layer	Description	Examples	CFO implication	CFO decision focus
Platform (infrastructure AI)	The foundational large models and APIs (LLMs, vector databases, agent frameworks) on which other tools are built	OpenAI GPT, Anthropic Claude, xAI Grok, Google Gemini, IBM WatsonX	These are not tools but *capabilities*. The CFO must understand where the enterprise's data flows into them, directly or through vendors	Long-term strategic alignment. Ensure data governance, security, and model transparency are adequate. Engage CIO and CISO to assess risk exposure and control frameworks
Application (embedded and specialized AI)	Finance applications embedding AI to automate specific workflows	Microsoft Copilot, Oracle Fusion AI, SAP Joule, Workday AI, Kyriba, BlackLine, Pigment	This is where the CFO's team works day-to-day; ROI and control are visible	Tactical investment prioritization. Evaluate ROI, speed of integration, and control impact. This is where most quick wins and measurable returns are found
Interface (assistive AI and agents)	Chat-based copilots, domain-specific assistants, and agents that orchestrate workflows	ChatGPT Enterprise, Microsoft 365 Copilot, Notion AI, internal AI agents	Where the finance team interacts directly with AI; this layer defines adoption experience and governance risk	Change management and user readiness. Define usage policies, access controls, and training. Focus on productivity gains and consistency in governance

- **Avoid redundancy.** Prevent multiple teams from deploying overlapping AI capabilities in different tools.
- **Manage governance boundaries.** Ensure auditability and explainability extend through all layers from data to decision.
- **Link ROI to architecture.** Tie each AI investment back to the right value horizon (short-term automation vs. long-term transformation).
- **Sequence adoption intelligently.** Introduce tools where integration and oversight are most manageable first, then scale upward.

This perspective helps ensure that AI adoption aligns with the finance function's mandate and reinforces that while AI may be everywhere in the stack, accountability must still flow to a single point: the CFO as the steward of financial integrity and strategic capital deployment.

The AI Coding Stack and Engineering Enablement

AI-augmented custom software development—utilizing developer copilots, code agents, and enterprise build platforms—enables the assembly of finance-specific tools, connectors, and agentic workflows on top of your data estate, forming an adjacency to the other three layers.

Typical components include:

- **Developer copilots and agents** that write/modify code and tests, refactor services, and scaffold integrations (e.g., GitHub Copilot and Copilot Agent).
- **Enterprise build platforms** for GenAI apps and agents on proprietary data (e.g., Databricks Mosaic AI, Snowflake Cortex).
- **SDLC governance for AI code** (secure development practices tailored to GenAI; model and component provenance).

Why It Matters

- **Velocity.** Controlled studies and field research show material productivity gains in coding tasks, often translating to faster time-to-value for internal tools and integrations.

- **Adoption is mainstream, but trust requires controls.** The 2024 Stack Overflow data shows ~76%+ using or planning to use AI in dev workflows; 2025 coverage highlights rising usage with persistent accuracy and trust concerns, underscoring the need for human review and secure SDLC.
- **From assistance to agents.** New "coding agents" can autonomously fix bugs or implement small features under review, accelerating maintenance and integration work—highly relevant when finance needs bespoke connectors or policy logic.

When the CFO Should Care

- **For large enterprises/S&P 1000.** Engineering enablement can reduce integration backlogs, accelerate policy automation, and support controlled internal agents. The "Build vs. Buy vs. Hybrid" section in the next chapter will explore this further.
- **For mid-market.** The opportunity with the coding stack allows for light customization and integration, where full internal builds are usually unwieldy or not cost-effective.

The CFO's AI Tool Map: Function-by-Function Overview

AI is no longer confined to a single tool or workflow; it's now on a path to touch nearly every process that moves through the CFO's office. From accounts payable to tax compliance, forecasting to procurement, AI has a multi-threaded capability that can be embedded in both the systems and the culture of financial operations.

Table 6.2 summarizes how AI is being applied across core and adjacent domains of the CFO's remit, showing the primary use, AI application, and a value lens through which each can be evaluated.

This table serves as both a capability inventory and a decision compass, enabling a CFO to:

1. **Identify where AI might already exist**—often hidden within ERP or collaboration tools.

Table 6.2 CFO AI Tool Map

Function	Primary use	AI application	Value lens (ROI focus)
Accounting and close	Reconciliation, journal entries, variance analysis, and close reporting	ML anomaly detection, automated reconciliations, and narrative generation tools	*Hard ROI:* reduced close cycle time and error rates *Strategic ROI:* improved control integrity
FP&A	Forecasting, scenario modeling, budget management, and board reporting	Predictive analytics, GenAI for commentary, and LLM-assisted scenario design	*Strategic ROI:* better decision quality, real-time insight, and faster scenario responsiveness
Treasury and cash management	Liquidity planning, investment management, and risk monitoring	Predictive forecasting, sentiment analysis for macro indicators, autonomous liquidity balancing	*Hard ROI:* working capital optimization *Strategic ROI:* improved risk anticipation and capital agility
Procurement and payables	Vendor management, invoice processing, purchase order matching	NLP-driven invoice parsing, RPA + AI exception handling, vendor risk-scoring models	*Hard ROI:* cycle time and cost savings *Governance ROI:* enhanced supplier compliance
Receivables and credit	Collections management, credit risk assessment, and cash application	AI-driven collection prioritization, customer payment behavior prediction, automated cash posting	*Hard ROI:* DSO reduction *Strategic ROI:* improved working capital predictability
Tax and compliance	Return preparation, reconciliation, audit documentation	Document recognition, rules-based automation, and regulatory update monitoring	*Hard ROI:* reduced audit prep time *Governance ROI:* enhanced compliance accuracy

Audit and risk management	Internal audit, control monitoring, and fraud detection	Continuous control testing, exception reporting, and predictive fraud analytics	*Strategic ROI:* lower risk exposure *Governance ROI:* improved assurance coverage
HR and payroll (finance-adjacent)	Payroll validation, workforce analytics, and planning	Predictive payroll validation, anomaly detection in compensation data	*Hard ROI:* process efficiency *Strategic ROI:* finance–HR data alignment
Travel and expense management	Expense policy enforcement and fraud detection	Vision and NLP models to extract and validate receipts; anomaly detection in claims	*Hard ROI:* reduced reimbursement errors *Governance ROI:* improved compliance visibility
Legal and governance (finance-adjacent)	Contract review, policy analysis, and risk documentation	Generative AI for clause extraction and summary; model-based policy compliance validation	*Strategic ROI:* faster cycle time *Governance ROI:* enhanced transparency in compliance processes

2. **Determine the tools for leveraging incremental value**—where small automation pilots can deliver measurable savings or free up capacity.
3. **Spot governance exposure**—the functions with sensitive data or regulatory implications that demand stronger oversight before AI scaling.
4. **Coordinate investment**—avoiding fragmented tool adoption across departments.

When layered over the ROI and prioritization frameworks developed in earlier chapters, this map helps establish a portfolio view of AI opportunities. Each cell represents a potential project, with different risk, maturity, and value potential.

- **Tangible (hard) ROI functions** (e.g., AP automation, close acceleration) are natural early-stage pilots.
- **Strategic (soft) ROI functions** (e.g., FP&A, treasury) mature later but yield long-term competitive advantage.
- **Governance ROI areas** (e.g., audit, compliance) ensure that efficiency gains do not come at the expense of integrity.

The CFO's Role in Tool Coordination

Finance and the CFO can't directly "own" every tool, but they do oversee the economic logic behind every implementation. Finance leaders should:

- Establish a central inventory of AI-enabled tools across functions.
- Require ROI accountability from tool sponsors (e.g., controller, treasurer, head of FP&A).
- Ensure data lineage and auditability for every AI-driven process that impacts financial reporting.
- Coordinate with the CIO and CISO to confirm that platform-level controls and vendor SLAs cover all tools in use.

By adopting a portfolio-level perspective, the CFO guarantees that AI implementation supports operational excellence and strategic insight, while maintaining control and compliance.

Embedded vs. Standalone Tools: A CFO's Integration Tradeoff

Understanding the finance AI ecosystem is only part of the task. The next step is to determine how these capabilities are integrated into the enterprise, whether through existing platforms or as standalone solutions. This distinction, between embedded AI and standalone AI solutions, affects both the speed of adoption and the level of strategic control.

In earlier stages of enterprise software, most features were built-in, and innovation followed vendor release cycles. AI has transformed that dynamic. Today, every major platform vendor is integrating AI capabilities, while a parallel market of specialized providers is developing focused, best-in-class applications. This presents a double-edged sword for the CFO: embedded tools offer seamless integration and lower risk, while standalone systems provide speed and expertise, but will often increase complexity.

In practice, no AI finance tool is truly self-contained. The distinction between embedded and standalone reflects functional scope and ownership, not system isolation. Both depend on shared data, governance, and integration standards. The difference lies in where control resides and how value is delivered.

The Core Tradeoff

Table 6.3 summarizes the key attributes of each approach from the perspective of finance leadership.

Table 6.3 Core Traits of Embedded or Standalone AI Tools

Attribute	Embedded AI (within existing platform ecosystem)	Standalone or specialized AI solutions
Speed to deploy	Fast—leverages existing ERP, EPM, or productivity environments	Slower—requires new integrations and data connections
Governance burden	Lower—inherits enterprise authentication, logging, and control frameworks	Higher—needs dedicated controls, access management, and assurance testing

(*Continued*)

Table 6.3 (Continued)

Attribute	Embedded AI (within existing platform ecosystem)	Standalone or specialized AI solutions
Customization potential	Limited—capabilities shaped by vendor roadmap	High—can be tailored to specific processes or data models
Lock-In risk	High—tied to platform vendor strategy and update cadence	Moderate—more portable, but dependent on integration APIs
Differentiation	Low—same capabilities available to all peers using the platform	High—can deliver unique processes and analytical models
Capital cost profile	Incremental—bundled within existing licenses or add-ons	Separate—subscription or build costs with variable scalability
Support and maintenance	Managed by vendor IT ecosystem	Requires internal oversight or third-party support
Time to value	Short—ideal for early ROI pilots	Medium—higher setup cost, but longer-term strategic upside

When Embedded AI Makes Sense

Embedded AI (e.g., Microsoft Copilot, Oracle Fusion AI, SAP Joule, or Workday's built-in ML tools) is the most natural starting point for many finance organizations. It offers immediate efficiencies without major architectural change. Because these tools reside within systems already under IT and audit control, the governance model is, likely, largely pre-existing.

CFO guidance:

- Use embedded AI for early-stage quick wins and low-risk automations that don't require data movement.
- Treat them as productivity multipliers, not strategic differentiators.
- Focus on governance assurance: confirm that embedded AI outputs follow the same review, approval, and documentation standards as manual processes.
- Use early success here to build credibility before scaling into more complex deployments.

These tools help demonstrate tangible ROI (e.g., reducing reporting cycles, streamlining reconciliations) while reinforcing the message that finance innovation can occur safely within established control environments.

When Standalone AI Adds Strategic Value

Standalone AI platforms, such as Kyriba for treasury, Ramp for payments, BlackLine for accounting automation, or Pigment for planning, delve deeper into specialized functions. They are ideal for organizations seeking competitive advantage, data-driven insights, or custom control logic beyond what embedded tools offer.

CFO guidance:

- Pursue standalone AI when the use case is material enough to justify integration effort, and when data readiness is high.
- Require the business case to quantify not only cost savings but also strategic and capacity ROI, such as improved decision velocity or risk anticipation.
- Establish joint oversight with the CIO for integration architecture and the CISO for data boundaries and model explainability.
- Mandate a pilot phase: verify that results produced in a standalone environment can be reconciled to official data and reporting sources.

Standalone AI offers flexibility by allowing the definition of processes and models that competitors can't replicate. However, this flexibility requires additional governance, particularly for model drift, data lineage, and third-party risk.

The Tradeoff in Practice

In a large enterprise, these decisions often mirror capital-allocation choices: embedded AI represents short-term operational gains, while standalone AI indicates long-term strategic potential. Both generate ROI, but on different timelines and with different governance needs.

For mid-market organizations, the distinction is just as important, even if their size varies. A finance team with limited IT resources may rely on embedded tools to gain early value safely, while selectively using standalone applications for processes that are both costly and recurring.

Ultimately, the AI-ready CFO must ensure that AI adoption aligns with business logic, not vendor momentum. Embedded tools will continuously evolve; standalone platforms will multiply. Without a clear integration strategy, you'll face redundant tools, fragmented data, and uncontrolled spending.

Integration Realities: Why Nothing Is Truly Standalone

Even so-called standalone AI systems in finance, treasury platforms like Kyriba, close-automation suites such as BlackLine, or FP&A and planning tools like Pigment cannot function in isolation. Each relies on stable integration with the organization's ERP, general ledger, data warehouse, and identity systems to access, validate, and update financial data.

For this reason, "standalone" should not be read as "independent." It denotes functional specialization and ownership, not technical isolation. Embedded tools extend existing enterprise systems, such as ERP modules, productivity suites, or collaboration platforms, while standalone tools deliver deeper functionality in a single domain. Both ultimately depend on the same data and control infrastructure.

The CFO should not decide whether to integrate, but how much integration risk to accept at a given stage of maturity. Embedded tools usually pose lower risk and deliver faster returns because they inherit governance and data controls from existing systems. Specialized or "standalone" tools offer greater strategic potential but require stronger data discipline, clearer ownership, and more cross-functional coordination with IT, risk, and compliance.

Tool Selection Logic: Linking to ROI and Quick Wins

Tool selection isn't just a technical task. It's a matter of capital discipline, directing limited investment capacity toward initiatives that balance return, risk, and organizational readiness. Viewed this way, every AI adoption choice can be traced back to these three questions:

1. **What type of value are we pursuing?** (Efficiency, insight, or differentiation)
2. **What level of organizational readiness supports that goal?** (Data, governance, or change management)
3. **What integration path delivers the outcome with the least disruption?** (Embedded vs. standalone vs. custom)

Aligning Tool Selection to ROI Horizons

Different categories of AI tools produce various types of ROI. Using the framework in Table 6.4, tools can be matched to the expected value horizon: short-term (efficiency), mid-term (insight), or long-term (strategic capability).

This framework links the type of tool to an expected financial return profile and timeline. The logic is: the farther out on the horizon, the greater the need for data maturity, change management, and governance depth.

Table 6.4 AI Tool Selection Framework

CFO objective	AI tool category	Example use case	Expected ROI type	Time horizon
Reduce manual effort	Embedded AI in ERP or productivity platforms	Invoice automation, expense validation, account reconciliations	Hard ROI—cost and time savings	<6 months
Enhance decision accuracy and speed	Specialized AI applications	Cash forecasting, FP&A automation, treasury risk modeling	Strategic ROI—improved decision quality	6–18 months
Transform capability and create differentiation	Custom or AI-agent solutions built on foundational models	Proprietary forecasting agents, dynamic pricing models, autonomous close systems	Long-term ROI—strategic advantage	18–36 months

Tool Maturity and Selection Discipline

Not all AI tools are created equal, nor are they equally ready for your organization. Maturity in this context is focused on evidence, reliability, and alignment with the organization's readiness to adopt, as seen in Table 6.5. Just as the ROI model distinguishes between short-term, mid-term, and long-term value, tool maturity will help determine where each investment belongs in the adoption sequence.

Tool maturity should directly influence capital allocation and governance intensity.

- **Emerging tools** demand smaller, reversible bets with strict validation.
- **Maturing tools** justify mid-term investments once controls are proven.
- **Proven platforms** anchor the long-term transformation portfolio.

By aligning maturity with the ROI horizon, the CFO keeps experimentation disciplined, risk visible, and capital working toward measurable, auditable value.

Sequencing by Organizational Readiness

Tool selection should also align with the organization's current stage on its AI maturity curve. A mid-market firm with limited IT resources might focus on embedded tools for automation and reporting. Meanwhile, a global enterprise could be prepared to test custom models or autonomous agents.

The right sequencing follows three readiness signals, as seen in Table 6.6.

By using these signals, the CFO ensures that adoption maturity determines timing.

Choosing by Value, Not Hype

Distraction is probably the single biggest risk in the current AI hype cycle. Vendors will put on impressive demos; analysts will point out trends; and peers will display flashy new implementations. The CFO must stay

Table 6.5 AI Maturity and Tool Selection

Maturity stage	Typical characteristics	CFO evaluation focus	Recommended use
Emerging tools	• Early-stage or Gen-1 products with limited enterprise deployments • Often positioned as pilots or proof-of-concepts • High innovation, low control maturity	• Governance risk: data handling, model explainability • Financial viability of vendor • Alignment with internal data-security requirements	Use selectively for experimentation and learning under tight governance. Require a Pilot Evidence Package before any scale-up
Maturing tools	• Demonstrated ROI in comparable organizations • Clear integration pathways with ERP/BI systems • Growing partner ecosystem and documentation standards	• Integration feasibility and audit-trail strength • Vendor service reliability • Total cost of ownership (TCO) including implementation and support	Prioritize for strategic pilots and walk-stage initiatives that extend automation into decision support
Proven platforms	• Enterprise-grade solutions with validated controls and audit certification (SOC 2, ISO 27001) • Stable APIs, service-level commitments, and reference clients • Embedded within established enterprise ecosystems	• ROI realization vs. modeled expectations • Change-management and adoption cost • Long-term lock-in exposure and upgrade cadence	Adopt for run-stage scaling and integration into core finance architecture. Use as foundation for multi-function optimization

Table 6.6 Organizational AI Readiness

Readiness dimension	Indicators	Implication for tool selection
Data and integration	Clean, unified data; stable ERP integrations	Enables movement from embedded to specialized tools
Governance and controls	Documented review and override mechanisms; defined model validation	Supports scaling into standalone or custom applications
Culture and capability	Trained users, cross-functional AI literacy	Allows transition toward agentic workflows and enterprise innovation

focused on the financial logic. If the return is unmeasured, it's speculation. If the risk is undefined, it's exposure.

To prevent technology enthusiasm from outpacing business rationale, CFOs should maintain a living tool evaluation matrix, updated quarterly, that tracks:

- Active tools under pilot or implementation.
- ROI categories and realization metrics.
- Governance maturity and audit assurance status.
- Integration complexity and dependency risk.

This portfolio view transforms AI adoption from a series of ad-hoc initiatives into a managed investment program, with each decision linked to an explicit financial hypothesis and a defined review process.

A Final Note About Low-Code and RPA: The Bridge to Intelligent Automation

Most finance organizations have most likely already begun their enterprise AI journey through RPA or low-code platforms such as UiPath, Power Automate, or Automation Anywhere. These systems handle deterministic, rules-based workflows to move data, match invoices, or reconcile transactions with high reliability but minimal AI.

As AI capabilities mature, these same tools are becoming a bridge layer between traditional automation and intelligent systems. They provide a familiar foundation for introducing ML or generative components without disrupting established processes. They can serve as a practical continuity path: extending efficiency gains while preparing data, workflows, and governance frameworks for more adaptive, probabilistic AI models.

Deterministic automation isn't obsolete; it's part of the infrastructure. While stabilizing processes today, they can lay the operational groundwork for AI-driven decision support tomorrow.

Note

1. Ranga Bodla (NetSuite/Oracle), interviewed by Glenn Hopper, Google Meet, December 16, 2025.

Further Reading

- National Institute of Standards and Technology, *Artificial Intelligence Risk Management Framework (AI RMF 1.0)*, 2023, https://www.nist.gov/itl/ai-risk-management-framework
- National Institute of Standards and Technology, *NIST AI RMF Playbook*, 2023, https://www.nist.gov/itl/ai-risk-management-framework/nist-ai-rmf-playbook
- Begum Karaci Deniz, Chandra Gnanasambandam, Martin Harrysson, Alharith Hussin, and Shivam Srivastava, "Unleash Developer Productivity with Generative AI," McKinsey & Company, 2023, https://www.mckinsey.com/capabilities/mckinsey-digital/our-insights/unleashing-developer-productivity-with-generative-ai
- McKinsey & Company, *How Gen AI will Reshape the Software Business*, 2024, https://www.mckinsey.com/industries/technology-media-and-telecommunications/our-insights/navigating-the-generative-ai-disruption-in-software
- McKinsey & Company, "Technology's Generational Moment with Generative AI: A CIO and CTO Guide," 2023, https://www.mckinsey.com/capabilities/tech-and-ai/our-insights/technologys-generational-moment-with-generative-ai-a-cio-and-cto-guide
- Curt Jacobsen, Erik Witte, Kaz Kazmier, and Oscar Villarreal. "Proven Strategies for Building Gen AI Capability," *McKinsey Digital*, 2025, https://www.mckinsey.com/capabilities/mckinsey-digital/our-insights/overcoming-two-issues-that-are-sinking-gen-ai-programs
- GitHub, *GitHub Introduces Coding Agent For GitHub Copilot*, 2025, https://github.com/newsroom/press-releases/coding-agent-for-github-copilot
- GitHub Blog, *Meet the New Coding Agent—GitHub Copilot*, 2025, https://github.blog/news-insights/product-news/github-copilot-meet-the-new-coding-agent/

- InfoWorld, *Spec-driven AI Coding with GitHub's Spec Kit*, 2025, https://www.infoworld.com/article/4062524/spec-driven-ai-coding-with-githubs-spec-kit.html
- GitHub Changelog, *Copilot Coding Agent is now Available in GitHub Enterprise Cloud with Data Residency*, 2025, https://github.blog/changelog/2025-08-27-copilot-coding-agent-is-now-available-in-github-enterprise-cloud-with-data-residency/
- Docs GitHub, *About GitHub Copilot Coding Agent*, https://docs.github.com/en/enterprise-cloud@latest/copilot/concepts/agents/coding-agent/about-coding-agent
- GitHub Blog, *GitHub Copilot Coding Agent 101: Getting Started with Agentic Workflows*, https://github.blog/ai-and-ml/github-copilot/github-copilot-coding-agent-101-getting-started-with-agentic-workflows-on-github/

AI Adoption and Disruption in Finance/Tools

- McKinsey & Company, *The Economic Potential of Generative AI*, 2023, https://www.mckinsey.com/capabilities/mckinsey-digital/our-insights/the-economic-potential-of-generative-ai-the-next-productivity-frontier
- McKinsey & Company, *AI-enabled Software Development Fuels Innovation*, 2025, https://www.mckinsey.com/industries/technology-media-and-telecommunications/our-insights/how-an-ai-enabled-software-product-development-life-cycle-will-fuel-innovation

Chapter 7

AI Partnerships and Platform Strategy: The Build–Buy–Hybrid Decision

Key Takeaways

- **Think partnership, not procurement.** AI vendors aren't tool suppliers, their products and services become embedded in your financial architecture. Choose them as you would a strategic partner: for trust, transparency, and resilience, not flashy sales pitches or convenience. The risk isn't buying the wrong tool; it's entering the wrong partnership.
- **Due diligence is governance in action.** Vendor diligence is where the CFO's fiduciary mindset meets AI's technical complexity. Evaluate vendors across four dimensions:

  - **Maturity**—Is the AI real, tested, and domain-relevant?
  - **Explainability**—Can you defend its outputs to auditors and regulators?
  - **Security**—Does it meet your CISO's standards and compliance obligations?
  - **Financial fit**—Do costs and ROI align with enterprise economics?
  - **Guiding principle**—Every vendor must withstand both technical and financial audit scrutiny.
- **Build, buy, or hybrid is an architecture decision.** Building vs. buying isn't binary. Taking a portfolio approach allows for strategic flexibility and options.
  - **Build** when AI touches proprietary data or differentiates your business.
  - **Buy** when the process is standardized and time-to-value matters.
  - **Hybrid** when you need both speed and control.
- **Align this sourcing decision with the embedded vs. standalone framework.** Embedded capabilities (close to core systems) often justify building or co-developing; standalone utilities favor buying.
- **Negotiate for optionality.** Contracts are where governance becomes enforceable. CFOs should secure:
  - **Data ownership** (your data, your rules).
  - **Outcome-based pricing** (pay for results, not consumption).
  - **Audit access** (retain explainability rights).
  - **Exit ramps** (no silent lock-in).
  - **Guiding principle**—Negotiate like you may need to leave the partnership, because someday, you might.
- **Collaborate without losing control.** Work shoulder-to-shoulder with the CIO, CTO, and CISO. They validate technical feasibility and security posture; you define financial guardrails and ROI thresholds. Collaboration ensures completeness, not dilution of accountability.

The Importance of Partnership

Selecting the right AI partner is one of the most consequential decisions a CFO will make in the early phases of adoption. These relationships increasingly define how data flows through the enterprise, how financial results are verified, and how confidently the organization can scale automation. While technology teams may lead implementation, the governance of these partnerships, how value is measured, risks are managed, and accountability is shared, ultimately sits with finance.

AI partnerships differ from traditional software procurement. Once embedded, they become part of the enterprise architecture, influencing the efficiency of close processes, the transparency of reporting, and the agility with which the organization can respond to new demands. Each choice shapes future cost structures, audit readiness, and the finance function's ability to innovate responsibly.

CFOs have been here before with ERP selection. You don't pick an ERP because a peer company picked it, or because it demos well. You pick it because it supports your workflows, your controls, and your data model, and because you can live with the implementation risk and the operating cost for years. AI vendor selection is the same muscle. The decision has to be anchored in what the tool can reliably do in your environment, how it ties out to system-of-record data, and what it takes to run it with an evidence trail, not what's popular in the market.

The risk, therefore, is not merely selecting the wrong tool, it's committing to the wrong partnership. A poor vendor decision does more than waste budget; it can erode credibility with the board and the executive team. If finance champions a platform that underdelivers or introduces compliance risks, the broader transformation agenda can lose momentum. Conversely, a disciplined, transparent selection process builds trust across the enterprise. It signals that AI adoption is being guided by the same fiduciary discipline that governs every major financial decision.

Part of the challenge lies in the asymmetry of information. Vendors live and breathe their products, while finance leaders are often encountering these technologies for the first time. Even seasoned executives can be swayed by a polished demo or a marketing claim that stretches the boundary between what is possible and what is production-ready. Without a structured evaluation framework, finance risks buying into aspiration rather than validated capability.

For most CFOs, this is a lived experience. Some automation initiatives stall when integration is harder than advertised, or when the promised efficiencies don't show up in cycle time, error rates, or rework. Others deliver meaningful results when the vendor acts as a strategic partner, helping compress close cycles, strengthen forecasting, and improve control consistency. Those contrasting outcomes reinforce a simple reality: partnership diligence is now a standing capability of the finance function, not a one-time project checkpoint.

Finance brings a unique lens to these relationships. Where a CTO might focus on scalability or model performance, the CFO evaluates governance performance, including the reliability of outputs, the defensibility of controls, and the sustainability of the commercial model. The core questions are pragmatic, but strategic:

- Can outputs be reconciled to underlying data and defended to auditors or regulators?
- Does the economic model align with capital-efficiency goals?
- Will the partnership preserve optionality as AI technologies evolve?

Each of these considerations ties directly to enterprise outcomes, predictability, working-capital efficiency, and risk assurance.

Ultimately, vendor diligence is an extension of the CFO's fiduciary role. A misstep here doesn't just result in a failed pilot; it might trap the enterprise in a multi-year contract that limits flexibility and drains confidence in innovation. But when partnerships are selected and governed with transparency, measurable outcomes, and contractual clarity, they become accelerators of transformation. They prove that finance can lead with innovation while protecting the integrity of the enterprise and are the CFO's first line of defense against wasted investment, reputational risk, and failed transformation.

Inside the AI Shift: A Vendor's View

To discuss the day-to-day realities of AI implementation inside finance organizations, I sat down with Ranga Bodla, Vice President at Oracle NetSuite, to get a closer look at how AI is being built into the tools finance teams use every day. Ranga is in a rare position: part strategist, part translator, working between product teams, CFOs, and operators trying to grow fast without breaking things.

NetSuite has been on the AI path for years. First with ML, now with GenAI embedded throughout the platform. But as Ranga said clearly in our chat, "The tech only works if the foundation is solid.

AI won't clean up bad data or fix sloppy workflows. What it *can* do is scale good ones—fast."[1]

A few of Ranga's thoughts include:

- AI falls flat without process discipline or data maturity.
- The CFOb (not the CIO) has become the natural driver of AI adoption.
- ERP rollouts taught us a lot about what makes AI fail or fly.
- There are specific kinds of use cases that build momentum inside finance teams.
- AI "prompting" is quickly becoming a skill you can't outsource.

Ranga's take is refreshingly clear-eyed: AI isn't magic, and it's not optional. He reiterates that it's already here, showing up in the tools you're using, whether you realize it or not.

His perspective, included throughout the book, reinforces the central theme: AI success in finance isn't about technology for its own sake. It's about operational readiness, strategic clarity, and a willingness to lead.

Building Confidence Through Vendor Due Diligence

If partnership selection sets the tone, due diligence is where the CFO earns the right to lead. It is the process through which finance distinguishes between promise and performance, translating technical claims into business reality. For many organizations, this step determines whether AI becomes a sustained capability or a stalled experiment.

AI tools can be marketed with confidence that sometimes exceeds their current maturity. Evaluating these offerings requires more than a checklist. It requires a structured lens for assessing readiness, reliability, and return. The CFO's role is not to validate algorithms, but to ensure that every AI relationship meets enterprise standards for control, transparency, and value creation.

The Four Dimensions of AI Vendor Readiness

CFOs can evaluate vendors across four dimensions (see Table 7.1) that together define enterprise readiness. These categories translate technical characteristics into financially relevant decision criteria.

Table 7.1 AI Vendor Maturity

Dimension	Purpose	Core questions for CFOs
AI maturity and capability	Validate whether the technology is truly AI-driven and fit for finance use cases	What models are actually in use, and how are they trained? Does the system adapt to new data or require manual rules? Are finance-specific workflows (GL, FP&A, audit) natively supported?
Explainability and governance	Ensure outputs can be trusted, audited, and defended	Can the vendor demonstrate audit trails and data lineage? Are decisions explainable under SOX/ICFR? Can humans review and override high-impact outputs?
Security and data protection	Protect sensitive financial and operational data	Is data encrypted in transit and at rest? What deployment options exist (SaaS, private instance)? Are certifications (SOC 2, ISO 27001) current? Is customer data used for model training?
Financial fit and strategic alignment	Connect the partnership to measurable business outcomes	What is the TCO over 24–36 months? Does the pricing model scale with usage or outcomes? Does the roadmap align with your finance transformation strategy?

These dimensions form a repeatable governance framework. They enable CFOs to engage confidently with technology leaders, asking different questions, but with the same rigor that defines investment, audit, and capital planning decisions.

AI Maturity and Capability. Many platforms now label themselves as "AI-powered," yet the range of actual intelligence varies widely. Some tools apply lightweight ML to rules-based workflows, while others deploy domain-tuned models capable of self-improvement.

CFOs should probe for evidence, not adjectives, superlatives, and empty promises. Request demonstrations using your own data, not vendor samples, to test adaptability. Ask whether the vendor's model has been trained on finance-specific datasets or repurposed from a general domain.

The presence of "verticalized copilots" (e.g., models fine-tuned for FP&A or treasury) often signals maturity, but domain specialization is only valuable if it translates to measurable accuracy and audit reliability.

Explainability and Governance. In finance, a model's output is only as useful as its audit trail. Black-box systems that generate forecasts or journal entries without clear logic introduce risk under SOX, ICFR, and other control frameworks.

CFOs should confirm:

- The tool provides audit logs capturing inputs, model paths, and outputs.
- Role-based access ensures data segmentation.
- High-impact tasks include human-in-the-loop review options.

A simple litmus test. Would you feel comfortable walking an auditor or regulator through how this system produced its result? If the answer is no, the solution may not be enterprise-ready.

Security and Data Protection. AI introduces new risk surfaces from data leakage to shadow-model training. Vendors must meet the same security and compliance standards as financial systems of record. Finance should validate:

- **Deployment flexibility.** Can data remain behind the firewall if required?
- **Encryption standards.** End-to-end encryption in transit and at rest.
- **Compliance certifications.** SOC 2, ISO 27001, or equivalent.
- **Incident history.** Has the vendor disclosed any prior breaches or data misuse?

For multi-jurisdictional operations, confirm data residency compliance (e.g., GDPR, CCPA). Many CFOs prefer private AI instances or "AI behind the firewall" architectures for sensitive workloads.

Financial Fit and Strategic Alignment. Due diligence is not complete without a financial and strategic lens. CFOs should model TCO over at least three years, incorporating licensing, integration, training, and maintenance. Ask:

- Does the pricing structure scale with usage, headcount, or outcomes?
- How does the vendor define ROI (e.g., time saved, accuracy improved, cost reduced)?
- Can success metrics be validated during pilot phases?

These evaluations ensure the vendor's economics align with enterprise realities rather than growth-stage aspirations. They also enable the CFO to benchmark vendors using familiar metrics: payback period, margin impact, and operating leverage improvement.

Red Flags to Watch. Some indicators warrant heightened caution:

- Claims of "autonomous finance" with no clear oversight or audit mechanism.
- Lack of reference clients in finance or audit-heavy industries.
- Vague responses on bias mitigation or hallucination controls.
- Reluctance to offer pilot contracts or performance-based pricing.

Don't worry about due diligence slowing progress. The need to safeguard value outweighs speed. Vendors' ability to answer these questions with clarity and evidence positions them as credible partners. Those who can't answer reveal gaps that will eventually surface under audit or operational pressure.

Vendor due diligence is where the CFO will separate marketing language from real capability. With GenAI in particular, vendors often present their platforms as intelligent or autonomous when in practice they are limited assistants or glorified scripts. A rigorous evaluation process ensures finance leaders can distinguish between what looks impressive in a demo and what will actually sustain audit-ready operations.

A Collaboration Framework: Working with the CTO, CIO, and CISO During Vendor Evaluation and Implementation

AI vendor diligence is a shared responsibility. No single function can evaluate financial value, technical feasibility, and risk posture in isolation. The CFO's role is to coordinate these perspectives so that every AI investment is justified by evidence, aligned with enterprise controls, and capable of scaling safely.

Effective collaboration will strengthen accountability. Finance defines the business case and risk tolerance; technology leaders validate how those expectations can be achieved without compromising data integrity or security.

Below, a potential framework is outlined for how the CFO, CTO, CIO, and CISO can coordinate through the vendor due-diligence process and post-pilot evaluation.

Phase 1: Before Vendor Engagement—Strategic Alignment

Purpose: Establish shared expectations before vendors are shortlisted. Early alignment on objectives, guardrails, and ownership prevents friction later in the process (see Table 7.2 for the full checklist).

Table 7.2 Vendor Due-Diligence CFO Focus

CFO focus	CTO/CIO/CISO contribution	Timing	Deliverables
Define the AI investment mandate—clarify ROI categories (efficiency, accuracy, insight) and capital allocation thresholds	Provide technical input on which finance workflows are feasible for AI based on data readiness and process maturity	Early planning sessions (one or two before RFP issuance)	AI investment charter co-signed by CFO, CIO, CTO
Identify governance guardrails—document compliance, data-residency, or control requirements that are non-negotiable	CISO outlines minimum security standards (SOC 2, ISO 27001, NIST AI RMF)	Before vendor list creation	AI governance baseline document
Agree on data ownership and responsibility—specify who controls model outputs, logs, and training data	CIO and CISO confirm feasibility of maintaining data control and segregation	Before RFP distribution	Data ownership statement included in RFP

These should be working sessions with the CFO setting financial objectives and acceptable risk thresholds; technology leaders define how those thresholds can be maintained in implementation.

Phase 2: During Vendor Evaluation—Technical and Risk Vetting

Purpose: Align due-diligence activities so that finance, technology, and security review vendors through their respective lenses and consolidate findings into a unified decision (see Table 7.3 for the full checklist).

Table 7.3 Technical and Risk Vetting

CFO focus	CTO/CIO/CISO contribution	Timing	Deliverables
Run the vendor evaluation scorecard—assess financial stability, operational capability, and governance maturity	CIO/CTO validate integration and performance claims; CISO reviews data handling, privacy, and model security	During RFP evaluation	Joint evaluation report with consolidated scoring
Require a pilot evidence package—validate vendor performance using the company's own data	CTO provisions a secure test environment; CIO/CISO define monitoring and anonymization protocols	Pre-pilot approval	Pilot governance plan (60–90 days) with agreed KPIs
Confirm budget and ROI accountability—align cost assumptions and funding	Provide infrastructure and support cost estimates for TCO modeling	Before contract signing	Pilot funding authorization memo jointly approved

Collaboration here is verification of parameters and timing. The CFO maintains investment authority while ensuring technology and risk peers confirm readiness and compliance.

Phase 3: Post-Pilot—Validation, Scaling, and Reporting

Purpose: Convert pilot results into documented value, risk evidence, and board-level reporting (see Table 7.4 for the full checklist).

Table 7.4 Validation, Scaling, and Reporting

CFO focus	CTO/CIO/CISO contribution	Timing	Deliverables
Assess pilot ROI results—compare achieved vs. modeled KPIs and reconcile deviations	CIO validates data integrity; CISO confirms control performance and incident logs	Immediately post-pilot	Pilot results report for executive or board review
Prepare board presentation—communicate financial impact, governance integrity, and next-stage investment needs	CTO/CIO/CISO provide technical appendices and attestations	Two to four weeks post-pilot	AI investment recommendation memo and board slides
Develop ongoing monitoring protocol—ensure sustained visibility into performance and risk	CTO/CIO/CISO establish monitoring dashboards and quarterly review cadence	Before full rollout	Quarterly AI steering committee review process

The CFO presents risk-adjusted financial results to the board, supported by technical and security attestations. This integrated validation reinforces credibility and strengthens future funding cases.

The Guiding Principle

This collaboration is not permission-seeking; it is due diligence.The CFO owns capital allocation and ROI accountability. Technology and security peers safeguard the integrity of the technological execution. Shared diligence ensures that AI investments create sustainable value without exposing the enterprise to unmanaged risk.

When this governance rhythm is established, the CFO can approach the next strategic question: whether to build, buy, or combine the best of both with confidence. Each option can be evaluated against the same cross-functional evidence base, ensuring the chosen path reflects both financial prudence and operational control.

AI Enterprise Security Threat: The Reality

The CISO's go-to move with most new enterprise technology is: "When in doubt, lock it out." With AI tools, the perceived threat isn't just external breaches. It's a fear that AI will "remember everything," leak confidential prompts, or expose sensitive data across teams. These fears have led to usage bans, especially in critical functions such as finance.

Here's the truth: with the right settings in place, enterprise-grade LLMs are as secure as your ERP, CRM, or cloud-storage tools. The bigger risk is avoiding them because of outdated fears.

Leading LLMs Meet the Same Compliance Standards as Traditional SaaS

The big four enterprise LLMs (OpenAI, Claude, Gemini, and Copilot) are SOC 2 Type II compliant. They provide encryption both at rest and during transit, strict tenant isolation, and customizable data-retention policies. Just like your ERP, accounting system, and payroll platform, these tools log access, enforce admin roles, and adhere to data residency rules.

AI "Memory" Isn't What You Think

Much of the worry about LLMs comes from a misunderstanding of how these tools process information. Three different types of data interaction are often mixed up:

- **Session context is temporary.** The model holds your prompt in working memory only long enough to generate a response.
- **Chat history or memory is optional and managed at the user or admin level.** For example, in ChatGPT Enterprise, memory can be completely turned off across the organization.
- **Model training data is what shapes the model's core knowledge during development.** The enterprise providers (OpenAI,

Anthropic, Microsoft) explicitly exclude your inputs from this process.

The AI doesn't "learn" from your data unless you give it permission. ChatGPT Enterprise enables organizations to set retention periods as low as zero days, with saved chats deleted manually or automatically from servers within a specified timeframe.

The Real Risk Is Doing Nothing

Widespread unauthorized AI use in the workplace has been confirmed by multiple industry surveys. Ban ChatGPT, and someone on your team will still copy sensitive data into a personal account, use free consumer versions with weaker security, or turn to unvetted AI options you've never heard of. The risk doesn't go away; it just moves underground where you can't monitor usage, audit conversations, or enforce data policies.

The core idea of this book is smartly integrating AI into the enterprise with effective guardrails: single sign-on (SSI), audit logs, access limits, and retention policies. Forward-looking finance teams are using LLMs to draft board materials, identify forecast anomalies, and declutter inboxes, all within secure, enterprise-grade environments.

Build, Buy, or Hybrid: Architecting the Finance AI Portfolio

The build–buy–hybrid decision mirrors the embedded vs. standalone discussion from earlier chapters, as both are architectural choices. Embedded vs. standalone determines *where* a capability resides within the enterprise stack; build vs. buy vs. hybrid decides *how* it is implemented and who controls the tools' development. Together, these decisions influence the finance function's balance of speed, control, and long-term flexibility. Ensuring coherence among these decisions ensures that architecture, ownership, and investment support each other rather than fragment the finance technology landscape.

With a valid use case and potential vendors passing initial due diligence, the next step is deciding whether to build an AI capability, buy it from an external provider, or blend both approaches. This is not a one-time choice. It is a portfolio decision that should evolve as data, talent, and tool maturity advance. Recent research from BCG, KPMG, and Gartner confirms that most enterprises now operate along this continuum rather than at either extreme.[2]

Building In-House

Let's start with the process that provides the highest level of control and differentiation, but requires the most significant investment in capability and governance. Building native AI capabilities will be limited to organizations with substantial resources for engineering and development. Often, these enterprises have a history of custom coding across their business, including investment and commercial banks like JPMorgan Chase or Goldman Sachs, and major retailers like Target or Wal-Mart.

Advantages

- **Competitive differentiation.** Models trained on proprietary data can produce unique insights. BCG notes this is often decisive when AI drives pricing, risk, or forecasting advantage.[3]
- **Data control.** Information never leaves enterprise boundaries, reducing compliance exposure.
- **Architectural flexibility.** In-house systems can be adapted without vendor dependency.

Challenges

- **Talent and cost.** Analysis from EY highlights the scarcity and expense of ML engineers and MLOps expertise.[4]
- **Time-to-value.** Building, validating, and operationalizing models can delay ROI by quarters or years.
- **Maintenance burden.** Retraining, monitoring, and governance generate ongoing cost and risk.

As an AI-ready CFO, regardless of your company's size, you should approach building an AI system like any other capital project, considering not only development costs but also long-term operational expenses and flexibility impacts.

Buying from Vendors

Most readers of this book will consider purchasing purpose-built or SaaS AI solutions, as they are typically the quickest way to achieve operational efficiency for standardized processes. The market for AI solutions is expanding at an astounding rate, which reinforces the reality that choosing the right vendor is going to be paramount in the build vs. buy equation.

Advantages

- **Speed to benefit.** Consulting group Insight Partners found that most finance-oriented AI suites can deliver measurable ROI within a single quarter.[5]
- **Vendor-owned maintenance.** Providers handle updates, retraining, and compliance certifications.
- **Standardization.** Established tools align with SOX/ICFR and ERP integration norms.

Challenges

- **Vendor lock-in.** Deep integration can restrict future flexibility.
- **Limited differentiation.** Competitors may use identical tools.
- **Data exposure.** Sensitive data may flow into external environments.

The CFO's buy decision needs to include the evaluation of the TOC over 24–36 months, including subscription escalators and switching costs. Linking pricing and service-level agreements (SLAs) to business outcomes such as cycle-time reduction or accuracy improvement should be part of purchase negotiations.

Hybrid and Co-Development Models (aka Blended Models)

Accounting leader KPMG and consultant Arion Research have recently argued that the binary "build vs. buy" framework is now outdated; instead, blended models dominate enterprise adoption.[6] Gartner describes these as ecosystems that combine embedded AI within existing systems with external AI services.[7]

Typical Blended Patterns

- **Platform + custom overlay.** Use a vendor platform for transactional automation and build proprietary forecasting or analytics layers on top.
- **Composable modules.** Integrate vendor APIs (e.g., optical character recognition, anomaly detection) with internal decision logic, an approach aligned with current composable enterprise trends.
- **Co-development partnerships.** Collaborate with vendors to train models on enterprise data while maintaining IP or data-use rights.

Advantages

- **Balanced ROI.** Combines vendor speed with internal differentiation.
- **Architectural flexibility.** Allows substitution of components as technology evolves.
- **Risk management.** Keeps sensitive data internal while leveraging external innovation.

Challenges

- **Integration complexity.** Requires a defined API and data-governance strategy.
- **Governance coordination.** Demands clear ownership among finance, IT, and security leaders.

The blended/hybrid model delivers option preservation. The CFO is able to maintain long-term strategic flexibility while capturing near-term value.

Decision Criteria for CFOs

Drawing on the research of BCG, EY, and Insight Partners, CFOs can evaluate each development path along four dimensions that parallel the embedded vs. standalone architecture framework (see Table 7.5).[8]

These dimensions can help finance leaders align sourcing with architecture. For example, embedded capabilities within ERP or reporting stacks often merit build or hybrid approaches to maintain control and compliance, whereas standalone utilities serving broad, standardized tasks may justify a buy decision.

Table 7.5 Build, Buy, or Blend Decision Grid for CFOs (Author Synthesis)

Dimension	Build	Buy	Hybrid/co-develop
Strategic importance	Core differentiator; proprietary advantage	Commodity or efficiency focus	Differentiation at edges; shared control
Data and compliance sensitivity	High—requires internal control	Moderate—vendor standards acceptable	Split—critical data internal, other data external
Capability readiness	Mature data/AI talent base	Limited internal expertise	Building capability while leveraging vendor strength
Time-to-value vs. flexibility	Slower start, greater adaptability	Rapid ROI, potential lock-in	Balanced speed with option to pivot

Source: Adapted from Boston Consulting Group (2018), EY Insights (2025), and Insight Partners (2025).[9]

Key Governance Checkpoints

Just like any technology purchase, continuous evolution in the market occurs. Today's leader might be tomorrow's laggard. To ensure these decisions adapt to changing conditions, leading firms follow a regular evaluation schedule.

1. **Post-pilot review.** Validate ROI and control outcomes before scale-up.
2. **Annual capability audit.** Reassess vendor dependency, model governance, and internal maturity.
3. **Reinvestment threshold.** Shift from buy to build when strategic importance or data sensitivity increases.

This approach reflects the market consensus that organizations should regularly review sourcing decisions as data assets, market maturity, and AI tools evolve.

Don't focus on designing the corporate AI infrastructure. Focus your attention on allocating capital, reducing risk, and maintaining flexibility. The aim is coherence: architecture choices (embedded vs. standalone) and sourcing options (build vs. buy vs. hybrid) should complement each other so that every AI investment enhances the enterprise's control environment and future adaptability.

As Gartner notes, "AI deployments rarely remain static. Finance leaders must design sourcing and architecture decisions that can blend, evolve, and recombine over time."[10] This mindset defines the AI-ready finance function: disciplined, data-literate, and built for change.

Negotiating Contracts and Avoiding Lock-In

Even when the tool and the vendor providing it seem to be the right fit, the terms of the purchase agreement or contract become another key factor in whether the relationship adds enterprise value or increases enterprise risk. The AI-ready CFO's negotiations with the vendor need to preserve financial control, ensure audit transparency, and maintain strategic optionality throughout the length of the contract.

Leading consulting firms Gartner, KPMG, and EY all observe that AI contracts demand a higher level of financial and technical literacy, as they connect the enterprise not just to a service but also to data pipelines, core models, and ongoing compute power consumption. This requires negotiation to be a cross-functional effort led by finance and shaped through collaboration with the CIO, CISO, and legal counsel to ensure alignment of commercial, technical, and security terms.[11]

It's important to break down the negotiation into three key parts: the CFO's mandate, core priorities (Table 7.6), and the process and functional roles (Table 7.7).

The CFO's Mandate

The CFO's objective in their negotiation with the vendor is threefold:

1. Align pricing to value delivered, not resource consumption.
2. Retain control of data and model outputs.
3. Embed exit and adaptability mechanisms that protect optionality.

Finance owns the economic model, but technology peers determine feasibility. The CIO and CISO should be involved to ensure that negotiated terms can be implemented within the enterprise's architecture and risk frameworks (see Table 7.6).

Table 7.6 Core Priorities in Contract Negotiations (Author Synthesis)

Negotiation area	Why it matters	CFO/C-suite tactics
Pricing structure	Many AI vendors price by tokens, API calls, or compute usage, which can inflate unpredictably with scale	• Push for tiered or outcome-based pricing tied to KPIs (e.g., invoices processed, forecast accuracy) • Require "spend visibility" dashboards and quarterly reconciliation rights • Lock escalation caps (<CPI + 3%) for multi-year deals
Data ownership and use rights	Financial data used in model training creates IP ambiguity and compliance risk	• Specify that all enterprise data and derivative models remain company property • Prohibit vendors from using client data to train external or shared models • Require written data-deletion and certification on termination
Auditability and explainability	Without contractual rights, access to logs or model decisions may be denied	• Mandate audit-trail access and model-explanation documentation • Align contract language to SOX/ICFR obligations • Include a clause for third-party audit cooperation
Service-level agreements	AI models degrade or "drift" over time; traditional uptime SLAs are insufficient	• Define service levels for model accuracy, latency, and retraining frequency • Establish penalties or remediation triggers if thresholds are missed

(*Continued*)

Table 7.6 (Continued)

Negotiation area	Why it matters	CFO/C-suite tactics
Security and compliance	AI systems expand the attack surface and may create cross-border data flows	• Require CISO sign-off on encryption, residency, and incident-response protocols • Include breach-notification timelines aligned with regulatory requirements
Change management and roadmap access	Vendor updates may alter functionality or compliance posture	• Insist on notice periods for major releases • Negotiate participation in customer advisory boards or beta programs
Exit and transition rights	Lock-in is the most common failure mode noted by Gartner (2025)[12]	• Build explicit termination for convenience after Year 1 with capped penalties • Require data export in open formats (JSON, CSV, Parquet) within 30 days of notice • Secure transition support obligations (knowledge transfer, parallel-run period)

Source: Adapted from [13]

AI vendor negotiation should follow a structured, CFO-led process coordinated with other executives (see Table 7.7).

Table 7.7 Negotiation Process and Cross-Functional Roles

Phase	Finance lead actions	CIO/CISO/ legal role	Deliverables
Pre-negotiation planning	Define target ROI, acceptable payback period, and TCO ceiling	Validate integration feasibility and security baselines	Negotiation objectives brief
Term-sheet development	Draft financial constructs (pricing, renewals, exit rights)	Add technical dependencies and compliance clauses	Unified term sheet reviewed by all functions

Phase	Finance lead actions	CIO/CISO/ legal role	Deliverables
Contract negotiation	Lead commercial discussions; quantify cost of each risk concession	Support with technical validation and risk commentary	Final contract draft with cross-functional sign-off
Post-execution governance	Monitor SLA compliance and cost performance quarterly	Run security audits and drift monitoring	Quarterly AI vendor performance report

This structure ensures accountability without unnecessary duplication of effort. The CFO remains the final approver of capital commitments, but each peer executive is responsible for assurance within their area.

Safeguards to Avoid Vendor Lock-In

Vendor lock-in often occurs due to the accumulation of subtle dependencies, such as custom integrations, proprietary data schemas, or opaque pricing tiers. To prevent it, CFOs can deploy four practical safeguards:

1. **Interoperability clauses.** Require open APIs and documented schemas enabling integration with other systems.
2. **Data-portability guarantees.** Demand export functionality in industry-standard formats at no extra cost.
3. **Modular contract design.** Segment contracts by function (e.g., forecasting, reconciliation) so underperforming modules can be replaced without dissolving the entire relationship.
4. **Periodic competitive benchmarking.** Reprice and test the market every 18–24 months. Gartner recommends benchmarking to preserve negotiation leverage and surface emerging alternatives.[14]

Practical Tactics and Potential Red Flags

Vendor negotiations in AI procurement carry unique risks that standard procurement playbooks don't always cover. The tactics and red flags below draw on patterns finance teams have encountered in real engagements.

Tactics That Strengthen the CFO's Position

- **Anchor negotiations in ROI evidence.** Use performance metrics from pilot phases as your valuation baseline.
- **Use competitive bids as leverage.** Maintain two viable options until signature.
- **Quantify risk as cost.** Translate vendor resistance (e.g., limited audit access) into explicit risk-adjusted cost in your model.
- **Document performance dependencies.** Require measurable KPIs in all marketing claims.
- **Stage commitments.** Start with a 12-month pilot or modular rollout before a multi-year term.

Notable Vendor Red Flags

- Refusal to provide reference clients in finance or compliance/audit-heavy industries.
- "All-inclusive" black-box pricing without transparency on consumption.
- Restrictions on data extraction or interoperability.
- Excessive auto-renewal clauses or unilateral price increases.
- Lack of clarity on model retraining schedules or change notifications.

Ultimately, vendor contract negotiation in the AI era is a team sport, with the finance leader serving as the captain. The CIO ensures architectural feasibility; the CISO protects data integrity; legal manages liability; but only the CFO balances financial exposure against strategic flexibility. The most successful AI-ready CFOs approach contracts as living instruments governed by metrics, reviewed against ROI, and designed for controlled exit.

Notes

1. Ranga Bodla (NetSuite/Oracle), interviewed by Glenn Hopper, *Google Meet*, December 16, 2025.
2. Philipp Gerbert, Sylvain Duranton, Sebastian Steinhäuser, and Patrick Ruwolt, "The Build-or-Buy Dilemma in AI," *Boston Consulting Group*, January 4, 2018, https://www.bcg.com/publications/2018/build-buy-dilemma-artificial-intelligence; Leanne Allen, "The Evolution of Build vs Buy," *KPMG*, 2023, https://kpmg.com/uk/en/insights/ai/the-evolution-of-build-vs-buy.html; Mary Mesaglio and Hung LeHong, "Build, Buy or Blend? Deploying AI in Your Organization," *Gartner*, March 31, 2025, https://www.gartner.com/en/articles/deploying-ai
3. Gerbert et al., "The Build-or-Buy Dilemma in AI."
4. Tim Morthorst, "Should Organisations Buy AI Systems or Build Them," *EY*, February 19, 2024, https://www.ey.com/en_ie/insights/ai/should-organisations-buy-ai-systems-or-build-them
5. Insight Partners, "Build versus Buy: Considerations for a Strategic Approach to Innovating with AI," *Insight Partners*, March 28, 2025, https://www.insightpartners.com/ideas/build-versus-buy-ai/
6. Allen, "The Evolution of Build vs Buy"; Michael Fauscette, "Build vs. Buy vs. Partner: Strategic Decisions for Agentic AI Capabilities," *Arion Research*, June 25, 2024, https://www.arionresearch.com/blog/no3hmo79kiasc549d2w39ksu1od9t3
7. Mesaglio and LeHong, "Build, Buy or Blend?"
8. Gerbert et al., "The Build-or-Buy Dilemma in AI"; Chris Watson and Scott McGowan, "How AI Navigates Third-Party Risk in a Rapidly Changing Risk Landscape," *EY Insights*, April 24, 2025, https://www.ey.com/en_gl/insights/consulting/how-ai-navigates-third-party-risk-in-a-rapidly-changing-risk-landscape; Insight Partners, "Build versus Buy."
9. Ibid.
10. Mesaglio and LeHong, "Build, Buy or Blend?"
11. Ibid.; Allen, "The Evolution of Build vs Buy"; Watson and McGowan, "How AI Navigates Third-Party Risk."
12. Mesaglio and LeHong, "Build, Buy or Blend?"
13. World Commerce & Contracting, *WorldCC Contracting Principles: AI and Algorithmic Contracting*, September 2024, https://www.worldcc.com/Portals/IACCM/WorldCC%20Contracting%20Principles.pdf
14. Mesaglio and LeHong, "Build, Buy or Blend?"

Chapter 8

Governance, Risk, and Finance–Control Alignment

Key Takeaways

- **Governance isn't bureaucracy. It's the operating freedom to scale responsibly.** For the AI-ready CFO, AI governance is SOX, ICFR, and COSO discipline applied to a new class of tools. The objective is simple: move fast without breaking auditability. Even in privately held companies, the logic holds. If AI touches close, forecasting, or reporting, it still needs ownership, review, and evidence.
- **Start with clarity and completeness.** Inventory every task where AI touches finance, including forecasting, reconciliations, disclosures, and approvals. Update your control matrices to reflect those AI steps so

review points, preventive limits, and evidence trails show up in testing. Tie each AI touchpoint to existing ICFR assertions and COSO components so nothing sits outside the control narrative.

- **Invest in reviewer capability.** Train control owners and reviewers to evaluate AI outputs: what looks reasonable, which drivers matter, how to read explainability artifacts, and when to escalate exceptions. Competent human review is still the strongest control in any AI workflow.
- **Build structure and oversight.** Stand up an AI governance committee that links finance, IT, model risk, and internal audit. Give it audit committee visibility, authority over change control, and ownership of the AI risk register. Use it to review monitoring results, drift signals, and remediation on a quarterly cadence.
- **Publish finance-specific AI policies that teams can execute.** Cover data handling, documentation, evidence retention, access, segregation of duties, change management, fallback procedures, and incident response. Define what "explainability sufficient for ICFR" means in your environment. Make vendor diligence a prerequisite before any tool enters a reporting or approval path.

When these disciplines are in place, governance becomes the scaling system. The same controls that keep reporting credible can also compress the close, improve forecast reliability, and reduce audit noise. Each model runs inside a defined control design with review, evidence, and monitoring, moving AI from experiment to infrastructure.

> Audit readiness starts with design... AI needs to be embedded in controlled workflows with traceable inputs... The notion of human verified automation is one of our core principles.[1]
>
> —*Tom Hood, AICPA/CIMA*

AI Through the Compliance Lens

For public companies, AI in finance is a compliance issue as much as a productivity play. Any tool that accesses financial data or influences reporting decisions has to stand up to SOX, ICFR, and PCAOB audit expectations. You can't separate AI adoption from the control environment.

Private companies face the same underlying risk, even if they don't have the same legal requirements. The difference is enforcement, not exposure. If AI touches the close, forecasting, approvals, or external reporting inputs, it still needs oversight that fits the company's existing control discipline.

Public company CFOs are stewards of investor confidence because they run the systems and processes that produce accurate, complete, and timely reporting. That responsibility doesn't change with AI. What changes is the risk surface. Generative tools that summarize close results, models that forecast reserves, or automations that clear invoices can accelerate work. If they generate undocumented outputs, omit required disclosures, or bypass review, they create SOX exposure.

Auditors and regulators have been direct. The PCAOB has warned that AI's "black-box" qualities, inconsistent outputs, and reliance on training data can undermine auditability.[2] The SEC has reminded issuers that if AI is material to operations or risk management, it may require disclosure in filings.[3] Companies can experiment, but they remain fully responsible for the accuracy of financial reporting.

That pushes the CFO's role past ROI and efficiency. The job is to design controls that keep AI-enabled workflows auditable, explainable, and documented. When AI proposes an entry, drafts disclosure language, or flags an exception, a qualified reviewer still has to validate it. The review needs to be logged, support needs to be retained, and the workflow needs to be defensible in SOX testing.

From this angle, governance is the enabler, not the obstacle. If finance can show auditors and regulators that AI-driven workflows are controlled, documented, and compliant, it can scale adoption with confidence. If governance is bypassed, the work often gets unwound at year-end when control gaps surface.

Governance Principles for CFOs

AI adoption in finance can't be separated from governance. Any system that influences financial reporting has to fit within established control frameworks. For CFOs, that means treating AI as another component of the control environment, held to the same standard as an ERP, a spreadsheet model, or a macro.

Four principles should govern any AI deployment in finance: transparency, accountability, auditability, and security.

- **Transparency.** Finance needs to explain what the tool is doing, what data it relies on, and how outputs flow into decisions. You don't need to understand model architecture, but you do need clear intent and traceable use. If a generative tool drafts disclosure language, the team should be able to show inputs, review steps, and explain how it ties to source data. Transparency keeps AI inside finance's control, not operating as an unexamined black box.
- **Accountability.** Responsibility doesn't move to the vendor or the algorithm. Under SOX and ICFR, management remains accountable for the accuracy of the financial statements, regardless of whether AI was involved. Policies should be explicit: the preparer and reviewer of an AI-assisted reconciliation or report carry the same responsibility as if they built it manually. Clear ownership prevents gaps when auditors ask who controlled the process.
- **Auditability.** AI use has to generate an evidence trail. Inputs, outputs, and overrides should be retained in a form that can be tested during SOX walkthroughs and PCAOB inspections. If AI flags unusual journal entries, the exception report and follow-up actions need to be logged and archived. If AI drafts a disclosure, retain the draft, reviewer comments, and final approved version as part of the period support. Without evidence, controls can't be tested.
- **Security.** Finance AI tools handle sensitive financial and operational data. Access controls, data residency, and vendor security need to meet company standards. That includes validating how vendors handle training data, whether outputs can be stored outside company systems, and whether the model runs in a private or behind-the-firewall setting. Weak security becomes a reporting risk if data integrity is compromised or access is mismanaged.

These principles map cleanly to familiar frameworks. COSO's five components are control environment, risk assessment, control activities, information and communication, and monitoring. The NIST AI Risk Management Framework (NIST AI RMF) includes "Govern," "Map," "Measure," and "Manage."[4]

AI governance doesn't require a new framework. It requires extending the ones you already run. Expand risk assessments to cover AI-specific concerns such as drift and data quality. Define clear human review points inside control activities. Monitor performance and error rates the same way you monitor other control metrics.

Embed this into day-to-day finance operations. Update policies, train reviewers to evaluate AI outputs, and report AI-related risks through the same channels you use for other control risks, including the audit committee. Don't push this to IT. This isn't infrastructure governance. It's financial reporting governance, and ownership belongs with finance leadership.

The Finance Profession's AI Reality Check

Tom Hood works at the intersection where practice meets standards. At AICPA/CIMA, with a focus on management accounting rather than audit, he has a front-row seat to how accountants, controllers, and CFO teams are adopting AI: what's working, what's stalling, and what firms can defend when auditors, boards, or regulators start asking questions. Tom provides the global, institutional, and profession-wide view that a vendor or practitioner may not fully grasp: the regulatory trends, the talent pipeline problem, and the early shape of guidance that will affect everyone in the profession.[5]

Tom sees the adoption of AI as an operational change that must withstand real-world scrutiny. Tom's perspective includes:

- The CFO agenda is shifting: AI isn't a "nice to have" experiment anymore; it's rising on leadership's priority list, which changes how finance must respond—more discipline, fewer science projects.
- What stops pilots from scaling? Not enthusiasm. Data shape and structure, and whether teams can get past finance's usual "COA-level" habits and into the detail that AI needs.
- How AI shows up inside the stack: especially the reality that AI gets embedded into ERP and core platforms, pushing finance toward redesigning workflows and decision paths, not just adding tools.
- Controls, audit trails, and accountability: the practical question underneath the hype—can you trace it, recreate it, and own it? Tom framed this as a design constraint, not a compliance afterthought.

- Liability and governance questions that aren't settled yet: what happens when AI touches reporting, who signs off, and what "acceptable" looks like as guidance evolves.
- The talent bottleneck: the shortage is real, and AI changes the shape of the organization and how people get trained—less apprenticeship-by-grunt-work, more deliberate skill-building and new competencies.

Throughout the book, Tom offers brief insights that bridge the theoretical and the practical. Every accountant is guided by the standards set by AICPA/CIMA. The organization is front and center in the conversation about how AI is used in the finance department and the impact it will have in the coming years.

SOX, ICFR, and PCAOB Audit Implications

SOX and ICFR underpin investor confidence in US public markets. AI tools used in finance have to operate within that framework. For CFOs, that means any AI used in financial reporting workflows belongs in the SOX 404 evaluation and needs to be tested as part of ICFR.

AI and the SOX Control Environment

SOX Section 404 requires management to establish and maintain internal control over financial reporting and to assess its effectiveness annually.[6] Auditors attest to that assessment. When AI is used in reconciliations, forecasts, disclosures, or approvals, those workflows fall within SOX scope. There's no carve-out for a "black box." If it affects the numbers or the reporting decisions, it's part of the control environment.

SOX has always come back to management responsibility. That responsibility stays with the CFO and controller, even when an algorithm performs the work. AI can assist, but it can't assume accountability.

ICFR Considerations

ICFR requires controls that provide reasonable assurance over accurate processing, protection of assets, and reliable reporting. Introducing AI changes the mechanics of control design in several common finance workflows:

- **Close and reconciliations.** If AI flags anomalies or recommends adjusting entries, the evidence needs to show who reviewed the output, what was done with it, and how the entry was approved. Without that chain, you have a control deficiency.
- **Forecasting and estimates.** Many accounting estimates depend on forecasts, including loan-loss allowances, impairment testing, and reserves. If AI produces the forecast, management still has to validate inputs, challenge assumptions, and document review. Using the output without an independent challenge won't hold up in testing.
- **Financial reporting.** GenAI can draft disclosures and summaries, but ICFR requires traceability back to source data and review by qualified personnel. The draft, review comments, and final approved version become part of the control documentation.
- **Approvals.** AI can clear routine items automatically, but compliance requires documented criteria, periodic testing, and monitoring. For flagged items, documentation needs to capture the reviewer's decision and rationale.

In practice, auditors will treat AI the way they treat spreadsheets and macros. They can improve efficiency, but they introduce error risk and need controls.

Audit Evidence and PCAOB Scrutiny

The PCAOB has emphasized that AI introduces new challenges for audit evidence. Models drift. Generative outputs can vary. Decision logic can be hard to explain. That raises the risk that evidence becomes insufficient, unreliable, or not reproducible.

The PCAOB's July 2024 focus on GenAI makes a simple point: engagement teams remain accountable for results and documentation even when AI is used in analysis.[7] Supervisors are expected to review AI-assisted work with the same rigor as any other audit evidence. For finance leaders, the implication is that AI-assisted outputs have to be retained, explained, and tied to supporting documentation in a form auditors can test.

Auditors will expect to see:

- Documentation of the AI tool's purpose, scope, and role in the process.
- Evidence of management review and approval of outputs, including overrides.

- Logs or reports showing inputs and outputs preserved for audit.
- Evidence that AI-enabled controls were tested in a non-production or parallel environment before reliance.

If those artifacts aren't available, auditors may conclude the control isn't operating effectively, which can escalate into a material weakness.

Segregation of Duties and Override Controls. Segregation of duties (SoD) is a core ICFR requirement. AI can weaken it because one system can be configured to initiate, approve, and record the same transaction. Without compensating controls, SoD collapses and the risk of error or fraud increases.

CFOs need workflows that reintroduce oversight when AI spans multiple steps. Examples include:

- If AI matches invoices and schedules payments, require manager review for high-value releases.
- If AI drafts journal entries, require review and approval above defined thresholds.
- If AI clears reconciliations, route exceptions to an independent reviewer.

Override controls also need to be explicit. If management can override AI decisions or outputs, define when overrides are allowed and what evidence must be retained. If overrides are informal or undocumented, auditors will treat it as a control gap.

PCAOB Guidance and Auditor Expectations. As of the end of 2025, the PCAOB has not issued AI-specific auditing standards, but its communications and existing expectations point to consistent themes.[8]

- **Human involvement is required.** Auditors expect a human in the loop who can evaluate AI outputs. AI doesn't replace professional judgment.
- **Methods must be transparent enough to evaluate reliability.** If AI is used to produce evidence, auditors need to understand what it did and why the output is dependable in context.

- **Parallel testing is expected before reliance.** Many firms encourage "shadow-mode" runs alongside the existing process to establish accuracy rates and support reliance decisions.
- **Documentation standards don't relax.** AI doesn't reduce the evidence burden. If it isn't documented, it didn't happen.

The practical takeaway is to treat each AI deployment as an auditable control. Update SOX narratives and control matrices, define review procedures, and archive evidence in a way that supports testing.

SEC Expectations. In 2024, the SEC's Division of Corporation Finance reminded issuers that if AI is material to operations or risk management, disclosure may be required under existing rules. This can include risk factors, MD&A, and board oversight disclosures. AI use in reporting workflows shouldn't only be controlled for ICFR purposes. It also needs to be assessed for external disclosure when it creates material risks to accuracy, compliance, or governance.

Specifically, the SEC has remarked:

> **Artificial Intelligence**
>
> Over the last year, we have observed a significant increase in the number of companies that mention artificial intelligence in their annual reports. These companies often discussed the topic in the risk factors or description of business sections, or both. There are also a number of companies that discuss the topic in their management's discussion and analysis (MD&A).
>
> As companies incorporate the use of artificial intelligence into their business operations, they are exposed to additional operational and regulatory risks. A number of existing rules or regulations may require disclosure about how a company uses artificial intelligence and the risks related to its use, including disclosure in the description of business section, risk factors, MD&A, the financial statements, and the board's role in risk oversight. In 2024, the Division staff will consider how companies are describing these opportunities and risks, including, to the extent material, whether or not the company:
>
> - clearly defines what it means by artificial intelligence and how the technology could improve the company's results of operations, financial condition, and future prospects;

- provides tailored, rather than boilerplate, disclosures, commensurate with its materiality to the company, about material risks and the impact the technology is reasonably likely to have on its business and financial results;
- focuses on the company's current or proposed use of artificial intelligence technology rather than generic buzz not relating to its business; and
- has a reasonable basis for its claims when discussing artificial intelligence prospects.[9]

The SEC has also stressed that boilerplate disclosures are inadequate. If AI presents a compliance, operational, or reputational risk, companies should describe how those risks are managed.[10] This puts pressure on finance leaders to ensure that AI governance frameworks exist not only in practice but also in documented, defensible form across the entire company.

Global Developments

AI governance and compliance oversight aren't limited to US regulators. The European Union's AI Act began taking effect in stages, starting in August 2025. The law classifies many financial AI applications as "high risk" because they can affect safety or fundamental rights. That category includes credit scoring, fraud detection, and other tools that influence financial outcomes. Compliance will require transparency, explainability, and human oversight. For multinational companies operating across jurisdictions, AI Act compliance isn't optional. It needs to be built into finance workflows and governance.[11]

Other jurisdictions are converging on similar expectations. The UK Financial Conduct Authority has published principles focused on AI fairness and accountability.[12] Singapore and Hong Kong have issued guidance for AI in financial services that emphasizes explainability and governance. Even if a company is US-listed, AI use in overseas subsidiaries can pull these requirements into scope.[13] Table 8.1 compares the major regulatory regimes and their practical impact on AI use in financial reporting.

Table 8.1 Overview of Regulatory Regimes and AI

Topic	**United States**	**European Union**	**Other regimes**
Scope	AI used in close, forecasting, reporting, or approvals falls under SOX/ ICFR. PCAOB audit evidence standards apply to any AI-assisted work. Disclosure may be required if AI use or risk is material	High-risk AI (e.g., credit, fraud, models that affect financial outcomes) requires risk management, transparency, and human oversight. GDPR adds strict data controls	Regulators emphasize explainability, accountability, and governance for AI in financial services. Local conduct rules and privacy laws apply
Governance	Treat AI as part of the control environment. Define ownership in finance, not only IT. Update SOX narratives and matrices for AI steps. Report AI risk to the audit committee	Document AI purpose, risk controls, human-in-the-loop, and monitoring. Map AI data flows to GDPR principles and records of processing	Maintain board-level oversight, model governance, and use policies. Align with local AI fairness and accountability guidance
Explainability	Auditors need to understand why an AI output is reliable. Keep models and outputs testable. Use explainability methods or alternative validations	High-risk AI requires explainability sufficient for users and regulators. Individuals may have rights to meaningful information about automated decisions	Supervisors expect firms to evidence model logic, challenge, and outcomes. Explainability is part of conduct and prudential reviews

(*Continued*)

Table 8.1 (Continued)

Topic	United States	European Union	Other regimes
Evidence trail	Retain inputs, outputs, drafts, exception queues, and reviewer sign-offs. Run parallel tests before reliance. If it isn't documented, it didn't happen	Keep technical documentation, risk assessments, data lineage, and monitoring logs. Evidence GDPR compliance for training and inference data	Maintain control testing packs, change logs, model risk files, and privacy impact assessments where relevant
Controls	Preserve segregation of duties where AI automates multiple steps. Add thresholds, secondary reviews, and override procedures. Periodically test auto-approval criteria	Implement human oversight, robustness testing, and post-deployment monitoring for high-risk AI. Align AI controls with GDPR access, purpose, and retention limits	Require human review for material decisions, change control for models, and monitoring KPIs. Follow local outsourcing/vendor rules for AI services
Disclosure	Consider risk factors, MD&A, and board oversight if AI is material to operations or risk management. Avoid boilerplate	Anticipate transparency obligations for high-risk AI and GDPR notices where personal data is involved	Provide clear disclosures where AI materially affects customers or controls, consistent with local listing and conduct standards
Security and privacy	Apply enterprise access controls, data residency, vendor diligence, and "behind-the-firewall" patterns for sensitive finance data	Meet GDPR security, minimization, and transfer rules. Validate cloud locations and subprocessors	Follow local data protection rules and cross-border transfer restrictions. Map AI vendors to third-party risk programs

Topic	United States	European Union	Other regimes
Monitoring	Track model error rates, drift, false positives, and exceptions. Escalate metrics to the audit committee. Retest controls after model changes	Ongoing monitoring for high-risk systems is expected, with documented retraining and incident handling	Supervisors expect continuous monitoring and timely remediation; internal audit should test AI controls periodically
CFO action list	• Inventory AI in finance • Update SOX documentation • Train reviewers • Build an AI risk register tied to ICFR • Prepare disclosure talking points	• Classify AI use cases by risk • Stand up human-in-the-loop and explainability • Align with GDPR for data • Plan for AI Act readiness	• Map local obligations • Harmonize global policy • Evidence governance in board papers and internal audit plans

Source: Data from [14]

Notes for Multinational Companies

Harmonize to the strictest common denominator: human oversight, explainability, documented testing, and full evidence trails. That reduces rework across regimes and keeps control design consistent.

For finance workflows handling sensitive data, prefer private or behind-the-firewall deployments. Log inputs, prompts, and outputs in company-controlled repositories so the audit trail doesn't depend on a vendor portal.

Build an AI risk register that maps each use case to SOX/ICFR controls and to local regulatory requirements. Review it with the audit committee on a quarterly cadence.

Three Primary Compliance Risks

The compliance exposure for finance leaders concentrates in three categories:

1. **Disclosure risk.** If AI is material to operations and isn't disclosed, companies invite SEC comment letters or enforcement risk.
2. **Control risk.** If AI outputs aren't reviewed, documented, and tested, they can create SOX control deficiencies and PCAOB findings.
3. **Regulatory divergence.** Multinationals may need to satisfy overlapping regimes, including SOX in the United States, the AI Act in the European Union, and global privacy requirements. That increases the burden of governance and raises the cost of inconsistency.

Implications

CFOs can't wait for AI-specific regulation to settle. Existing rules already apply. The SEC expects material AI risks to be disclosed. The PCAOB expects audit evidence to be sufficient and reliable, whether AI was involved or not. Global regulators are converging on explainability and oversight. AI can improve efficiency and insight, but it doesn't change the standard. Management remains fully accountable.

Bias, Explainability, and Accountability

Bias and model opacity aren't just ethical issues. They create compliance risk that can undermine SOX, ICFR, and the reliability of audit evidence. CFOs should treat bias testing and explainability as control activities, embedded in the same framework used for other reporting risks.

Data bias shows up when training or inference data is incomplete, stale, or not representative. In finance, that can distort forecasts used in estimates or drive automated approvals that violate policy. Process bias shows up when model features act as proxies for irrelevant or sensitive factors, or when the model overweights sources with weak quality controls.

Outcome opacity is the black-box problem: outputs that look plausible but lack a rationale the team can defend to auditors.

Management should be able to explain how a model behaves in practice for its intended use, show that it performs fairly within that context, and demonstrate that qualified reviewers evaluated and approved outputs before they influenced reporting. Evidence needs to be retained and reproducible.

The CFO's objective is straightforward: make every model explainable, every output reviewable, and every decision reproducible.

Explainability: Knowing What the Model Did and Why

Explainability closes the gap between data science and financial accountability. CFOs don't need to master algorithms. They need proof that model logic can be demonstrated and challenged.

Choose the method that fits the decision:

- For overall behavior, use summaries such as feature importance or partial dependence to show which inputs drive results.
- For specific outputs tied to material estimates or disclosures, retain local explanations using tools such as SHAP or LIME to show why a specific prediction or narrative was produced.

SHAP quantifies how much each input contributed to a prediction using a game-theory approach to allocate impact across variables.[15] LIME builds a simpler local model around a single prediction to show which features most influenced that outcome.[16]

Store the evidence where auditors will look. Explainability artifacts belong in the period support package, not on an analyst's laptop. They should be version-controlled and linked to the financial statement line items they influence.

Translate technical findings into finance language. Use short narratives or sensitivity tables that show key drivers and the direction of effects, including how revenue, volume, or cost inputs moved the forecast.

Bias and Performance Testing: Proving Fairness and Stability

Bias testing is a control activity. Before a model supports a financial output, finance needs to:

- Validate stability by comparing current outputs to baseline periods.
- Check for bias by reviewing results by segment or cohort to identify distortive patterns.
- Test sensitivity by measuring how small input changes affect results and where outliers break the logic.
- Document frequency and follow-up by rerunning tests after any model, data, or prompt change and archiving results, reviewer sign-offs, and remediation actions.

If tests fail or thresholds are breached, pause reliance until the issue is corrected and retested.

Human Oversight: The Required Control

A practical rule is "AI may propose, but finance must dispose." Outputs that affect reserves, disclosures, or exception handling require documented human review as part of ICFR.

Record the output, reviewer comments, tie-outs to source data, and final approval. Treat the review as a formal control step with defined ownership, approval thresholds, and evidence requirements.

> Whatever they do with AI, they want to make sure there is a **human in the loop**... it needs to be **auditable**—we have to justify and recreate how we got to the answers.[17]
>
> —*Tom Hood, AICPA/CIMA*

Change and Drift Management: Treat AI Like Code

AI models change as data shifts, business conditions move, and parameters or prompts get updated. Over time, those changes can create model drift, where outputs diverge from expected results. If drift isn't detected and controlled, it can degrade reporting reliability.

Manage AI the way you manage other systems inside finance's control environment:

- Route all parameter, data, and prompt changes through ticketed change control.
- Run parallel tests before a new version goes live and compare outputs to the prior version.
- Monitor for drift, including unexpected changes in accuracy or driver behavior, and pause reliance when limits are exceeded.
- Retain versions, approvals, and monitoring logs as permanent records.

Security and Privacy: Protect the Data Path

AI in finance will touch sensitive and proprietary data, so it needs the same security standards applied to ERP and reporting systems:

- Prefer private or behind-the-firewall deployments for sensitive workflows.
- Log prompts, inputs, and outputs.
- Enforce role-based access and run quarterly access reviews.
- For vendor-hosted models, require audit-ready logs, data residency alignment, restrictions on vendor training using company data, and deletion clauses with defined timelines.

GenAI: Additional Guardrails Needed

Generative models add exposure because outputs can vary and can sound credible even when they are wrong. Apply explicit controls:

- Retain the prompt, retrieved context, and raw output for each task.
- Prefer RAG that surfaces source documents for tie-out.
- Maintain a red-team prompt library of known failure cases and retest it after each model update.
- Treat any AI-drafted disclosure as preparer output. Require ledger tie-outs, authoritative-source validation, and checklist review before approval.

Audit Readiness and Assurance Controls

Audit readiness comes down to evidence that can be tested without interpretation or technical translation. Each reporting period, assemble a self-contained audit pack that includes:

- Model version, parameters, and deployment approval.
- Data refresh date and validation sign-off.
- Explainability outputs such as feature importance, sensitivity tables, or driver narratives.
- Bias and stability test results with reviewer sign-offs.
- Exception queues with reviewer notes and dispositions.
- Change tickets, drift monitoring logs, and any fallback activations.
- Access and security logs for sensitive runs.

Evidence should live in the company's control documentation, not in personal folders or vendor portals. If it isn't documented, it won't be relied on in SOX testing.

Accountability and Roles

Audit readiness starts with ownership (Table 8.2). Each finance model needs defined roles that tie directly to SOX controls and the model inventory.

Table 8.2 Roles and Responsibilities in AI Audit Readiness

Role	Responsibility
Model owner (finance)	Maintains documentation, ensures testing, and control operation
Reviewer/approver (finance)	Performs and records reviews of AI outputs that affect reporting
Model risk or internal audit	Provides independent challenge and periodic validation for high-risk uses
IT/data teams	Manage environments, enforce access, preserve version history
Audit committee	Oversees governance structure and receives quarterly reporting on AI control performance

This structure makes accountability visible and defensible, the same standard applied to any key control under ICFR.

Mapping to COSO and ICFR

Auditors will expect to see AI controls expressed through frameworks they already use. Mapping AI assurance activities to COSO's five components demonstrates that these systems sit squarely inside the existing governance structure (Table 8.3).

Table 8.3 COSO Risk Framework and AI Controls

COSO component	AI control activity
Control environment	Defined ownership, policies, tone from the top
Risk assessment	Inclusion of bias, drift, security, and misuse in the risk register
Control activities	Explainability testing, bias checks, human review, and change control
Information and communication	Model inventory, evidence packs, audit-committee reporting
Monitoring	Ongoing drift metrics, bias retesting, and independent internal-audit reviews

Source: Adapted from [18]

By aligning AI oversight to COSO and ICFR, finance can prove that every algorithmic control meets the same standards of design, implementation, and operating effectiveness as any manual or automated control in the reporting process.

Stop Criteria: Knowing When to Pause Reliance

Even well-governed models can degrade. CFOs should define explicit stop triggers that suspend reliance on AI until revalidation is complete:

- Material drift or unexplained change in feature importance.
- Failed bias or stability tests without timely remediation.
- Missing or incomplete review and approval evidence.
- Security or access breaches that could compromise data integrity.

When the stop criteria are triggered, revert to the fallback or challenger process, document the event, and notify the disclosure and audit committees. The fallback is the prior approved manual or deterministic process used to maintain reporting continuity, while the challenger model is an independent benchmark that runs in parallel to validate accuracy. Both assure that financial reporting remains controlled even when an AI model is paused or under review.

Note that stopping reliance on the AI output is not a failure; it is evidence that the control environment functions as designed and offers an opportunity to improve the resilience and performance of the models used.

Risk Framework: The AI Risk Register for Finance

Most finance teams within publicly traded companies already maintain a risk register under COSO's ERM framework and SOX 404/ICFR documentation.[19] An AI risk register is simply an extension of those existing processes, bringing AI into the same structure used for operational, financial, and compliance risks. For private firms, the register serves the same purpose as mitigating AI-related risks that could harm the business, even though it may not be required to do so.

Purpose

The AI risk register has two goals:

1. Inventory every place AI touches finance workflows.
2. Link each AI use case to its risks, controls, evidence, and accountable owner.

This single source of truth lets the CFO show auditors, the board, and regulators that AI adoption is governed, documented, and testable within the company's established control environment.

Alignment with Existing Risk Frameworks. Below we map common AI governance requirements to the risk frameworks most finance teams already have in place. This alignment helps avoid building parallel structures and instead layers AI controls into existing processes.

Existing frameworks	How an AI risk register fits
COSO ERM (2017)—governance and culture, performance, review and revision[20]	The AI register documents how AI risks are identified, assessed, mitigated, and monitored using the same categories and reporting cadence as the enterprise risk register
SOX/ICFR—internal control over financial reporting[21]	Each AI use case that affects financial reporting is included in the SOX control matrix. The register links risks (e.g., data drift) to specific ICFR controls and evidence
NIST AI RMF (2023)—govern, map, measure, manage[22]	The register operationalizes NIST's four-function cycle: govern = policy and ownership; map = identify use case and context; measure = assess model performance and bias; manage = implement mitigations and track them

This alignment ensures the register doesn't create another silo; it plugs directly into the CFO's existing risk infrastructure.

Structure of the Register

Each register entry will mirror what auditors already expect to see in risk documentation (see Table 8.4).

Table 8.4 AI Risk Framework Alignment Matrix

Field	Example
AI use case	Generative tool drafts MD&A disclosure
Risk category	Reporting accuracy
Potential impact	Material misstatement in external filings
Mitigation/control	Human review and tie-out to ledgers + GAAP (Generally Accepted Accounting Principles) checklist
Evidence/testing	Review notes, checklist, versioned drafts
Owner	Director of external reporting
Status/next review	Operating effectively—Q4 retest scheduled

For transactional AI use (e.g., expense scanning), the pattern is identical, except that the risk type and owner change.

How It Works in Practice

To see how this governance structure operates in a real workflow, consider a typical AI deployment cycle. The steps below trace the process from initial alignment through ongoing monitoring:

1. **Inventory and classification.** Finance lists all AI tools in use across close, forecasting, and reporting.
2. **Risk assessment.** Each tool is evaluated for likelihood and impact within existing COSO or ERM scoring scales.
3. **Control mapping.** Mitigations are tied to SOX/ICFR controls already tested by internal audit.
4. **Ownership and monitoring.** Named control owners review evidence quarterly; exceptions flow to the audit committee.
5. **Continuous update.** The register is updated with new deployments, model changes, or regulatory developments each quarter along the same cadence as other SOX documentation.

Management and Board Value

When AI is embedded in finance workflows with proper governance, the value extends beyond operational efficiency. The following points capture how these capabilities translate into outcomes that matter to management and the board:

- **For auditors.** The register shows that AI risks are identified, controlled, and evidenced under the same standards as traditional financial processes.
- **For the board and audit committee.** It demonstrates disciplined adoption as AI is being scaled inside the governance system, not around it.
- **For management.** It surfaces maturity gaps, highlights where mitigations are weak, and gives finance a forward-looking view of where to invest in stronger controls or automation.

The AI risk register is not a new compliance burden, it is the familiar COSO and SOX discipline applied to a new class of tools. By embedding AI risks into the existing register, CFOs can speak the language of auditors and regulators while giving their teams a practical roadmap for safe, scalable adoption.

The Guardrails and Control Design

Controls come first. Tools come second. That order keeps AI from creating surprises in the close, the forecast, or the filings. Guardrails are simply the design choices that let finance capture the benefits of AI without losing the discipline, evidence, and segregation that underpin SOX and ICFR.

Guardrail 1: Scope and Use-Case Definition

AI performs best (and remains easiest to control) when it operates within clear, narrow boundaries. Start with limited, well-understood tasks such as drafting variance explanations or flagging duplicate invoices. These are easy to verify and create clean evidence trails. Avoid deploying AI where it can directly post or approve transactions until reliability and controls are proven. A tight scope keeps both control design and audit testing straightforward and offers a path to scale responsibly.

Guardrail 2: Embedded Human Review

Every AI workflow must include a documented human checkpoint. When a model drafts a disclosure, an accountant reviews it, links it to the ledger, and checks it against the GAAP checklist before giving approval. If a model proposes an accrual, the preparer evaluates the supporting evidence and signs off before posting. These review steps should be outlined in the control matrix, specifying the reviewer, their authority, and the evidence provided. While a model can assist with preparation, management remains responsible for judgment and approval.

Guardrail 3: Segregation of Duties

Automation does not alter the fundamental principle of segregation of duties. A system that processes invoices, codes them, and routes them for payment cannot also approve or release those payments. Maintain a clear separation between data processing, approval, and payment release, supported by robust access controls. For any automated approval logic, set conservative thresholds and regularly test the rules to confirm they operate as designed. This helps prevent control failures where one automated process takes on multiple conflicting roles.

Guardrail 4: Logging and Evidence Trail

Logging is not optional. It is proof that the control operated. Retain the inputs, model outputs, final decision, and reviewer sign-offs for every AI use case. For generative tools, store the prompt and retrieved context; for forecasting models, store the version, data slice, and comparative output vs. prior periods. If logs reside in vendor systems, export periodic snapshots to company-controlled repositories so auditors can access them. Logs form the foundation of SOX testing and PCAOB expectations for evidence.

Guardrail 5: Change Control and Model Updates

Treat AI like code. Any adjustments to parameters, data sources, or prompts should undergo a formal change-control process. Run parallel tests before deploying a revised model into production. Compare its outputs with the previous version using real data and clarify any differences. If a change impacts a key control, get explicit approval from the control owner before using it. Document the reasons, test outcomes, and approvals, this safeguards both audit records and business continuity.

Guardrail 6: Fallback and Challenger Methods

Every AI-enabled process needs a documented fallback, a manual or deterministic method that keeps reporting controlled if the model fails, behaves inconsistently, or exceeds tolerance thresholds. Where it's practical, keep a challenger model running in parallel as an independent benchmark. If drift or anomalies show up, pause reliance, revert outputs to the fallback, and begin remediation. That preserves continuity without weakening assurance.

Guardrail 7: Access Control and Security

Access needs to be tightly controlled. Limit who can run models that influence reporting, view sensitive inputs, or change configurations. Perform role-based access reviews at least quarterly. If a vendor hosts the model, require audit-ready logging, data residency alignment, and clear user activity records in the contract. Weak access controls can turn an operating issue into a compliance violation.

Guardrail 8: Model Performance and Drift Monitoring

AI reliability can degrade, so monitoring can't be optional. Track operational metrics that finance can act on, including accuracy, exception aging, reviewer adjustments, and cycle time. Retest on a set cadence and after major updates to detect drift, behavior changes driven by new data or changing conditions. When drift exceeds thresholds, suspend reliance and revalidate. This fits both the NIST AI RMF "Manage" function and COSO's "Monitoring" component.

Guardrail 9: Vendor and Third-Party Risk

If an external model sits in a reporting workflow, treat the vendor as a critical service provider. Review SOC 1 or SOC 2 Type II reports, subprocessors, and data-handling procedures. Contracts should limit vendor training on company data, define deletion timelines, and guarantee access to audit-ready logs. If a vendor can't meet these standards, keep the use case behind the firewall or outside ICFR scope.

Guardrail 10: Data Governance and Lineage

Model reliability follows data quality. Use controlled sources tied to systems of record. If a model relies on external or operational data, add a reconciliation step before outputs enter a financial control path. Document data lineage end to end: origin, transformations, model version, and the slice used for the run. Treat data source or schema changes as model changes and revalidate before reuse.

Guardrail 11: Parallel Runs and Pilot Validation

Before relying on an AI model in production reporting, run at least one shadow cycle alongside the current process. Compare outputs, analyze variances, and document explanations. Move to reliance only when accuracy is demonstrated and controls are operating as designed. Parallel runs create the audit trail that supports management assurance and PCAOB review.

Using the Guardrails

Map these guardrails to the control framework you already run. Preventive controls define what the model can't do without a human gate. Detective controls flag anomalies and route them to a reviewer. Automated controls clear routine items. Manual controls handle judgment calls and anything material. Tie each guardrail to COSO components and to the control matrix so it shows up in walkthroughs and testing, not as a separate AI concept.

The examples below concretely illustrate the design choices:

- In accounts payable, the model flags duplicate invoices and out-of-policy expenses. The guardrails make segregation of duties explicit. The role that reviews exceptions can't also release payments. Auto-approvals stay limited to low-value invoices from approved vendors with a clean history. Exceptions route to a manager, and the manager documents the decision and rationale. Logs retain flagged items, dispositions, and periodic test results so the control can be reperformed and audited.
- In external reporting, the model drafts a footnote summarizing routine movements. The draft remains output for the preparer—not a final document. A reporting manager ties it back to the ledger, runs it through the GAAP checklist, and signs off. Prompts and retrieved context are stored with the period support. Any change to the template or model routes through a ticket, a parallel run, and control-owner approval before finance relies on the new version.

Notes

1. Hood, interview, December 16, 2025.
2. Public Company Accounting Oversight Board, "Spotlight: Staff Update on Outreach Activities Related to the Integration of Generative Artificial Intelligence in Audits and Financial Reporting," July 2024, PDF, accessed November 1, 2025, https://pcaobus.org/documents/generative-ai-spotlight.pdf

3. Erik Gerding, "The State of Disclosure Review," *U.S. Securities and Exchange Commission*, June 24, 2024, https://www.sec.gov/newsroom/speeches-statements/gerding-statement-state-disclosure-review-062424
4. National Institute of Standards and Technology (NIST), *Artificial Intelligence Risk Management Framework (AI RMF 1.0), NIST AI 100-1* (Gaithersburg, MD: US Department of Commerce, January 2023), https://nvlpubs.nist.gov/nistpubs/ai/NIST.AI.100-1.pdf
5. Hood, interview.
6. Sarbanes–Oxley Act of 2002 § 404(a), codified at 15 U.S.C. § 7262(a) (accessed November 1, 2025), Cornell Law School Legal Information Institute; and Securities and Exchange Commission, Regulation S-K, Item 308, "Internal Control over Financial Reporting," 17 C.F.R. § 229.308 (accessed November 1, 2025), Electronic Code of Federal Regulations.
7. PCAOB, "Spotlight: Staff Update on Outreach Activities Related to Generative AI."
8. Ibid.
9. Gerding, "State of Disclosure Review."
10. Ibid.
11. European Parliament, *Artificial Intelligence Act*, European Parliament Think Tank, September 2, 2024, https://www.europarl.europa.eu/thinktank/en/document/EPRS_BRI(2021)698792; European Union, *The EU Artificial Intelligence Act*, accessed November 5, 2025, https://artificialintelligenceact.eu
12. UK Financial Conduct Authority, *AI Update*, 2024, https://www.fca.org.uk/publication/corporate/ai-update.pdf
13. Darren Grayson Chng, "Global AI Governance Law and Policy: Singapore," *International Association of Privacy Professionals*, July 16, 2025, https://iapp.org/resources/article/global-ai-governance-singapore; Gibson Dunn, "Hong Kong Monetary Authority Issues Guidance on Gen-AI Use in Customer-Facing Applications and Use of Artificial Intelligence in Tackling ML/TF," *Gibson Dunn*, September 19, 2024, https://www.gibsondunn.com/hong-kong-monetary-authority-guidance-on-gen-ai-use-in-customer-facing-applications-and-use-of-ai-in-ml-tf/
14. Sarbanes–Oxley Act of 2002 § 404(a), codified at 15 U.S.C. § 7262(a); PCAOB, "Spotlight: Staff Update on Outreach Activities Related to Generative AI"; European Parliament, *Artificial Intelligence Act*; UK Financial Conduct Authority, *AI Update*; Grayson Chng, "Global AI Governance Law and Policy: Singapore"; Gibson Dunn, "Hong Kong Monetary Authority Issues Guidance on Gen-AI Use."
15. Scott M. Lundberg and Su-In Lee, "A Unified Approach to Interpreting Model Predictions," *arXiv*, May 22, 2017, accessed November 5, 2025, https://arxiv.org/abs/1705.07874

16. Marco Tulio Ribeiro, Sameer Singh, and Carlos Guestrin, "'Why Should I Trust You?': Explaining the Predictions of Any Classifier" (*Proceedings of the 22nd ACM SIGKDD International Conference on Knowledge Discovery and Data Mining*, KDD '16, San Francisco, CA, 2016), accessed November 5, 2025, https://www.kdd.org/kdd2016/papers/files/rfp0573-ribeiroA.pdf
17. Hood, interview.
18. Committee of Sponsoring Organizations of the Treadway Commission (COSO), *Enterprise Risk Management*, accessed November 6, 2025, https://www.coso.org/guidance-erm
19. COSO, *Enterprise Risk Management*; Sarbanes-Oxley Act of 2002 § 404(a), codified at 15 U.S.C. § 7262(a).
20. COSO, *Enterprise Risk Management.*
21. Sarbanes–Oxley Act of 2002 § 404(a), codified at 15 U.S.C. § 7262(a).
22. NIST, *Artificial Intelligence Risk Management Framework (AI RMF 1.0).*

Chapter 9

Realistic Timelines: 90-Day Wins to Two-Year Scaling

Key Takeaways

- **AI readiness becomes real only when it is executed through structure, evidence, and rhythm.** This chapter defines that structure: the minimum-governance pilot (MGP).
- **Each MGP is a contained 90-day cycle that proves value, documents control, and creates the evidence base for scale.** Linked together, MGPs form the architecture for developing a long-term roadmap that delivers measurable ROI and governed innovation.
  - In the first 90 days, success comes from precision: narrow scope, clear metrics, and visible output.

- By six months, momentum grows through replication, each connected MGP reuses prompts, evaluation methods, and evidence packs to extend AI across adjacent processes.
- From 12 to 24 months, wave planning turns these building blocks into a managed program. Each wave (quick wins, core processes, and decision support) advances only when the prior cycle's ROI, governance, and adoption are proven. Continuous oversight, not point-in-time review, is the hallmark of maturity.
- ROI validation, evidence creation, and compliance checks run inside every MGP, allowing course correction before small issues become structural failures.

- **Leadership shapes the duration of a project.** The CFO maintains support through open communication, quarterly evidence reports, and transparent governance practices. As AI advances into decision-support territory, board-level oversight and enterprise-wide replication naturally follow: the same rigor that proved successful in the finance function becomes the model for the entire company.
- **The AI-ready CFO's role is to achieve proven progress and build trust.** Not to innovate endlessly, but to implement AI through carefully managed successes one at a time.

From Readiness to Execution

The previous chapters defined what it means for a finance function to be ready for AI. Chapter 6 addressed the tool landscape: how to select capabilities that solve real finance problems, assess maturity, and distinguish between embedded features and dedicated applications. Chapter 7 focused on partnerships and how to structure relationships with vendors and technology teams so the organization keeps flexibility and control as solutions evolve. Chapter 8 established the governance model: how AI activity is documented, evidenced, and managed within existing SOX and control frameworks.

With those foundations in place, the AI-ready CFO now needs a clear plan for action. This chapter provides that plan. It translates readiness into delivery through defined time horizons that align with how finance already operates: the 90-day quarter, the one-year cycle, and the two-year roadmap. It focuses on what to do first, how to organize work, and how to expand responsibly once early results are proven.

Specifically, this chapter shows how to:

- Deliver measurable results in the first 90 days through well-scoped pilots.
- Build an operating cadence that combines speed with governance discipline.
- Apply a repeatable pilot structure, the MGP, to produce evidence and avoid scope drift.
- Extend success through "copy-with-variation" methods that scale AI across adjacent processes.
- Plan a 12- to 24-month program that turns individual pilots into a managed capability.

The objective is straightforward: establish a realistic, auditable path from first proof to scaled impact. What follows is a playbook for delivering AI adoption in finance with precision, discipline, and credibility.

Establishing Credibility: Quick Wins and Early Proof

Every finance transformation starts with trust. Teams that have experienced ERP migrations, BI implementations, or automation projects remember how long it took for benefits to materialize. Those experiences left a mark: caution born from fatigue. When a new initiative comes up, especially one that promises transformation, the first question is rarely about strategy. Instead, it's: "When will this make my work better?"

Finance leaders share that skepticism. The CFO's role is to demand evidence before scale. That's why quick wins matter. They demonstrate value early, quell the resistance, and build confidence that AI can improve and accelerate finance's work without adding risk.

However, the psychology of change management can't be ignored. Finance departments are not blank slates; they carry a collective memory of past programs that consumed resources before producing results. Maybe an ERP migration that took years, or BI dashboards that provided insights only after months of data cleanup. These experiences have taught finance professionals that new systems often create much more work before they reduce it. Quick wins can help change that narrative by showing measurable benefits within weeks, not years.

A bit of history reinforces this truth. The "big-bang" ERP strategies of the 1990s and 2000s promised complete transformation with one massive rollout. Many ended with budget problems, missed deadlines, and delayed benefits. Over time, finance learned that phased delivery works better because each stage shows progress, issues surface early, and momentum builds through evidence of success.

AI adoption demands the same pragmatism, if not more. Its outputs can be abstract, its behavior unpredictable, and its learning process unfamiliar. Demonstrating value quickly makes it more tangible. Until teams see an AI tool cut reconciliation time or produce a draft variance explanation that reads accurately, it is all just theoretical.

The right early project is scoped small, produces a visible output, and measures improvement against a clear baseline. Examples might include using GenAI to draft narrative variance commentary, detecting duplicate invoices, or creating the initial draft of board-pack analysis. These are modest tasks, but powerful demonstrations. They show that AI can save time, strengthen controls, and improve finance work immediately.

Quick wins change the psychology of adoption. They replace cautious hope with observed progress. They tell the team, "This time, the improvement is real."

Why AI Needs Quick Wins Even More

AI introduces additional pressures, making early results critical. First, the novelty factor plays a role. GenAI doesn't resemble ERP or BI. Its outputs can seem abstract or unpredictable to those without technical training. Providing a quick, practical result helps keep the conversation grounded in reality.

Second, finance teams operate in a regulated environment. They can't simply experiment for months without demonstrating that controls are in place. An AI pilot that shows not only efficiency but also compliance with existing review processes reassures auditors and managers that the technology can be trusted within current frameworks.

Third, the external environment creates a sense of urgency. Executives are reading about AI breakthroughs in the press and asking what their teams are doing with it. They expect to see tangible results in a short period. Quick wins enable CFOs to respond with actual progress rather than speculation.

Finally, unlike complex ERP systems, AI adoption is more accessible than ever before. Many tools can be tested without full-scale enterprise integration. Copilots and simple SaaS platforms can create value within days. This reduces the barrier to quick wins and eliminates excuses for delays. If a finance team cannot demonstrate value in the first quarter, stakeholders may question whether the program is even viable.

What Counts as a Quick Win?

The right quick win is small, scoped, and measurable. It addresses a real pain point and produces an output that stakeholders can see. It doesn't require extensive data engineering or deep integration into core systems.

Examples in finance may include:

- Drafting narrative explanations for variance analysis using a generative model. The CFO can compare the AI-generated draft against the analyst's version within weeks.
- Automating the flagging of duplicate invoices in accounts payable. The measurable result is errors prevented.
- Using AI to draft the first version of board-pack commentary. Executives see the output directly, which makes the benefit visible.

These are steppingstones, not final goals. Each small win builds trust and adds capacity, setting the stage for tackling more complex initiatives like rolling forecasts or speeding up the close process.

Organizational Dynamics: Buy-In Through Proof

Executive sponsorship is important, but adoption takes hold only when managers and staff participate in the work. Many employees worry AI will take their jobs. Quick wins help reset that concern. When technology handles repetitive tasks and people keep judgment and decision-making, the story changes. Staff start to see AI as a tool that tightens their work, instead of threatening their roles.

When a group benefits from a pilot, they often become its strongest supporters. A team that saves 20 hours a month on manual reconciliations will be quick to flag where the next pilot should run. Those advocates help build momentum across the organization.

Avoiding the Trap of Overpromising

A common change-management failure is creating a gap between what's promised and what's delivered. A leader may declare that a new system will cut close time in half within six months. When the results don't show up, the program loses credibility.

A better approach is to treat adoption as a series of proofs. State what the pilot will deliver in the first 90 days. Separate what will take 12 months or longer. Set expectations that scale and maturity take time, while evidence of value should be visible in the first quarter. This keeps credibility intact and keeps the team engaged.

Operating Model: Agile for Finance AI

Early proof is only meaningful if it can be repeated. That requires a delivery model built for learning and control. For finance, the answer is a tailored form of Agile: structured enough for compliance and light enough to iterate without adopting Scrum or SAFe in full.

Traditional project management assumes predictability. AI work rarely behaves that way. Results evolve as models learn and data improves. An Agile-style rhythm lets finance teams test, adjust, and deliver progress in short, visible cycles. The cadence should fit finance operations: frequent review, documented evidence, and continuous improvement.

In practice, "Agile for finance" is a governed operating rhythm. Work moves in short cycles with measurable deliverables, constant feedback, and clear accountability.

What "Agile" Means in This Chapter

Agile is a delivery approach built for work where you can't predict outcomes upfront. Instead of long planning cycles followed by a single large release, Agile breaks work into short, time-boxed cycles that produce a usable deliverable each round.

In a finance AI context, Agile typically includes:

- **Short cycles (weekly or bi-weekly).** The team ships something tangible each cycle, even if it's small.
- **Defined roles and accountability.** Clear owners for requirements, build/configuration, validation, and sign-off.
- **Review and measurement every cycle.** Each output is reviewed against agreed success criteria (accuracy, time saved, exception rates, control evidence).
- **Tight feedback loop.** The team incorporates user feedback and performance results immediately, reducing surprise later in the project.
- **Governed iteration.** Changes are logged, approvals are explicit, and evidence trails are maintained so improvements don't weaken controls.

Agile doesn't mean moving fast without structure. It means making measurable progress through repeated, controlled cycles so you learn early, limit wasted effort, and scale what works.

Adapting Agile Principles to Finance AI

Traditional project management relies on extended planning phases followed by large releases. That approach works poorly for AI because results vary, data often needs adjustment, and vendor capabilities keep changing. A plan made months in advance can be stale before it's executed.

Agile fits better because it keeps decisions close to evidence. Finance teams can run a short cycle, review outputs against defined acceptance criteria, log exceptions, and either tighten the workflow or stop the work before costs compound.

In finance terms, think of this as "prove the benefit early, then invest more." Instead of building a large AI system for forecasting, start with a sprint to produce a draft revenue commentary using historical data. Route it through the normal review and approval path. If it ties out and the time savings are real, improve it in the next cycle. If not, the cost of failure stays limited.

This cadence also helps set expectations. Executives are used to quarterly financial updates. Weekly or bi-weekly cycles create a steady drumbeat of visible progress, so stakeholders don't wait months to learn whether a pilot is working.

Culturally, the message is simple: no one has to master AI overnight. The work is built around controlled learning, with each cycle tied to measurable value and a clear control point.

Roles, Cadence, and Responsibilities

For an Agile framework to work in finance, responsibilities have to be explicit. Each role maps to a control point or operating need in the department:

- **Executive sponsor.** Usually the CFO. Provides authority, removes barriers, and keeps the program aligned with business priorities.
- **Product owner**. Often a finance transformation lead or senior manager. Owns the backlog, defines the problem to be solved, and validates that outcomes match business needs.
- **Project manager (similar to scrum master).** Keeps the cadence on track, manages dependencies, and routes communication.
- **Data lead**. Owns data access, quality, and lineage. Ensures the AI system is working from reliable sources.
- **Compliance lead.** Brings SOX, ICFR, or other control frameworks into the work. Reviews logs and evidence so the output can stand up to audit scrutiny.
- **IT or integration partner.** Manages connections between systems and oversees security.
- **Process owners.** Leaders in accounts payable, FP&A, or reporting who validate outputs against real workflows.

Not every organization staffs these as full-time roles. In smaller teams, one person may carry multiple responsibilities. The requirement is coverage: each role is assigned so essential functions don't get missed.

Cadence is as important as roles. Weekly or bi-weekly sprint reviews are the heartbeat. These are brief sessions where the team demonstrates a working output to stakeholders. The rule is simple: show the thing. Even if it's rough or only covers part of the workflow, it creates accountability and gives stakeholders evidence that the work is moving.

In addition to sprint reviews, a monthly steering meeting with executives supports the larger decisions. That's where the CFO and senior leaders decide whether to expand a pilot, rescope it, or retire it. The combination keeps everyone aligned without adding unnecessary bureaucracy.

Essential Artifacts and Guardrails

Agile often prioritizes working software over heavy documentation. For finance AI projects, documentation is a control requirement. These artifacts aren't busywork. They create the evidence that lets work be audited, controlled, and repeated.

- A prompt library is a core artifact. AI workflows rely on prompts, and small wording changes can produce different outputs. Versioning keeps prompts stable and reviewable. The library should record what's used, who created it, and when it was last updated.
- The runbook is another artifact. It documents the end-to-end workflow, including inputs, outputs, and exception handling. The purpose is continuity. If a staff member leaves, the process still runs, and auditors can see how the system works.
- The evaluation report functions as the scorecard. It tracks accuracy, error rates, latency, and cost per run, giving stakeholders an objective basis to decide whether the AI is outperforming the manual process it replaced.
- A decision log complements the report by recording each time a human intervenes to approve, edit, or override an AI output. This record maintains transparency and shows that oversight stays in place.

All of these items feed the evidence pack: a unified record of inputs, outputs, logs, and approvals for each reporting cycle. When auditors or regulators ask how a variance explanation was created, finance can point to a single file that ties the output back to its sources and reviews.

These artifacts strike a balance. They keep the work agile by focusing on what finance needs to run and defend the process. The guardrails (detailed in Chapter 8) ensure agility doesn't weaken control. Every workflow should include a human review step. Every run should produce a log. Every system should have a rollback plan. These rules limit risk while letting the team move at a reasonable pace.

Before starting a sprint, the team also needs agreement on what "done" means. In a forecasting pilot, "done" might mean the AI produces a revenue forecast narrative with 90% alignment to the analyst's version and that the output has been reviewed and approved by a manager. Without a clear definition of done, projects can drift and disputes can surface over whether the work is complete.

An "Agile for finance" framework that's practical enough to run allows finance leaders to deliver AI pilots quickly while maintaining accountability. The roles clarify ownership. The cadence keeps progress visible. The artifacts create the evidence needed for controls. Together, they form an operating model that produces results without losing discipline.

The First-90: Project Selection Criteria

The first project sets the tone for everything that follows. Pick the right one, and the organization sees immediate evidence that AI can help. Pick the wrong one, and skepticism returns before the program begins.

A good first project is modest in scope but clear in intent. It uses existing data, works within current controls, and delivers visible, measurable results. Automating tasks like duplicate-invoice detection, drafting variance comments, or speeding up reconciliations are practical examples. They demonstrate value without needing system-wide integration or extensive data engineering.

> Find a specific, contained use case where you can rapidly learn and gain confidence... and keep repeating it.[1]
>
> —*Ranga Bodla, NetSuite*

Complex forecasting or AI-driven close acceleration might be tempting, but they belong further down the roadmap. The first quarter should demonstrate feasibility, not scale. A pilot that saves staff 20 hours per month, or cuts error rates in half, does more for credibility than an unfinished multi-system integration at year-end.

Defining success upfront is non-negotiable. The CFO should set clear expectations: what the project will improve, how that improvement will be measured, and what evidence will confirm it. When results arrive, there is no debate about whether progress was real.

A quick win doesn't need to be transformational. It needs to be visible, verifiable, and aligned with the finance team's rhythm. In the first 90 days, proof of concept is proof of capability.

Consider accounts payable. Few areas in finance generate as much routine, repetitive work, and few are as well documented. A pilot that uses AI to detect duplicate invoices is focused enough to deliver quickly, measurable in its ability to prevent errors, and transparent because every flagged invoice can be reviewed by staff and reported to leadership. It also integrates smoothly within existing approval processes, allowing auditors to validate it without designing new controls. Within weeks, the finance team has evidence of cost savings and hours saved, and the CFO can highlight a practical example of AI making the department more reliable.

Variance commentary is another great example. Finance teams spend many hours every month creating explanations for budget-to-actual differences. A generative model can be prompted to generate a first draft using historical data and simple business rules. Analysts still review and edit, so there's no risk of releasing unchecked text, but the time saved is clear. Executives see that commentary is delivered more quickly, and staff see that AI handles the most routine parts of their work. Here, the pilot's value is not just efficiency but also perception: the team learns that AI can assist them without undermining their expertise.

These examples highlight an important principle. The first measure of impact is whether the project saves staff time, prevents errors, or produces outputs that stakeholders can rely on. If a pilot saves 20 hours a month in reconciliations, or removes a set of duplicate payments from the cycle, that counts as impact. The scale can come later. Early projects prove that value is possible at all. No one should expect an AI pilot to eliminate millions in costs or cut the close in half in its first quarter.

Visibility is a key factor in selecting quick wins. Early projects must clearly show results so stakeholders can observe them. A variance commentary pilot provides text that executives can easily understand. An anomaly detection pilot offers a list of transactions for audit review. Visibility is important because perception impacts momentum. A project that saves time but lacks visible output is harder to promote than one that executives can directly experience.

Careful selection helps avoid the risks of poorly executed initial projects. The first-90 project isn't about scale or strategic transformation. It's about proof. It shows that AI can be used in finance in a way that's practical, measurable, and controlled.

The 90-Day Plan

The first 90 days of an AI program serve as the proving ground. By this time, the finance leader has established an operating model and selected a project that qualifies as a quick win. What's still missing is rhythm. Without a clear cadence, projects tend to drift. Deadlines are missed, and what was intended to be a short pilot can turn into a year-long experiment. The discipline of a 90-day plan helps prevent that drift. It sets expectations, keeps stakeholders engaged, and produces evidence at a pace that matches how finance already functions.

Why 90 Days?

The 90-day timeframe naturally aligns with finance rhythms. Companies are built around quarters, and investors expect updates accordingly. Executives are used to evaluating performance at quarter's end. Creating pilots that follow the same schedule simplifies their assessment and explanation. After three months, the CFO can report not only on earnings but also on whether an AI pilot delivered tangible results.

The timeframe is also psychologically significant. It is long enough to move past the novelty of a new tool and into the actual workflow, but short enough to keep the urgency. People stay motivated when they know the evaluation is weeks rather than months or years away; 90 days is a period that commands attention without overloading staff.

Month 1: Mobilizing the Pilot

The first 30 days set the foundation. The project team needs clarity on scope, data, and responsibilities. The current baseline needs to be established: how long a process takes today, how many errors occur, and what it costs. Without a baseline, improvement cannot be demonstrated later.

Mobilization also means involving the right people working through potential bottlenecks. CFO sponsorship may clear obstacles, but the day-to-day work belongs to process owners, analysts, and compliance staff. Naming project owners at the start prevents confusion later. Data access is often the first bottleneck. Even for small pilots, the team needs a defined dataset to work with. The key is to select data that is representative but manageable. Trying to connect every source system in the first month creates unnecessary delays.

The mobilization period also allows for agreement on what success will look like. Defining success upfront gives the entire project team a shared target.

Month 2: Proving the Concept in Real Workflows

In the second month, the pilot should come to life. The aim isn't perfection, but something tangible that can be used and critiqued. Don't make promises; show the output.

In practice, this involves creating the smallest functional version of the workflow and deploying it to users. If the project focuses on variance commentary, analysts should start reviewing AI-generated drafts by the middle of the second month. For invoice detection, AP clerks should be validating flagged invoices against their usual checks. The goal is to integrate the AI tool into the workflow quickly enough to evaluate its usefulness and identify any weaknesses that need fixing.

Evaluation begins during this stage, not at the end of 90 days. Outputs are compared against baselines to see if the expected benefits are emerging. At this stage, staff start to form opinions. If AI saves them time, they will become advocates. The pilot must produce visible, useful outputs at this stage or it risks losing momentum.

Month 3: Expanding and Deciding

As 90 days approach, it's time for refinement and decision. With a working slice of the workflow in place, the team can expand. For invoice detection, that might mean moving from one vendor set to three. For commentary, that might mean generating drafts for both revenue and expense accounts. Remain conservative; test the system performance at slightly larger scales without losing control.

Collate project documentation to give the CFO confidence that the pilot has been managed properly and prepare the ground for any audit questions. Prompts should be versioned, decision logs should be complete, and evidence packs should be ready.

Then comes decision time: Is the pilot ready to scale? Should it pause for further refinement? Or is it time to retire the project?

- Scale means committing resources to expand the workflow across more processes or departments.
- Pause means the concept has promise but requires more data or adjustment.
- Retire means the pilot did not deliver value and should be closed cleanly.

Any of these outcomes is acceptable. Failure is ending the pilot drifting with no decision.

Discipline Beats Speed Alone

Don't try to do too much in the first 90 days. As leaders see initial results, they might want to add more use cases or expand the scope immediately. Resist the urge to satisfy them. Focusing on one project, demonstrating it thoroughly, and making a clear decision at the end builds trust. For the AI-ready CFO, the 90-day plan sets a steady rhythm in a fast-paced, sometimes chaotic process, helping ensure AI adoption progresses at a pace that matches the tempo of finance.

The Minimum-Governance Pilot: The Building Block of AI at Scale

The use of AI at the enterprise level cannot scale through grand launches. Scaling depends on the successful implementation of a series of disciplined, repeatable units that connect experimentation and institutionalization.

The concept of the MGP is simple: each MGP is a self-contained cycle that demonstrates value, records control, and builds the evidence base for the next expansion, paving the way for finance to shift from isolated pilots to an operating system for AI.

Why the MGP Exists

The finance department can't afford uncontrolled experimentation, but it can't wait for perfect certainty either. The MGP resolves that tension. It applies the 90-day delivery cycle and the ROI discipline of finance within a governance framework that is light enough to move quickly but strong enough to satisfy audit.

Each MGP answers three questions:

1. Does this use case create measurable value?
2. Can it operate safely within our controls?
3. Is it repeatable across other workflows?

When a pilot answers these questions with a "yes," it can establish a pattern, and that pattern becomes scale.

The Structure of an MGP

Every MGP has five linked components:

1. **Readiness.** Data access, owners, and success metrics confirmed before work begins.
2. **Thin-slice delivery.** A small but functional piece of the workflow that can run in production conditions within 90 days.
3. **Evaluation.** Accuracy, latency, and cost tracked against the baseline ROI agreed at launch.
4. **Evidence.** Prompts versioned, outputs logged, human reviews captured, and all artifacts consolidated in an evidence pack.
5. **Decision gate.** Scale, refine, or retire based on verified results.

These five components set the operating pattern that connects the different parts of the CFO's AI agenda.

Each MGP carries forward the lessons of:

- **Tool selection.** Each pilot anchored in a defined use case that solves a measurable problem.
- **Partnership and governance.** Every role, control, and evidence requirement is explicit from the start.
- **ROI and value.** Each cycle launched with a baseline and evaluated on real results.
- **Agile delivery.** Short iterations that learn and improve rather than promise perfection.

An MGP is the fundamental unit of AI implementation. Each 90-day cycle is a self-contained opportunity to validate a business case, ensure compliance, and improve the model for scaling. Together, multiple MGPs weave the fabric of an AI-ready finance function, growing but remaining under control, continuously learning while maintaining evidence, and compounding value through repeatable success.

How the MGP Connects Strategy to Scale

The CFO's roadmap consists of many MGPs linked in sequence:

- **Phase 1.** One or two MGPs focused on quick-win use cases such as variance commentary, duplicate-invoice detection, or reconciliations. These establish proof and credibility.
- **Phase 2.** Copy-with-variation. Replicate successful MGPs across adjacent processes to build momentum.
- **Phase 3.** Wave planning. Combine multiple MGPs into broader programs such as forecasting or close acceleration.

Every completed MGP leaves behind assets: validated prompts, performance metrics, evidence packs, and refined governance practices. Together, these assets form the organization's AI control fabric and the institutional knowledge that enables efficient, safe scaling.

The Role of ROI in Every MGP

Because finance lives by numbers, every MGP begins with a quantified hypothesis of value:

- **Efficiency ROI.** Hours saved, error rates reduced, throughput increased.
- **Effectiveness ROI.** Faster insight generation, improved forecast accuracy.
- **Control ROI.** Reduction in manual checks or audit exceptions.

At the end of the cycle, these metrics are compared to baseline. Even small improvements create a cumulative return when repeated across dozens of workflows. The CFO uses MGP results to justify continued investment with hard data, not promises.

How to Use the MGP

The MGP is both a design pattern and a management unit for the AI-ready CFO.

- **As a design pattern,** it tells you how to construct each pilot: small, measurable, governed.
- **As a management unit,** it gives you a common language with IT, compliance, and the board: "We are running three MGPs this quarter; one is scaling, one is paused, one retired."

Over time, this vocabulary changes the conversation. AI no longer appears as a series of disconnected experiments; it becomes a controlled portfolio of MGPs, each with its own ROI, evidence, and owner.

The Discipline Behind the Name. "Minimum governance" doesn't mean minimal control. It means no unnecessary control. It is designed to insert the least structure required to produce credible evidence. That discipline is what makes scaling possible. It prevents the sprawl of unverified tools while keeping innovation alive. Each MGP should leave a documented trail that allows finance to move quickly and answer the auditor's questions in a single file.

Evolution of AI within the organization should take place inside this framework. If an idea is worth testing, it deserves an MGP. If it can't meet MGP standards, it's not ready for finance.

From Pilot to Scale

When used consistently, MGPs form a scaling architecture for an AI-ready finance function:

- **Proof** in the first 90 days.
- **Momentum** through repetition and variation.
- **Maturity** through accumulation of evidence and ROI.

From 90 Days to Six Months: Building Momentum Through Connected MGPs

Once a pilot proves its value in the first 90 days, the next step is to extend it. As noted before, scaling doesn't mean jumping directly to enterprise-wide adoption or taking on the most complex workflows. The more reliable approach is to link proven MGPs together, applying their tested structure to adjacent processes. This copy-with-variation method builds momentum while preserving the discipline that made the first pilot succeed.

The logic follows directly from the structure of the MGP itself. Every completed pilot already contains the ingredients for replication: prompts that generate outputs, evaluation criteria that measure success, and controls that capture evidence. Rather than starting from scratch, the finance team can reuse and adapt them for a new context. The result is a project that feels familiar, is faster to implement, and carries less risk because the underlying MGP framework is already proven.

Each pilot leaves behind tangible assets: prompt libraries, evaluation templates, metrics, and evidence packs. These artifacts are not administrative byproducts; they're the infrastructure needed to scale. When reused in new contexts, they shorten setup time, reduce design variability, and signal to compliance that governance remains intact. In this way, finance can evolve from one proof to a portfolio of proofs in a structured progression rather than a leap of faith.

Three Early MGP Extensions

Consider how three early MGPs might evolve within six months:

- **AP expansion.** The initial MGP detects duplicate invoices, and the next iteration uses the same framework for purchase-order matching or vendor-statement reconciliation. The logic, identifying anomalies through pattern comparison, remains the same. The dataset and thresholds shift, but the prompt structure, review process, and evidence pack are reused. Because staff already know the process, adoption is immediate and the audit trail stays consistent.
- **Variance commentary series.** A pilot that began with revenue accounts extends naturally to expenses, then to cash flow. Each MGP

uses the same narrative-prompting method, review cadence, and evaluation metrics. Analysts develop confidence through repetition, while executives see AI's contribution expand across core FP&A deliverables.

- **Reconciliation and close acceleration.** After anomaly detection proves effective in AP, the next MGP could apply the method to intercompany reconciliations or accrual testing. The workflow is different, but the verification logic is identical: flag, review, document. This progression connects transactional speed with period-end accuracy and provides a visible bridge between operational and reporting improvement.

Connecting the MGPs

Each connected MGP strengthens the organization's AI-driven foundation. Prompt libraries become more comprehensive; evaluation reports compile benchmarks; evidence packs demonstrate consistency. Auditors and executives alike can begin to see the pattern: results are reproducible, governance remains stable, and value is quantifiable.

By the six-month mark, the finance function will have completed several MGPs, each building on the last. Teams will have seen AI in action across multiple processes; leadership will have evidence that adoption boosts both reliability and efficiency. The organization will have established the rhythm of scaling with repeated progress through repetition, learning through evidence, and building confidence through control.

This pattern, illustrated in the 24-month roadmap, shows how 90-day MGPs become the building blocks in a continuous cycle of readiness, delivery, and evidence review. It's the operating rhythm that naturally extends into the one- and two-year horizons.

The 12- to 24-Month Program Roadmap: From MGP Portfolio to Program

The first six months of AI adoption focus on proving concepts and expanding them to related workflows. By the one-year point, the CFO needs to shift perspective from pilots to full programs. The question changes from "What did we test?" to "How do we integrate AI into finance as a managed capability?" The 12- to 24-month roadmap provides that framework by demonstrating to stakeholders that AI is not just a series of experiments, but a disciplined development process based on MGP cycles.

The guiding principle at this stage is wave planning. Instead of treating each new use case as a separate initiative, leaders group related MGPs into deliberate waves, similar to rolling-wave planning used in Agile and portfolio management. Near-term work is detailed, while later waves stay flexible for adjustments as results come in.

Wave 2: Core Process Expansion (Months 12–18)

The finance function applies the MGP framework to more central workflows like close acceleration, cash forecasting, and collections prioritization. These projects are more complex and have a broader impact, but the structure remains the same: readiness, thin slice, evaluation, evidence, decision gate. Artifacts from previous MGPs, like prompt libraries, evaluation reports, and evidence packs, serve as templates, reducing both risk and cycle time.

Wave 3: Strategic Decision Support (Months 18–24)

By this stage, finance is prepared to implement AI where it influences decisions, not just processes. Rolling forecasts, scenario modeling, and capital allocation analysis become part of the agenda. The CFO transitions from sponsoring pilots to designing a governed AI capability that connects multiple MGPs into a cohesive program.

Ongoing Review

Each wave includes continuous gate reviews. Before advancing, teams validate that:

- Data quality and access remain sufficient.
- Control and evidence frameworks are intact.
- Users report measurable improvements.

These reviews occur within every MGP cycle, ensuring that ROI validation, evidence collection, and governance oversight continue throughout the roadmap. If a pilot underperforms or fails a control test, it's refined or retired before the next wave progresses.

This approach embodies the Agile concept of progressive elaboration: planning near-term work precisely, evaluating progress regularly, and adjusting long-term goals as insights and maturity develop. Meanwhile, the roadmap stays flexible as business priorities shift and technology advances, but its value lies in the discipline it enforces. Stakeholders can see that AI adoption is managed, measured, and governed over time.

After two years, a finance function following such a roadmap will have integrated AI across multiple processes, from transactional automation to planning and decision support (see Table 9.1). More importantly, it will have built a repeatable operating model: a portfolio of MGPs, each providing ROI and evidence of control, collectively forming the foundation for ongoing innovation.

How to Read the Table

- **Each cell** represents an active MGP or cluster of linked MGPs (90-day blocks).
- **Waves** group those MGPs into strategic themes: quick wins → core processes → decision support.
- **Continuous oversight** is an always-on thread; the CFO, compliance, and data teams evaluate ROI and governance during every sprint, not only at quarter-end.
- **Failure or misalignment** in any MGP triggers an immediate redesign or suspension—no waiting for a year-end review.

Avoiding Common Failure Modes

Even well-designed programs can falter. When AI initiatives in finance stall, the problem rarely lies in the technology itself. It stems from gaps in scope, governance, or follow-through. The AI-ready CFO needs to anticipate these failure modes and prevent them before they erode credibility.

Table 9.1 24-Month Evolution of AI in Finance (MGP-Based Roadmap)

Timeframe	Wave/focus	Finance operations	FP&A	Compliance and IT	Executive/ governance	Continuous oversight and evaluation
0–3 months (Q1)	Wave 1: quick wins/MGP launch	Launch MGP #1: duplicate-invoice detection (AP)	Launch MGP #2: revenue variance commentary	Validate data sources; establish logging and prompt versioning	CFO sponsors program charter; define ROI baseline	*Readiness review*: confirm data quality and ownership *ROI tracking begins*: collect initial savings and time metrics
3–6 months (Q2)	Wave 1 extension: connected MGPs	Extend to PO matching and vendor reconciliation (MGP #3)	Extend commentary to expenses and cash flow (MGP #4)	Evaluate data security; test integration with ERP	Executive steering review of first ROI data and compliance logs	*Evidence review*: evaluate accuracy and control artifacts *Continuous ROI validation* during each sprint
6–12 months (Q3–Q4)	Wave 2: core processes/ operational scale	Launch MGP #5: close acceleration	Launch MGP #6: cash forecast automation	Expand monitoring to transaction and forecast models	CFO presents progress to board; align on next-wave investment	*Ongoing ROI validation* for each MGP *Control audits* at MGP closure points. Failing ROI or governance prompts redesign before scale

Timeframe	Wave/focus	Finance operations	FP&A	Compliance and IT	Executive/ governance	Continuous oversight and evaluation
12–18 months (Q5–Q6)	Wave 2 expansion: high-value workflows	Extend close acceleration to multi-entity reporting	Extend forecast automation to scenario modeling	Implement data lineage tracking; upgrade prompt library controls	CFO defines AI center of excellence; formalize program metrics	*Continuous evidence review* each quarter *ROI reforecast* based on maturity metrics
18–24 months (Q7–Q8)	Wave 3: decision support/ strategic integration	Embed AI in working-capital optimization and risk analytics	Integrate AI into capital allocation and rolling forecasts	Deploy governance dashboard linking MGP metrics to audit controls	CFO evolves from program sponsor to AI architect; report on enterprise ROI	*Governance checkpoints ongoing*: verify data ethics, controls, and model reliability *Re-evaluate ROI* for underperforming MGPs before renewal

Overreach. Here, ambition grows faster than readiness. Teams try to automate the close or redesign forecasting before smaller pilots prove stable. Data gaps arise, and complexity overwhelms governance. The safeguard is structural: stay within the boundaries of the MGP. Each 90-day cycle must have a clear business case, controlled data, and defined decision gates. Scaling follows evidence, not enthusiasm.

Neglect of Controls. The desire for speed can lead teams to skip documentation and reviews. When prompts are changed without recording them, or outputs aren't logged, even valid results become hard to defend. Every MGP should generate a complete evidence pack including prompts, outputs, approvals, and ROI metrics that are ready for review at any time. That evidence is the proof that sustains ongoing innovation.

Drift. Drift occurs when pilots linger without closure. Teams keep tweaking models rather than deciding whether to scale or stop. This drains capacity and fosters skepticism across the organization. To prevent drift, define "done" at the start. When an MGP completes its cycle, assess it against baseline metrics. If it meets its goals, move on to the next MGP; if not, revise or retire it. Momentum relies on closure.

The three traps of overreach, neglect, and drift are not exclusive to AI, but AI accelerates their exposure. The same discipline that guides finance must also guide AI transformation: defined scope, consistent controls, and timely decisions. When these principles are followed, AI programs remain credible, auditable, and trusted by those who rely on their results.

Consolidating Support: Sustaining Momentum and Trust

Technical progress matters little if people don't believe in it. Sustaining support is what turns an AI initiative into a durable capability. The CFO leads this work successfully through evidence, transparency, and inclusion.

Different groups engage from different perspectives:

- Executives focus on alignment to strategic goals and return on investment.
- Compliance and audit care about control integrity and traceability.

- IT and security want safe integration with existing systems.
- Finance managers and analysts want tools that remove routine work while preserving judgment.

CFOs must communicate with each audience in their language. Executives review consolidated ROI data and productivity results. Compliance examines the evidence packs and control documentation. IT participates in architecture and risk assessments. Analysts see early prototypes and assist in refining prompts. When each stakeholder can point to tangible results, support naturally strengthens itself.

Create Champions. The most convincing advocates are practitioners who use the tools every day. A manager who saves 20 hours a month or an analyst whose forecasts become more accurate builds more trust than any presentation. Involve these champions early; let them test, suggest improvements, and share results. Their credibility supports the overall story.

Communicate Throughout the Cycle. Support fades when communication is inconsistent. View engagement as an ongoing part of the MGP cycle. Each 90-day review should include not only performance metrics but also a communication output: sharing results with staff, ensuring compliance, and updating leadership. Being open about what worked, what didn't, and what's coming next fosters trust more quickly than polished success stories.

Use Governance as Proof. The carefully developed governance artifacts, like prompt libraries, decision logs, and evidence packs, are not just internal or compliance paperwork. They serve as communication tools. This documentation clearly demonstrates how AI operates within control frameworks and reassures skeptical stakeholders that innovation remains accountable.

Extending Support to the Board and the Enterprise

As AI moves into Wave 3, the CFO's communication responsibility expands far beyond the finance function. At this point, AI begins to influence forecasts, capital allocation, and possibly elements of external reporting. These areas sit squarely within the board's oversight role and often intersect with regulators and investors. The CFO must therefore establish a board-level briefing rhythm that mirrors the MGP cadence: concise, evidence-based updates every quarter that summarize ROI realization, control integrity, and risk posture.

Boards don't need the technical detail, but they do need assurance that:

- Each AI initiative operates within established governance frameworks.
- Control owners remain accountable.
- Model performance and audit evidence are reviewed continuously, not annually.

This communication discipline converts potential anxiety about AI risk into confidence that the CFO is managing innovation with the same rigor applied to capital markets and disclosure controls.

Beyond Finance

Mature MGPs can serve as templates for enterprise adoption. Procurement, HR, and supply-chain teams can tailor the readiness, thin-slice, evaluation, evidence, and decision-gate framework to their specific areas. The CFO's governance example sets the tone for responsible AI scaling across the organization: disciplined, measured, and auditable.

By demonstrating that AI can operate safely in finance, the most scrutinized function, the CFO builds a framework for enterprise trust. Over time, evident progress and steady governance turn support into confidence. The CFO's credibility becomes the company's assurance that AI improves performance without raising risk, and that finance can innovate without losing control.

The success of an AI program in finance depends as much on people as on technology. Even a well-designed pilot will struggle if executives remain unconvinced, if compliance feels excluded, or if staff see the tool as a threat. Gaining support requires a deliberate strategy that considers each group's interests and builds trust through evidence and participation. Without this, early pilots risk being dismissed as experiments without lasting impact.

Note

1. Bodla, interview, December 16, 2025.

Further Reading

- Accenture, *Transforming Finance Now: Getting Your Finance Transformation Off the Ground, Accelerating, and Taking It Higher*, accessed November 7, 2025, https://www.accenture.com/content/dam/accenture/final/capabilities/technology/technology-innovation/document/Accenture-Finance-Transformation-New.pdf

  Why included: Practical framing for finance operating-model evolution and staged transformation (quick wins → scaling → reinvention), which maps well to wave planning.

- Atlassian, "Agile Quarterly Planning: 8 Steps to Start Long-term Agile Planning," accessed November 7, 2025, https://www.atlassian.com/agile/agile-at-scale/long-term-agile-planning

  Why included: Clear practitioner explanation of rolling/quarterly planning and roadmap mechanics that mirror a 90-day governance rhythm.

- Gartner, *Propel AI Capabilities with the Finance AI Maturity Model.* By Mark D. McDonald. Research report, June 26, 2024. Accessed November 7, 2025. (Available via Gartner or authorized reprint channels.)

  Why included: Provides a finance-specific AI maturity framing and roadmap logic that can be aligned to quarterly operating cadence.

- Harvard Business Review Analytic Services, *Maintaining Momentum on Digital Transformation: CIOs Share Strategies to Sustain Speed.* White Paper, 2022. Accessed November 7, 2025, https://enterprisersproject.com/sites/default/files/2022-01/hbr_maintaining_momentum_digital_transformation.pdf

  Why included: Useful evidence base on sustaining transformation pace, adoption dynamics, and change fatigue—good support for "quick win → momentum" arguments.

- Institute of Management Accountants (IMA), *The Impact of Artificial Intelligence on Accounting and Finance: A Global Perspective.* Report, January 2024. Accessed November 7, 2025, https://in.imanet.org/research-publications/ima-reports/the-impact-of-artificial-intelligence-on-accounting-and-finance

  Why included: CFO/accounting-specific discussion of AI adoption barriers plus ethical/governance considerations that reinforce oversight and accountability themes.

- McKinsey & Company, "Charting a Path to the Data- and AI-Driven Enterprise of 2030." *McKinsey Quarterly*, September 5, 2024. Accessed November 7, 2025. https://www.mckinsey.com/capabilities/tech-and-ai/our-insights/charting-a-path-to-the-data-and-ai-driven-enterprise-of-2030

Why included: A credible "roadmap"-style source for enterprise AI transformation sequencing.

- ModelOp, "The EU AI Act Is Approved: What Is the Minimum Viable Governance That Global Enterprises Need to Comply With Regulatory Requirements?" March 21, 2024. Accessed November 7, 2025, https://www.modelop.com/blog/minimum-viable-governance

  Why included: A concrete industry articulation of "minimum governance pilot" concepts that parallel lightweight governance patterns.

- Project Management Institute and Agile Alliance, *Agile Practice Guide* (Newtown Square, PA: Project Management Institute, 2017). Accessed November 7, 2025, https://www.pmi.org/standards/agile

  Why included: Establishes rolling-wave planning and progressive elaboration principles with an authoritative standards anchor.

Chapter 10

Redesigning Finance Workflows for AI

Key Takeaways

- **Finance speeds up when work stops ricocheting between people and spreadsheets.** Close, forecast, and board decks all have the same failure modes: sloppy handoffs, rework, and missing context. A solid workflow carries the numbers and the "why" forward, so nobody's hunting inputs at 9 p.m. AI pours gasoline on whatever you built, so build something worth speeding up.
- **A current-state map turns opinions into timestamps.** Write down what actually happens: who touches the file, where it sits, when it moves, and what triggers a review. Do it at the messy level (e.g., forecast refresh, AP exceptions, revenue cutoffs), where the bodies are buried. Then you've got a baseline you can measure and argue from.

- **Friction is data. Treat it that way.** Approval pileups, "send me the latest version," and shadow spreadsheets point to fuzzy decision rights and brittle trust. A quick barrier scan shows where oversight turns into gridlock and where people babysit broken flow. Once you can name the choke points, you can fix them.
- **Controls belong inside the workflow, not stapled on after.** Let evidence collect as the work runs: source docs linked, fields captured, confidence flagged, reviewer actions logged. Set clear thresholds so routine items move and higher-priority risks get a human set of eyes. Ensure the new workflows are supported in an audit room.
- **Progress comes from one lane done cleanly, then copied.** Pick a lane like forecast refresh, connect the data, run it for a few cycles, and watch the rework drop. Then reuse the same pattern for monthly variance write-ups or the reporting package. Keep the scorecard short, like eight or ten measures, and let the repeat playbook do the work.

> AI is not a shortcut. You still have to fix your data. You still have to fix your processes. If you've got bad workflows, it's not going to fix them.[1]
>
> —*Ranga Bodla, NetSuite*

Workflow Design for an AI-Ready Finance Function

Every finance executive knows the rhythm of the close or forecast cycle: late nights, cascading spreadsheets, systems strained under load, and endless Slack threads asking when the numbers will be ready. Despite decades of technology investment, the work still feels like a grind because most workflows were built for a pre-digital era: they're optimized for control, not flow. As a result, finance teams spend more time moving data than interpreting it.

But now, with AI, we are starting to see faster analysis and automated reporting in production workflows. But we still hear regular reports of failed AI implementations. That's because just adding an algorithm to a flawed process is not transformation. All that does is accelerate chaos and speed up inefficiency! The AI-ready CFO understands that the real challenge is structural: how work flows, who owns it, and how decisions are made. Before AI can improve performance, the underlying workflows need to be redesigned for speed, accuracy, and judgment.

Earlier chapters introduced the language of AI along with its economics, governance, and deployment logic. Only after understanding how AI transforms forecasting, reporting, and decision support can the finance leader grasp a deeper truth: sustainable value depends not on tools, but on the organization's ability to work differently. We begin with workflows because they serve as the bridge between technology and people. When these flows are redesigned, the organization itself starts to change.

Mapping these workflows might seem dull compared to pilots and POCs, but this is exactly the discipline that distinguishes experimentation from business value. When finance leaders track how data originates, transforms, and reaches board reports, they identify the true constraints on performance: bottlenecks, duplications, and overreliance on individual reviewers. These frictions aren't due to a lack of talent; they are outcomes of legacy design. Once they're visible, they can be redesigned so automation enhances control rather than diminishes it.

This mapping work also provides a quantitative baseline. If the month-end close currently takes 12 days and involves hundreds of manual touches, improvement can be measured objectively. CFOs aren't persuaded by anecdotes; they respond to evidence. Establishing that "before" state is what allows AI's "after" to be proven in hard numbers.

GenAI raises the stakes. It thrives on language, context, and synthesis, which are exactly the qualities that finance workflows generate in large amounts. But its outputs are only as reliable as its inputs. A model may produce a narrative report in minutes, but if the underlying data or approvals are flawed, the result is worse than useless. So, redesign has to move from a technical task to a leadership priority. It involves assigning people to areas where judgment is needed, embedding controls where risk is greatest, and ensuring every automation step produces evidence suitable for audit.

Global surveys reinforce this sequence. According to Gartner's 2024 CFO Agenda Survey, 72% of finance leaders cite fragmented workflows and inconsistent data ownership as the main barriers to unlocking AI's potential.[2] AI doesn't fail because of weak models; it fails because of outdated workflows. Redesigning them is the groundwork for performance, governance, and trust.

This chapter illustrates how to map the current state of processes, people, technology, and data. It then identifies the barriers that hinder finance, introduces design principles for AI-enabled workflows, and presents a repeatable playbook for transforming core processes across FP&A, accounting, and reporting. The aim is to enhance the human element of the process, focusing their expertise on generating insights rather than just managing administration.

The finance department has always evolved by adopting new tools, moving from ledgers to spreadsheets to ERP systems. AI is simply the next tool. This time, the difference is that the CFO must redesign how work is done, not just decide which technology to use. It marks the next stage in building an AI-ready organization, where understanding drives redesign, and vision becomes operational reality.

Map the Present, Before You Automate the Future

Every CFO who's experienced a system implementation recognizes the pattern: we address what's visible, automate what we understand, and then realize we never truly knew how the work was actually happening in the first place. After the strategy, ROI, and tooling discussions of the earlier chapters, the next step in leadership is gaining visibility. Before redesigning for AI, you must understand what you are currently running—your operational blueprint.

Gartner's 2024 Process Optimization in Finance study revealed that 72% of CFOs identify "poor end-to-end visibility of workflows" as the main reason why automation projects fall short.[3] The conclusion is straightforward: without a clear baseline, AI only speeds up what's already broken.

Process Flows: Seeing Work as It Really Happens

Documenting "how" work gets done is not just administrative busywork; it's the foundational act of leadership discipline. In most finance organizations, official process charts often don't reflect actual practice. Data moves through hidden handoffs, manual uploads, and unspoken dependencies. Mapping these flows, the "who touches what, when, and why" turns stories into facts.

A process map isn't one-size-fits-all. A forecast refresh looks different from an accounts payable process, but both share key elements: inputs, decisions, outputs, and owners. The goal isn't to create a perfect diagram. Instead, illustrate the actual sequence of steps the team follows so bottlenecks and redundancies become clearly visible.

As part of this exercise, CFOs should identify where controls are triggered (e.g., approvals, reconciliations, and evidence logs) because these checkpoints will define how to embed governance as AI automation is implemented.

The CFO's role is to insist on truth over myth. Ask your teams to depict the process as it truly runs, not just as policies describe it. When you see the full swim-lane view, you often discover that less than 30% of cycle time is "touch time," with the rest spent waiting, reworking, or dealing with approval delays. Deloitte Finance Reimagined 2024 reports a 27% average reduction in close time for firms that visualized end-to-end workflows before automating.[4]

Data Lineage: Tracing Numbers to Their Source

Finance lives and dies on data credibility. Every number tells a story. From its origin through its changes to its current state, tracking that history reveals duplicates, conflicting versions, and control weaknesses. When CFOs can see each step—from the source system to entry in a spreadsheet to use by a BI tool—they can also understand where AI should or shouldn't be trusted.

True leadership at this depth reflects accountability, not micromanagement. Data lineage clarifies ownership by showing which parts of the flow belong to finance, IT, or the business units. That clarity is a critical component for future automation governance.

People Dependencies: Finding the Human Bottlenecks

Even the most automated process hides human choke points. A single controller approving every accrual, or a manager editing every board narrative, are habits that create invisible queues with visible delays. Mapping reveals them without blame. It gives CFOs the evidence to redesign roles and approvals by risk tier and by efficiency, rather than tradition.

The key question for leadership is: Does this review preserve value or just safeguard tradition? When the answer is tradition, it's time to redesign the process.

Technology Landscape: Exposing the Manual Bridges

Most finance functions rely on a patchwork of ERPs, spreadsheets, and point solutions. While vendor presentations often show seamless integrations, they're frequently maintained through manual exports and email attachments. Mapping out the existing systems, their data, and how they connect reveals the "swivel-chair" work your team does every day, where data swivels between automated and manual entry.

This visibility enables the CFO to make smarter investments, including funding new APIs and data connectors, instead of adding another reporting layer. Data links and integration are often-overlooked backbones of every successful AI deployment.

Baseline Metrics CFOs Should Track

Many of these signals already exist within your systems. They just haven't been viewed through a process perspective. ERP logs, workflow tools, and ticketing platforms record timestamps, approvals, and rework every day. The AI-ready CFO highlights what's already visible and leverages it to drive change:

- **Cycle-time duration.** Days from trigger to completion (close start to close sign-off).
- **Touch vs. queue time.** Proportion of active work to waiting.
- **Manual touches per transaction.** Journal entries, reconciliations, approvals.
- **Error or exception rate.** Frequency of rework.
- **Control evidence capture.** Percentage of steps automatically logged.

Quantifying these metrics turns intuition into management data. When you know the baseline, you can prove progress.

Blueprinting the current state isn't an operations exercise; it's a visibility exercise in service of leadership. It forces CFOs to see the structure of accountability, the reality of capacity, and the quality of data on which every forecast, filing, and board decision rests.

AI can't fix what you can't see. Map the present, and you give your organization a strong foundation to build on for the future.

The Barrier Scan: Turning Friction into Design Insight

Once finance leaders map their workflows, the picture that emerges is both clarifying and, probably, quite uncomfortable. Visibility highlights inefficiencies. The next step is to identify barriers. This isn't to assign blame, but to understand the patterns that may appear. Barriers are often not isolated mistakes; they're signs of deeper structural issues. Recognizing them clearly is how CFOs develop a blueprint for change.

Human Bottlenecks: When Oversight Becomes Obstruction

Finance prides itself on precision, but many of its processes rely on a narrow chain of approval that trades control for delay. Controllers who sign off every reconciliation, FP&A leads who must validate every forecast adjustment, or CFOs who personally edit each board narrative all contribute to satisfying risk appetites, but they drain momentum.

The leadership insight: bottlenecks are design choices, not personal flaws. They reveal where decision rights are too centralized and where trust in the process has eroded. Redesign begins by redistributing accountability: approvals tiered by risk, reviews sampled by exception, and systems configured to document evidence automatically. Oversight must shift from sequential to simultaneous if finance is to move at digital speed.

Structural Friction: The Hidden Tax of Fragmented Systems

Every CFO recognizes the quiet grind of "swivel-chairing," where analysts export data from ERP systems, modify it in Excel, upload it to BI dashboards, and reconcile again when the numbers don't match. None of this provides insight. It just wastes hours and increases the chance of errors.

This friction is the operating tax of an environment built around tools, not workflows. But the truth is, fragmentation causes delays. Mapping reveals where data jumps, where formats fail, and where teams double-check the same numbers repeatedly. The solution is architectural: streamline data paths, invest in connectors (APIs, event triggers), and establish a single source of truth for every recurring output. AI can't fix broken architecture; it just exposes it more quickly.

Context Loss: When the Story Detaches from the Evidence

Numbers seldom speak for themselves. As data moves between systems or is reformatted for presentation, the links to its original evidence often break. By the time figures appear in variance reports or board decks, the audit trail has become thinner, and teams spend hours reconstructing what happened and why.

Context loss is more than just inefficiency; it's a major credibility risk. GenAI relies on traceable data. Without it, models create narratives that are disconnected from reality. The AI-ready CFO must consider "explanation integrity" as a key control factor. Build workflows where context follows the data, and every variance, driver, and source is automatically tagged and logged. When evidence and narrative stay connected, AI can accelerate understanding rather than amplify confusion.

Cultural Inertia: The Habit of Inefficiency

Over time, the monthly scramble becomes a badge of honor. Teams are praised for "getting it done," not for questioning why it's so hard to accomplish in the first place. Inefficiency becomes invisible because it's been normalized. PwC's 2024 Global CFO Survey found that 68% of finance leaders cite "change fatigue and legacy comfort" as the most significant barrier to digital transformation.[5]

This is the key insight: culture is the most difficult part of redesigning a workflow. Habits of heroics and crisis management weaken the discipline needed for automation. The CFO's role is to set a new rhythm that values process health over personal endurance. Shift success metrics toward predictability and insight, not rescue efforts and face time. Cultural inertia shifts when leaders reward transparency rather than improvisation.

Tool Gaps: When Technology Outpaces Design

It's easy to blame tools for slow cycles, but most technology issues originate from design misalignment. Legacy ERPs coexist with modern point solutions; integrations exist in theory but aren't always realized in practice. BCG's Finance Transformation Playbook (2024) states that 60% of automation underperformance results from "partial integration and unowned workflows."[6] The core problem isn't the software; it's ownership. Who's responsible for the design?

Leadership should understand that governance is weak when systems depend on people to manually fill gaps. CFOs should see integration not just as an IT issue but as a control design issue. Each data transfer is a risk for failure, and every successful transfer needs to be automated, with proof recorded by design.

Cultural and Control Overlap: When Compliance Adds Drag

Finance's risk culture can swing too far. It's a well-intentioned instinct: add more reviews, more sign-offs, more eyes. But those layers of manual checking often create the illusion of safety rather than the reality of it. Automated logs already capture much of what those steps aim to confirm.

Good leadership knows the difference. Controls should serve the mission, not smother it. Governance works best when it's built into the flow of work, not stacked awkwardly on top.

The core point starts here: risk management has to evolve with how work actually gets done.

> Workflow barriers are not issues to be fixed in and of themselves. They are signals about how the system was originally designed. Each one points to a decision about trust, ownership, or risk that was made in a different era. Recognizing those decisions clearly is the first step toward changing them for AI.[7]
>
> —*Michael Bayer, Wasabi*

The barrier scan provides honest feedback. It replaces frustration with data, turning friction into valuable design insights. Each bottleneck reveals a trust gap. Each manual handoff shows a lack of proper integration. Every layer of rework uncovers doubts about ownership. The CFO's role is to interpret these signals and guide a redesign plan, one that shifts exhaustive motion to smooth flow and constant vigilance to clear visibility.

Redesign Principles: Don't Automate the Past

Each barrier identified earlier offers insight into how the finance function's workflows must be rebuilt. Bottlenecks point out areas where trust affects decision-making. Fragmented systems expose design flaws. Cultural inertia reveals where leadership focus has shifted. An AI-ready CFO sees these signals as a blueprint for redesign. The goal is not just to automate faster but to create processes that flow more smoothly, manage risks more intelligently, and adapt as conditions change.

Leaders who only focus on speeding up existing processes miss Henry Ford's famous lesson. He is credited to have said that if he had asked his customers what they wanted, they would have said "faster horses," not automobiles.[8] The same mindset persists in finance: too often, we try to automate outdated workflows instead of creating new ones. True progress involves rethinking the design itself, not just making the inefficient faster.

Principle 1: Stream Once and Reuse Everywhere

Finance teams repeatedly rebuild the same datasets. Reports, variance analyses, and forecasts often pull the same information in different formats. Each extraction raises the risk of errors and wastes hours that could be better spent on analysis.

The goal of the AI-ready CFO should be to extract data from a single, structured "system of record" that automatically updates and supplies every downstream process. When a close package, variance report, and forecast all originate from the same data stream, reconciliation is eliminated, and generating insights becomes quicker. McKinsey's 2024 Finance Redesign Report found that firms with unified data pipelines reduce reconciliation efforts by over 40%.[9]

Principle 2: Turn Unstructured Inputs into Structured Information

Much of finance still runs on free-text emails, ad-hoc explanations, and inconsistent templates. Unstructured information resists automation and weakens auditability.

Standardized templates, controlled input forms, and tagged commentary fields make data understandable for both people and machines. This setup enables AI to generate variance narratives, summarize trends, and connect explanations directly to evidence. The CFO's role is to establish these standards so the system can interpret and reuse every input without losing context.

Principle 3: Automate the Flow, Not Just the Task

Many automation efforts stop at the task level. They speed up one step but ignore what happens before or after. A faster invoice scan is progress, but not transformation, if approvals still crawl through email or postings wait on manual entry. The real gains come from flow. Each completed action should trigger the next, with information moving cleanly through the system.

Gartner's 2024 CFO Design Framework backs this up: companies that automate the flow, not just the task, nearly double their cycle-time improvements. Automation works best when handoffs move as fast as the work itself.[10]

Principle 4: Right-Size Human Oversight

Legacy processes tend to treat every transaction as equally risky. The result is predictable: low-value items get bogged down in manual reviews, slowing the system and pulling skilled staff away from decisions that actually require judgment. A better design distinguishes oversight by risk tier. Low-risk transactions can be approved automatically and sampled after the fact. Medium-risk items might go through dual review. High-risk or judgment-heavy cases always reach a human.

The CFO defines these thresholds and makes sure the evidence is captured along the way. Oversight stays strong, but attention shifts to where it matters most.

Principle 5: Establish Guardrails for GenAI

Generative models can produce convincing but incorrect or unverified results. They add value only when based on controlled data and used within clear boundaries.

CFOs must ensure that every AI output can be traced to its source data, that prompts originate from approved libraries, and that all activity is logged. Governance, data privacy, and model explainability belong within the workflow, not outside it. Guardrails make AI safe, repeatable, and auditable qualities that finance cannot compromise.

Applying these principles also positions finance to take advantage of GenAI's strengths while mitigating its weaknesses. AI is best at language generation, synthesis of structured data, and interaction through natural language. It is weaker at arithmetic precision, deterministic calculations, and policy enforcement. By structuring inputs, grounding outputs, and keeping humans in the loop, redesigned workflows direct AI toward the tasks it performs well while protecting the function from its limitations

Principle 6: Measure, Learn, and Adjust

Workflows are dynamic. After redesigning, they require ongoing monitoring and adjustment. Incorporating feedback loops helps teams track how automation performs over time and identify where exceptions tend to occur. Metrics like cycle time, error rate, and exception recurrence support continuous refinement. The AI-ready CFO views redesign as a continuous capability, not just a one-time project.

Redesigned Workflow Examples

The following examples show how redesigned workflows perform in real finance operations. Each one walks through a specific scenario, from the trigger that starts the process to the output the team acts on.

Variance Commentary

In the traditional process, analysts typically pull actuals into spreadsheets, calculate variances, and collect explanations via email. A redesigned version might begin with a single structured data pull, standardized driver tags, and AI-generated first-draft narratives linked to evidence. Analysts review and edit, and the system logs every change automatically. The cycle compresses from weeks to days, with full traceability.

Accounts Payable

Many AP departments used to receive invoices in various formats and manually entered them into the ERP. A new process can implement digital intake, OCR, and AI-based extraction to classify data and automatically match it to purchase orders. Low-value invoices within limits are posted immediately; exceptions are routed to reviewers with confidence scores attached. This enhances control and doubles throughput. AP analysts can now focus on review and reporting, rather than data entry.

These brief examples only show the goal, not the many steps needed to get there. Achieving this level of integration requires disciplined sequencing, data readiness, and collaboration with technology teams. The CFO's role is to guide this process and make sure AI automation advances only as far as data quality, governance, and controls allow. This idea has been emphasized repeatedly throughout the book. Redesign is not an immediate change; it's a managed evolution toward these target workflows.

These principles carry important leadership implications. Redesign is as much about behavior and investment choices as it is about process.

- **Challenge established habits.** Teams may resist standardizing inputs or shifting approvals, insisting that long-standing controls should remain untouched. The AI-ready CFO must show that controls are not being removed but rebuilt to be both stronger and more efficient.
- **Invest in the connective tissue.** Seamless automation depends on APIs, data pipelines, and integration layers that rarely attract attention but determine whether AI can scale. These less-visible investments often produce the greatest long-term returns.
- **Reframe the people story.** Redesign is not about reducing headcount. It is about redirecting talent toward analysis, scenario testing, and judgment—the work that defines finance as a strategic partner.

A workflow redesign helps the AI-ready CFO move from insight to action. Each principle turns a point of friction into a rule that builds flow, trust, and speed. When workflows run on structured data, measured risk, and clear evidence, AI becomes a natural part of how finance operates. These principles form the foundation for using GenAI safely and effectively. The next section explores how to put them into practice.

The Flow-to-Factory Playbook: Turning Redesign into a Pattern of Transformation

The principles help define what good workflow design looks like. A playbook will turn those ideas into a repeatable pattern. Everything that follows draws directly from the methods, guardrails, and measurement concepts introduced earlier. It arranges them into an easy-to-apply sequence. It is a blueprint you can reuse each time a workflow is ready for redesign.

After successfully rearchitecting a single process, the next challenge is scaling. Progress stalls if each improvement is seen as a one-time project. A repeatable method turns each redesign into a pattern that others can follow. The result is a finance function that can continually improve, one lane at a time.

The factory metaphor is intentional. A well-managed factory doesn't improvise; it applies consistent standards, quality checks, and feedback loops to every unit it produces. The same discipline can guide workflow redesign. Each process follows the same set of steps, evaluated against the same outcomes, so that improvements become predictable and transferable.

Six-Step Playbook

1. **Choose a single lane.** Start with a narrow focus. Select a workflow that matters but has limited regulatory or reputational risk (e.g., variance commentary, a forecast update, or accounts payable intake). Focusing on one area creates visible progress and builds internal support before addressing high-stakes processes. Evidence creates momentum; statements only describe it.
2. **Baseline the current state.** Every improvement starts with measurement. Capture the current process: where time is spent, where errors occur, where people intervene. Once you have that baseline, proof replaces opinion, and credibility builds naturally.
3. **Carve the backbone.** Set up data connections and integrations that remove manual handoffs. These could include APIs, event triggers, or shared data models. This phase often involves collaborating with IT or data teams and affects the stability of the redesign. Frequently, it is the hidden infrastructure or connective tissue that produces the visible results.[11]

4. **Insert AI use where it fits best.** Once the backbone is stable, integrate AI-led automation and GenAI where they enhance speed or intelligence. Examples often include generative models for drafting narratives, anomaly detection in reconciliations, or invoice classification. AI is never the initial step; it only speeds up the existing structure. AI should strengthen the design, not replace missing elements.
5. **Embed controls by risk.** Redesign should enhance, not weaken, controls. Set approval processes based on materiality: low-value items are auto-approved and sampled later; mid-range transactions go to dual review; high-risk items always require human judgment. Automatically collect evidence at each step. Controls stem from good design, not delays.
6. **Measure and iterate.** Monitor performance starting from the first cycle. Compare cycle time, manual touches, and exceptions to the baseline. Share results openly. Success spreads when people see it. Adjust thresholds or automation triggers as data collects. Repetition turns progress into culture, a pattern seen in transformation programs that maintain measurable gains over time.[12]

Composite Example: Forecast Refresh

The forecast refresh illustrates what's now achievable in leading finance organizations, even if every implementation takes its own unique path. Consider a hypothetical scenario that incorporates the most advanced practices emerging across the market.

At a mid-sized technology company, the CFO begins by targeting forecast refreshes. Analysts spend roughly two weeks each quarter updating models, slowed by manual data pulls and reconciliation issues. When the team maps the process, they find that more than half the time goes to chasing inputs from business partners and reformatting spreadsheets.

Following the playbook, the CFO selects forecast refresh as the first priority. A single data pull from the ERP and CRM replaces multiple requests, and baseline calculations are automated. GenAI drafts narrative explanations of forecast changes by comparing actuals to prior projections and flagging significant deviations. Thresholds are set so that minor changes flow through automatically, while material shifts require analyst review.

Results are tracked over three cycles. Forecast refresh time drops from two weeks to four days, and analyst hours spent on data prep fall by 70%. Encouraged by the outcome, the CFO applies the same playbook to monthly variance reporting and sees similar gains.

While this is a hypothetical case, similar advances are underway today in many large enterprises. The story serves to illustrate what becomes achievable when structure, controls, and disciplined iteration come together.

The idea behind the playbook is to assist in transforming the redesign of your workflows from a series of isolated projects into a repeatable program. Each completed workflow becomes a template for the next. Over time, finance can develop an internal factory for improvement with consistent methods, shared data standards, and measurable outcomes. This consistency needs to be protected, ensuring that every new design follows a similar rhythm of mapping, measurement, and iteration. When that rhythm is established, the organization is ready to let AI operate safely within it.

GenAI in the Workflow: Where It Helps and Where It Doesn't

AI has positioned finance at the crossroads of data, risk, and strategy. CFOs now authorize billions in investments for data centers, AI chips, and related technology services. The technology itself is advancing fast, yet its value still depends on context. In some areas, GenAI is already reshaping how work gets done. In others, it remains untested, unreliable, or risky. Seeing both realities clearly is what allows finance leaders to harness its potential while setting the boundaries that keep it safe.

Where It Helps

GenAI succeeds when the problem is language-heavy, pattern-based, and grounded in reliable data. Finance has many of these domains.

- **Narrative generation and synthesis.** Models can summarize key drivers, prepare variance commentaries, or draft the first version of a management discussion. When the inputs come from structured data and standardized tags, AI accelerates what analysts already do. Gartner's

2025 Finance AI Adoption Study reports that 71% of finance leaders now use or plan to use generative tools for narrative automation within the next 18 months.[13]

- **As an interface to corporate data systems.** Instead of waiting for analysts to pull a report, executives can query financial data directly: "Show me the change in gross margin over the last three quarters and explain the drivers." A properly integrated system can return not just the numbers but also a draft explanation with links to evidence. GenAI's natural-language layer can reduce friction between business leaders and finance.
- **Classification and matching.** Invoice categorization, account mapping, and expense review lend themselves to pattern recognition. Models can propose classifications or surface anomalies that human reviewers confirm. Deloitte's 2025 Finance Automation Outlook found that early adopters reduced manual review time in AP and AR by 30% while maintaining control accuracy.[14]
- **Document summarization.** Parsing contracts, policies, or audit notes and highlighting exceptions is now a proven use case. It saves staff hours on routine reading while improving consistency.
- **Forecast insight generation.** When trained on structured scenario data, GenAI can highlight drivers or trend narratives for review. The Wharton Budget Model (2025) projects that finance teams combining structured data with generative insight could see productivity gains of 18–22% over the next three years.[15]

In each of these examples, AI enhances speed and communication but doesn't replace analysis. The key to success is design. The data must be structured, the model grounded, and the output reviewed by accountable humans.

Where It Doesn't

GenAI still struggles where precision, regulation, or judgment must dominate.

- **Where deterministic outputs are required.** Journal entries, consolidations, and statutory calculations require absolute precision that stochastic models cannot guarantee. These remain the domain of rule-based automation and human oversight.

- **Policy and materiality judgments.** Determining disclosure thresholds or accounting treatment involves contextual reasoning, not pattern recognition. These tasks rely on human interpretation informed by AI-generated analysis, not on decisions made by AI.
- **Sparse or confidential data.** When information cannot be safely shared or lacks historical volume, AI predictions degrade quickly. Keeping sensitive data behind secure boundaries remains mandatory.
- **Ambiguous or multi-source processes.** When inputs vary across business units or formats, AI can often amplify inconsistencies rather than resolving them. Clean integration and standardization must precede automation.

MIT Sloan Management Review (2024) found that organizations using generative models in unstructured or low-data contexts experienced error rates five times higher than those operating in standardized environments.[16] Protiviti's CFO Survey (2025) echoed this, noting that most failures stemmed from "inconsistent input design and unclear ownership of verification."[17]

Why Humans Must Stay in the Loop

GenAI expands capability; it doesn't replace judgment. Human review ensures context, ethics, and credibility. No model can guarantee these qualities. The most advanced organizations are building human-in-the-loop systems where AI drafts, people decide, and evidence is logged automatically.

Yale Budget Lab's 2025 research on AI and labor allocation found that the biggest productivity increases happen when human review time shifts from manual data processing to analytical validation.[18] Analysts spend less time searching for data and more time verifying its meaning. Leadership needs to create workflows that maintain this balance: automation for efficiency, humans for understanding.

A Design Rule for Using GenAI

GenAI thrives in well-structured environments. And it fails where ambiguity lives. The heuristic is simple: design first, automate second, verify always. From there, a clean data foundation, clear role boundaries, and embedded controls turn AI from a novelty into infrastructure.

AI isn't a plug-in; it's a participant in the workflow you design. Deloitte's 2024 State of Generative AI in Finance found that teams embedding AI into redesigned workflows, not layering it onto legacy ones, achieved 25% faster close cycles and higher audit confidence.[19]

Example: Finance Narrative Generation. The boundary between helpful and risky use of GenAI keeps moving, but it hasn't vanished. Vendors are rolling out finance-specific models that handle numbers more cleanly and understand domain language. They make fewer arithmetic errors and stay closer to the facts. Even so, the CFO's job hasn't changed. The integrity of reporting still comes first. The CFO's job is to decide where AI adds clarity and where human judgment still leads.

One use case stands out. In redesigned workflows, AI can now draft narrative updates for reports by pulling structured data from the ERP, blending it with key drivers from the warehouse, and producing first-pass commentary for each cost center. Analysts follow by reviewing, editing, and approving the drafts before they're added to the final report. The payoff is clear: less manual writing, faster cycles, and full audit traceability.

In this setup, the line is easy to see. The model translates what the numbers mean. The math still happens in the systems built for it. Deterministic systems still handle computation and control totals. That separation is what keeps the process responsible. AI works best as a drafting partner and interpreter, not as the accountant itself.

GenAI is most valuable when it functions within a structured environment and under supervision. It converts data into language, speeds up review processes, and enhances capacity, but only when the foundational work of redesign, measurement, and control is already in place. Its purpose in finance is not to replace human thinking but to enable humans to think faster and with better evidence. As models advance and governance improves, AI will increasingly serve as a dependable partner in well-designed workflows of the AI-ready organization.

Three Patterned Use Cases

Redesign principles and the flow-to-factory playbook come alive when applied to real situations where AI can add value. It is one thing to describe principles in the abstract and quite another to see them reshape familiar workflows. To illustrate, let's step into three different corners of finance: FP&A, accounting, and reporting. Each example shows a distinct pattern where AI fits in the redesign and how humans remain central. These examples are composite sketches of practices emerging across leading organizations.

Analytical: Variance Commentary. Budget vs. actual reporting cycles have always strained the finance function. Analysts chase data across teams and systems, consolidate spreadsheets, and draft variance explanations line by line but the narratives vary widely in style and depth. In redesigned workflows, structured deltas and driver tags feed a generative model that produces first-pass commentary and scenario summaries. Analysts review, edit, and approve; the system records every change and links each statement to its source data.

The real value shows up in how work is done. Reports become consistent, commentary aligns across divisions, and insights arrive faster. Every business unit now describes results in the same analytical frame, and finance leadership can compare commentary across divisions without translation. Time saved becomes time reallocated for sensitivity testing, assumption review, and forward analysis. AI accelerates the thinking process, giving analysts more bandwidth for judgment.

Transactional: Accounts Payable Exception Handling. Accounts payable automation has matured, but exceptions still consume human effort. Missing purchase orders, duplicate invoices, and policy exceptions create manual queues that delay month-end close. In advanced environments, AI classifies invoices, detects anomalies, and ranks exceptions by confidence score. Routine items process automatically; outliers move to reviewers with context attached.

The payoff is precision and control. Audit logs show exactly who touched what, and exception volumes decline as models learn from prior resolutions. Teams no longer chase the same issues repeatedly and they have time to focus on genuine risk issues or supplier relationships. AI becomes part of the controls infrastructure, raising issues early and documenting every decision for audit support. The finance function gains reliability, not just throughput.

Communication: Management Reporting and Disclosure Preparation. Financial reporting is where finance translates numbers into a cohesive story for executives, investors, and regulators. The challenge has never been generating content, one glance at an annual report confirms that. The issue is time and alignment. The days before a board meeting often feel like a race against the clock: reconciling numbers, formatting slides, and drafting narratives at the last minute. Redesign changes that rhythm completely. Data is ingested continuously from financial and operational systems, fed into standardized templates, and combined with AI-generated drafts of commentary. Reviewers add context, adjust tone, and sign off.

Instead of a frantic sprint, the board book becomes the product of a controlled, auditable process that runs in the background. Executives receive information sooner, and finance leaders arrive at the meeting focused on strategy rather than survival.

Each example starts with a process that's slow and manual. Each is redesigned with structured data, AI drafts, risk-based controls, and human oversight. The result is faster cycles, stronger evidence, and more meaningful work for finance professionals. This new efficiency is great, but more importantly, credibility is enhanced. Variance commentary becomes consistent and evidence-backed. Invoices are processed without delay and with clear audit trails. Board reporting shifts from an exercise in formatting to a source of trusted insight.

These examples show where AI creates lasting value, within the core workflows that run finance every day. Start with one. Apply the playbook. Measure what changes. Then carry the pattern forward. Over time, the organization shifts from manual cycles to a continuous, AI-enabled flow of information, with judgment and accountability still anchored in people.

Humans in the AI-Ready Workflow: Your Finance Team Should Not Be Replaced

While AI may change how finance operates, it doesn't replace the reason finance exists. The promise of automation has never been to make people obsolete; it's been to make their judgment more valuable.

In the rush to implement generative models, some organizations have mistaken efficiency for reducing headcount. This seems logical on paper: fewer employees plus faster systems equals lower costs. However, the data and the lived experiences of finance leaders tell a different story. Automation without human interpretation becomes fragile. Models may compute perfectly, but they cannot recognize when they are wrong or explain why results matter. The CFO's job is to keep financial judgment sound, even as the pace increases.

Evidence for Human Value

Research from consulting and academic institutions now confirms that finance functions that emphasize human–AI collaboration outperform those relying solely on automation. McKinsey's 2025 State of AI in Finance survey found that 72% of CFOs who implemented AI tools reported increased demand for higher-level analytical and strategic skills, while only 9% cut staff. These organizations achieved measurable productivity improvements (e.g., about 20% faster cycle times) without sacrificing oversight or decision quality.[20]

Deloitte's 2025 Finance 2025 update succinctly describes this shift: "Automation is redefining work, but the audit trail still ends with a person. Accountability cannot be automated."[21] Even in highly automated environments, audit and control still depend on human verification. As AI becomes more integrated into financial workflows, the value of people who understand context, ethics, and consequences increases.

Research from BCG's 2025 AI–Human Collaboration Playbook shows the pattern clearly. When AI handles the first draft and humans refine it, insight cycles shorten by roughly a third, and management trust rises.[22] Machines generate information, and humans turn it into decisions. The difference is measurable and repeatable.

From a macroeconomic view, Yale's Budget Lab (2025) found that productivity gains from AI were highest when firms "redeployed, not reduced" their workforce. Institutional knowledge and collaboration amplified output. Replacing experienced staff erased tacit knowledge, the kind of contextual intelligence no model can infer.[23] Wharton's Budget Model (2025) reached a similar conclusion. Organizations that retrained finance professionals to work alongside AI achieved nearly twice the ROI of those that focused on automation and reduction.[24] The gains came not from faster processing but from stronger scenario design, interpretation, and communication.

The pattern is consistent across studies. AI extends what teams can know, but people remain the source of insight. The strongest finance functions are those where human expertise and machine intelligence evolve together.

The Three Domains of Human Advantage

If automation is the engine, people remain the steering system. Finance will continue to depend on human intelligence across three dimensions: analytical judgment, control stewardship, and communication.

Analytical Judgment. AI can identify anomalies or correlations, but it can't assess their significance in the full business context. Humans bring intent, experience, and storytelling to numbers. Analysts and finance leaders interpret the reasons behind a variance or forecast change. They understand when a deviation indicates opportunity rather than risk, or when a pattern shows timing rather than performance. Judgment isn't a data function. It's a consequence function. Without human interpretation, finance merely reflects the past instead of guiding the future.

> I'm not here just to provide data—I'm here to help people make better decisions.[25]
>
> —*Marcos Bento, Wasabi*

Control Stewardship. AI enhances detection and accuracy, but humans are still accountable for control. Accountability demands ownership, which in turn requires people. Even as systems automatically produce audit evidence, finance professionals must define acceptable risk, validate exceptions, and decide when to override automation. Control stewardship is based on discernment and judgment, knowing when rules need interpretation. Deloitte's Finance 2025 report states that "the ultimate control remains human review."[26] The more advanced the technology, the more vital that human judgment becomes.

Communication and Storytelling. GenAI can write, but it doesn't understand real-world context. It can assemble sentences, but it can't prioritize which story the board should hear first. Finance's role is to derive meaning from numbers, not just generate them. Humans provide tone, emphasis, and context, the elements that turn data into insight and guidance. Wharton's 2025 study found that finance teams using generative tools to support human-written narratives, rather than replace them, produced more consistent messaging and gained higher confidence scores from investors.[27] Machines may draft, but people decide what message the draft should convey.

These three domains aren't stale relics of the pre-AI era. They are the areas where human intelligence amplifies machine efficiency. Each supports the other: judgment shapes analysis, stewardship maintains control, and communication transforms insight into impact. Together, they ground finance in its enduring human purpose and ensure that intelligence, whether artificial or organic, serves judgment, not the other way around.

Upskilling and Redeployment

CFOs who view AI as a way to enhance the workforce rather than cut it are already leading the way. Reassigning talent to roles that require analytical, control, and communication skills maintains a competitive edge and boosts organizational resilience. McKinsey's 2025 survey predicts that 70% of finance organizations will need to retrain more than half their staff within three years.[28] The focus is on building smarter systems by investing in people's skills. Upskilling current professionals strengthens institutional knowledge and helps ensure that the finance function stays a source of human judgment in a more automated world. We'll get into more detail on this topic in the next chapter (see Table 10.1).

Automation now monitors transactions, detects anomalies, and builds evidence trails in real time. Governance, however, still begins and ends with people. Every control framework reflects human judgment about which risks matter most, what thresholds to set, and when an exception deserves attention.

As AI becomes part of financial workflows, the human role grows even more central. Machines bring consistency. People ensure integrity.

Table 10.1 The Human Advantage in the AI-Ready Finance Function

Human skill domain	Purpose in the AI era	Relevant finance roles	Value to the organization
Analytical judgment	Interpreting AI outputs, weighing business context, distinguishing noise from signal	• FP&A analyst/ finance business partner • Scenario modeling lead • Forecast integrator	Ensures that insight equals understanding. Converts data into direction and identifies the "why" behind financial performance
Control stewardship	Applying discernment to risk and compliance decisions that automation alone cannot resolve	• Control steward/SOX coordinator • Evidence architect/audit liaison • Exception analyst	Maintains legitimacy and trust in automated workflows. Defines thresholds for human review and validates system integrity
Communication and storytelling	Translating analysis into narrative for executives, boards, and investors; ensuring coherence across reports	• Narrative editor/ management reporting lead • Investor relations analyst • Prompt librarian/ knowledge curator	Aligns financial story with data reality. Strengthens decision quality and organizational alignment through clear, consistent communication

The audit trail lives in code, and accountability lives with those who interpret it.

The next stage of audit and governance is about equipping auditors, controllers, and finance leaders to interpret technology's output with clarity and purpose.

Controls and Governance: Making Auditors Comfortable

Speed without control isn't progress. Finance has a fiduciary duty that goes beyond just providing timely figures. The CFO must produce numbers that can withstand scrutiny from auditors, regulators, and boards.

AI offers new opportunities for efficiency and accuracy, but it also raises questions about transparency and accountability. Governance cannot be an afterthought. Governance design is the discipline that ensures innovation strengthens, rather than erodes, trust.

Automation might execute a control, but only people can define one. Every threshold, approval, and rule reflects human judgment about what constitutes acceptable risk. AI magnifies the importance of that judgment because AI outputs are only as sound as the logic humans embed within them. The PCAOB's 2025 guidance makes human control over AI explicit: AI can expand evidence, but the assessment of sufficiency remains a human responsibility.[29] The AI-ready CFO must treat governance as the human conscience of automation.

Visibility and Traceability. AI governance begins with knowing where it operates. Finance leaders need a clear, living inventory of every model, automation, and workflow that involves financial data. The list should include the purpose, data sources, owners, and change history. This "model register" helps prevent shadow AI (untracked and unauthorized tools that can undermine control) and provides auditors with a single reference point for how automation affects financial reporting.

Transparency continues through evidence bundling. Each automated output should include its own documentation: data inputs, prompts or configurations, model version, and reviewer approval. Both COSO and Deloitte's 2025 AI control frameworks emphasize the principle of automatically capturing evidence at the moment of creation.[30] When auditors ask, "How was this result produced?" the answer should be visible in the log, not reconstructed by memory. The most dependable audit trails are those created as work is performed.

Explainability completes the visibility chain. Finance can't rely on black-box narratives that offer conclusions without proof. Any AI-influenced or derived explanation, such as "higher headcount costs drove the variance," must link directly to supporting data like payroll files or staffing records. This not only satisfies regulatory expectations but also builds internal confidence. The C-suite trusts insights they can verify.

Control Integrity. Traditional controls—such as segregation of duties, access restrictions, and change management—still form the foundation of governance. AI just changes the surface area of exposure. Systems must preserve role-based access, ensuring analysts cannot alter their own reviews and that controllers maintain authority over final sign-offs. Experimental models should be used in sandbox environments separate from production data to prevent contamination of reporting systems.

Governance over controls is as much cultural as it is technical. The urge to bypass controls "just this once," for speed, must be countered through effective workflow design. Automation should support discipline, not just convenience. A well-designed workflow minimizes the temptation to bypass controls out of fear of delay because compliance should be embedded directly into the process.

Continuous Review. Automation doesn't eliminate the need for monitoring, but it does modernize it. Instead of manually sampling transactions, finance teams can test the automation process itself. If invoices below a certain threshold are auto-approved, a rotating percentage should be reviewed regularly to ensure accuracy. If GenAI drafts variance commentary, reviewers should periodically compare those drafts to raw data to verify reliability. This feedback loop keeps the system honest and stops small errors from escalating into systemic issues.

Periodic validation also demonstrates good stewardship. Deloitte's 2025 Governance Benchmark found that organizations embedding these "audits of the automation" reduced remediation efforts by 40% and cut audit cycle time nearly in half.[31] Continuous review builds resilience and keeps governance grounded in evidence.

Governance Beyond the Firewall. Governance also extends beyond internal systems. Many AI capabilities now operate through external platforms or vendors, which auditors treat as service organizations. Reviewing each provider's SOC 2 Type II or equivalent attestation has become a standard expectation under both COSO and PCAOB 2025 guidance.[32] The CFO's responsibility is to confirm that these reports are current, understood, and mapped to internal controls. Outsourcing automation does not outsource accountability. The Big Four firms now encourage clients to maintain a central repository of SOC 2 attestations for all critical AI and automation vendors and to assign ownership for ongoing review to the controller or internal audit. This simple practice gives auditors confidence that external dependencies are governed with the same rigor as internal processes.

Recommended Best Practice: Evidence Packaging from the Start

Because AI workflows produce data continuously, governance has to be part of the design from the start. One effective approach is to treat every automated decision as an evidence package, a complete record that captures source documents, extracted fields, confidence scores, and reviewer actions.

The structure may seem heavy at first, but it pays off quickly. When questions arise, the record is already there. Audit teams can test directly from the system of record, and finance avoids the scramble to rebuild missing support. Embedding evidence creation into each process turns governance into a source of speed and confidence instead of delay.

Design for Assurance

A common failure in automation programs is treating controls as something to add after achieving efficiency gains. The better approach is to ask governance questions during the design phase.

- What evidence will this process generate?
- Who owns approval at each stage?
- How will we demonstrate explainability?
- Where will logs reside, and how will they be secured?

Asking these questions early helps AI shift from a compliance risk to a compliance asset. When governance and automation are developed together, control quality improves even as cycle times decrease.

AI may make finance faster, but only governance makes it credible. Controls remain the language of trust between the function and its stakeholders. The finance organization that embeds visibility, traceability, third-party assurance, and review into every intelligent workflow not only satisfies the auditors; it improves its own resilience. The auditor's question has not changed: Who is accountable? AI will alter how the evidence is created, not who signs the responsibility line. Today's goal with AI should no longer be to balance speed against control, but to design systems in which the two advance together.

Proving Value: The Dashboard That Shows It Worked

Every corporate transformation program ultimately comes down to proof—did it work? Finance has a deep discipline in measurement, but AI adoption introduces a new test—do the numbers show progress that others can trust? The CFO must prove that automation, redesign, and intelligence have made finance faster, sharper, and safer, all without compromising credibility.

The best way to demonstrate this is with a dashboard (see Table 10.2) that links every claim of improvement to verifiable evidence, providing a structured view of speed, accuracy, control, and human contribution, grounded in the baselines set at the start.

This dashboard is more than a project report. It serves as finance's scorecard for enterprise AI maturity. When the CFO shares it, they demonstrate the success of finance's own redesign and set the example for how progress should be measured across the organization.

Table 10.2 Success Dashboard: The Dimensions of AI Value

Dimension	Representative metrics	Source/ evidence	Purpose and interpretation
Speed and efficiency	• Close cycle time • Forecast refresh duration • Manual touches per transaction	ERP and FP&A system logs	Demonstrates operational improvement and capacity creation. Shorter cycles confirm that automation translates into usable time, not just faster clicks
Accuracy and insight quality	• Forecast variance vs. actuals • Data-quality score • AI model precision rate	FP&A platforms and data-validation reports	Shows that redesign enhances decision confidence. Lower forecast variance proves AI improves foresight, not just output speed

(*Continued*)

Table 10.2 (Continued)

Dimension	Representative metrics	Source/ evidence	Purpose and interpretation
Control and governance	• % transactions with evidence packages • # audit exceptions • % AI vendors with current SOC 2 Type II attestations	Audit logs, compliance dashboards	Confirms that control integrity scales with automation. Links vendor governance to internal assurance—proof that oversight extends beyond the firewall
Human contribution	• Analyst hours redeployed • Training hours per employee • Scenarios analyzed per quarter	HR analytics and planning records	Validates that automation amplifies, not replaces, people. Increased analytical output shows talent moving from manual to strategic work

Metrics should use the baselines captured during initial workflow mapping and be updated quarterly. Executive dashboards display summary trends; operational teams monitor detailed breakdowns. The goal is not to achieve a single data point, but to tell a story of continuous improvement.

How to Read the Dashboard. When these metrics are reviewed together, they tell a complete story:

- **Speed** proves operational impact.
- **Accuracy** proves intelligence.
- **Control** proves trust.
- **Human contribution** proves sustainability.

The boards should see the dashboard as evidence that AI provides enterprise value while preserving assurance. Auditors need to view it as a control tool. Your team needs it to recognize that their work now generates higher-level insights. Each audience interprets the same data through its own perspective, but all read the same report.

Designing the Dashboard: The AI-Ready CFO's Six-Step Runbook

Building the AI dashboard is an operating discipline. Follow these six steps to turn metrics into a living system that proves value, sustains credibility, and scales across the enterprise (see Table 10.3).

Table 10.3 CFO Six-Step Runbook

Step	Action	Leadership focus	Typical owner
1. Confirm baselines	Lock the pre-automation values for each key metric—close days, forecast variance, exception rate, and analyst hours	Establishes the "before" picture against which every gain is measured	CFO sponsor/ FP&A lead
2. Assign owners	Designate a single accountable owner for each metric. Link ownership to existing process leadership roles	Creates clarity and accountability. A metric without an owner is a number without meaning	Controller, FP&A director, HR analytics lead
3. Wire data feeds	Connect each metric to an automated data source (ERP, FP&A system, audit log, HRIS). Avoid spreadsheets or manual entry	Ensures data integrity and reduces bias in reporting	Data engineering/ finance systems
4. Set cadence	Define how often metrics update and who reviews them. Operational dashboards monthly; executive versions quarterly	Keeps results visible and avoids "after-the-fact" analysis	CFO staff/ FP&A
5. Define thresholds and actions	Establish R-Y-G bands and escalation paths. When a metric turns red, document who investigates and what remedial step follows	Converts the dashboard from observation to management	Process owners/ internal audit

(*Continued*)

Table 10.3 (Continued)

Step	Action	Leadership focus	Typical owner
6. Publish and review	Produce two synchronized views: one-page executive summary for the board, detailed dashboard for the finance team. Review trends, not just points	Reinforces that measurement is leadership, not oversight	CFO/finance leadership team

Tip: Keep the initial dashboard simple, focus on eight to ten metrics across speed, accuracy, control, and human contribution. Expand only after three stable reporting cycles.

From Finance Proof to Enterprise Practice. Measurement is a form of leadership. When finance defines, tracks, and publishes metrics for AI success, it sets the tone for how the rest of the enterprise should evaluate it. The AI-ready CFO must become the organization's credibility anchor, the executive who insists that progress be both visible and verifiable.

Across industries, surveys conducted in 2025 by McKinsey, Gartner, and Wharton all emphasize the same point: companies that evaluate AI adoption with balanced dashboards combining process, control, and human metrics achieve higher returns and sustain adoption longer than those that focus solely on cost savings.[33] Measurement discipline serves as a cultural bridge between the pilot phase and reaching enterprise scale.

The dashboard gives finance a visible way to lead. It tracks enterprise AI maturity with the same discipline used for financial performance. When the CFO shares it, they demonstrate the results of finance's own redesign and set a standard for how progress should be measured across the organization.

Notes

1. Bodla, interview, December 16, 2025.
2. Gartner, Inc., *CFO Agenda 2024: Top Priorities for Finance Leaders*. Research Report (Stamford, CT: Gartner, Inc., 2024).
3. Gartner, Inc., *Process Optimization in Finance: Gaining End-to-End Visibility for Automation Success*. Research Report (Stamford, CT: Gartner, Inc., 2024).
4. Deloitte Development LLC, *Finance Reimagined 2024: The State of the Modern Close*. Research Report (New York, NY: Deloitte, 2024).

5. PwC, *2024 Global CFO Survey: Navigating the Complexity of Digital Transformation*. Research Report (London: PricewaterhouseCoopers, 2024).
6. Boston Consulting Group, *Finance Transformation Playbook: From Experimentation to Business Value*. Research Report (Boston, MA: Boston Consulting Group, 2024).
7. Bayer and Bento, interview, December 17, 2025.
8. Patrick Vlaskovits, "Henry Ford, Innovation, and That 'Faster Horse' Quote." *Harvard Business Review*, August 29, 2011, https://hbr.org/2011/08/henry-ford-never-said-the-fast
9. McKinsey & Company, *2024 Finance Redesign Report: Building Unified Data Pipelines for Digital Excellence*. Research Report (New York, NY: McKinsey & Company, 2024).
10. Gartner, Inc., *The CFO Design Framework: Moving from Task Automation to Workflow Flow*. Research Report (Stamford, CT: Gartner, Inc., 2024).
11. Deloitte Development LLC, *2024 Finance Automation Survey: Uncovering the Hidden Backbone of Digital Transformation*. Research Report (New York, NY: Deloitte, 2024).
12. Boston Consulting Group, *CFO Transformation Guide: Strategies for Sustaining Measurable Gains*. Research Report (Boston, MA: Boston Consulting Group, 2024).
13. Gartner, Inc., *2025 Finance AI Adoption Study: The Shift Toward Narrative Automation*. Research Report (Stamford, CT: Gartner, Inc., 2025).
14. Deloitte Development LLC, *2025 Finance Automation Outlook: Precision and Efficiency in Transactional Cycles*. Research Report (New York, NY: Deloitte, 2025).
15. Penn Wharton Budget Model, *The Projected Impact of Generative AI on Future Productivity Growth*. Research Brief (Philadelphia, PA: University of Pennsylvania, September 8, 2025).
16. MIT Sloan Management Review, *Artificial Intelligence and the Limits of Unstructured Data*. Research Report (Cambridge, MA: MIT Press, 2024).
17. Protiviti, Inc., *2025 Global Finance Trends Survey: The CFO's Guide to AI-Ready Governance*. Research Report (Menlo Park, CA: Protiviti, Inc., 2025).
18. The Budget Lab at Yale, *Evaluating the Impact of AI on the Labor Market: Current State of Affairs*. Research Report (New Haven, CT: Yale University, October 2025).
19. Deloitte AI Institute, *The State of Generative AI in Finance: Q4 2024 Pulse Survey*. Research Report (New York, NY: Deloitte, 2024).
20. McKinsey & Company, *The State of AI in 2025: How Organizations are Rewiring to Capture Value*. Global Survey Report (New York, NY: McKinsey & Company, 2025).
21. Deloitte Development LLC, *Finance 2025 Revisited: Digital Transformation and the Human Element*. Research Report (New York, NY: Deloitte, 2025).
22. Boston Consulting Group, *AI–Human Collaboration Playbook: Scaling Intelligence Across the Enterprise*. Research Report (Boston, MA: Boston Consulting Group, 2025).

23. Yale Budget Lab, *Impact of AI on the Labor Market.*
24. PWBM, *Projected Impact of Generative AI.*
25. Bayer and Bento, interview.
26. Deloitte, *Finance 2025.*
27. PWBM, *Projected Impact of Generative AI.*
28. McKinsey & Company, *Beyond the Pilot: Retraining the AI-Ready Finance Workforce.* Research Report (New York, NY: McKinsey & Company, 2025).
29. Public Company Accounting Oversight Board (PCAOB), *Guidance on the Use of Artificial Intelligence and Technology-Assisted Analysis in Audits.* Standard-Setting Update (Washington, DC: PCAOB, 2025).
30. Committee of Sponsoring Organizations of the Treadway Commission (COSO) and Deloitte, *Realize the Full Potential of Artificial Intelligence.* Guidance Report (New York, NY: COSO, 2025).
31. Deloitte Development LLC, *2025 Governance Benchmark: Strengthening AI Assurance and Internal Controls.* Research Report (New York, NY: Deloitte, 2025).
32. COSO and Deloitte, *Full Potential of AI*; PCAOB, *2025 AI Guidance.*
33. McKinsey, *State of AI in 2025*; Gartner, *2025 Finance AI Adoption Study*; PWBM, *Projected Impact of Generative AI.*

Chapter 11

Leading, Organizing, and Upskilling the AI-Ready Finance Team

Key Takeaways

- **Organizational structure determines AI velocity.** Whether you build a center of excellence, embed AI specialists across finance, or blend both approaches, the model you choose should match your leadership style and business context. There's no universal blueprint, but there is a wrong answer: leaving it undefined.
- **Role clarity and workforce readiness can't be afterthoughts.** Scaling AI means evolving existing positions, defining new competencies, and building fluency that spans finance, data, and AI systems. The goal is a team that understands what the tools do and why they matter.

- **Training works when it's sequenced, not dumped.** Upskilling programs that try to cover everything at once tend to cover nothing well. Start with foundational literacy, then layer in hands-on capability-building that shifts the team's mindset from task execution to analysis and control.
- **If you can't communicate AI's value, you haven't created it.** Measurement frameworks and executive reporting aren't just governance checkboxes. They're how you build organizational confidence in AI adoption and maintain the mandate to keep scaling.
- **Leadership style matters less than leadership lens.** The traits that show up consistently in high-impact AI initiatives aren't about a particular management philosophy. They reflect a way of evaluating AI that keeps finance projects anchored to outcomes.

> Getting the data team inside the CFO office... is important because the major focus of the team is not to work on data for data's sake. It's to add value to the company.[1]
>
> —*Marcos Bento, Wasabi*

Evolving the CFO's Organization

By this stage in the book, the reader has learned how to identify AI opportunities, govern them responsibly, and translate early pilots into repeatable workflows. This is the technical essence of the AI-ready CFO. Now, attention needs to turn to leadership and the CFO's ability to build a finance function that can evolve and scale the programs that work, develop new capabilities, and demonstrate the value of these AI investments to executives and the board. This chapter focuses on the structural and cultural adjustments that make an AI-ready finance team most effective. The CFO is the driving force behind designing the AI-driven organization and developing the skills its employees need. Their leadership is needed to measure and contextualize success in financial terms, and then communicate it with clarity and confidence.

Organizational Design Models

An AI-enabled finance function is not going to resemble the one many CFOs entered early in their careers. Transaction volume persists, but much of the manual touch will have disappeared. The center of gravity shifts toward analysis, controls design, compliance assurance, and business partnership. Teams may be smaller in some areas and larger in others; in either case, adaptability becomes a defining characteristic. Finance professionals must combine their domain expertise with fluency in data and automation. Achieving this shift requires organizational intention across structure, roles, skills, and culture.

> It's not the CTO or CIO leading the AI charge. It's really got to be people more in tune with the business itself—especially the CFO.[2]
>
> —*Ranga Bodla, NetSuite*

Organizational design is one of the CFO's most effective tools for ensuring that AI enhances performance without weakening oversight. Although company size, industry, and system complexity will impact final structures, three patterns tend to define how finance teams might address AI and its evolution in the department: the center of excellence, the hub-and-spoke, and the fully embedded squad.

The Center of Excellence. The center of excellence (CoE) focuses AI and automation skills within a single team that sets standards, assesses use cases, and develops reusable components. A CoE might create a standard approach to variance commentary or develop prompt templates that analysts across regions can adopt.

This structure excels at maintaining discipline. Standards are established quickly, evidence packages stay consistent, and institutional knowledge remains—even when employees depart. Organizations under heavy regulatory oversight or with many subsidiaries often favor this uniform approach.

However, centralization also creates distance. A CoE can feel disconnected from everyday tasks, and business units may face delays or receive generic solutions. For example, a CoE in a global consumer products company could show both results: the London-based CoE might enhance controls and boost audit outcomes, while the Asian units experience slow adoption. Centralization must be combined with clear intake procedures, service-level expectations, and intentional outreach across the organization.

The Hub-and-Spoke. The hub-and-spoke model blends standardization with local adaptability. The "hub" consists of a small team of dedicated professionals within the CFO or controller's office that sets governance expectations and maintains policies and templates. "Spokes" are the individual professionals housed within FP&A, controllership, or AP that adapt AI tools to local needs.

The hub maintains consistency while the spokes ensure relevance. This model is especially effective for mid-market companies that have limited central resources but significant operational diversity.

In a small professional services firm, it might look like this: a two-person hub documents evidence standards and naming conventions, while each department designates a spoke representative.

Fully Embedded Squads. In the embedded model, each finance subfunction has its own AI-powered analysts working nearby without a central team. This is often the best choice for smaller companies that can't support a centralized team. A lean manufacturer might train a staff accountant to create invoice-matching automation while giving a forecasting model to an FP&A analyst.

One strength of this approach is responsiveness. But it can also lead to inconsistency. Without shared documentation and regular alignment, each analyst might develop processes differently, making audits more complicated and slowing future scaling. A small startup using this model could face this issue during its first public audit, resulting in inconsistent documentation and months of reconciliation. Embedded models work best when combined with clear documentation expectations and routine cross-team reviews.

Choosing the Right Model. Although each design offers benefits and tradeoffs, the core principle remains the same. A strong organizational structure for finance is essential. It drives innovation, prevents fragmentation, and assures executives, auditors, and regulators that finance has maintained control over its processes. Ultimately, the CFO's leadership style will shape the decision. Which model best suits the leader you are?

Roles, Competencies, and the AI-Ready Workforce

As organizational models evolve, role clarity becomes a crucial tool for turning structure into action. Employees need to understand how AI impacts their responsibilities, which decisions they still own, and how their efforts fit into the larger control framework. Clear roles also communicate to auditors, investors, and regulators that finance remains responsible for the processes AI now supports. On the other hand, ambiguity creates gaps where control weakens, accountability becomes unclear, and progress slows.

Therefore, avoid introducing exotic titles that could complicate HR structures or cause unnecessary questions during audits. Titles like "Finance Data Scientist" or "Machine Learning Architect" may sound innovative, but they don't clearly communicate what someone is responsible for. Extending current roles is more effective. For example, a staff accountant who documents AI controls is easily understood by auditors; a "neural network specialist" doing the same is not. The goal should be to enhance familiar roles with new responsibilities, not to reinvent the organizational chart.

A key trait of an AI-ready finance team is a broad, shared understanding of systems, finance, and data. Every employee should understand how AI impacts their work, what the system does, when judgment is necessary, and how to raise concerns. When this kind of understanding is shared throughout the staff, from junior analysts to senior directors, AI can be used confidently and responsibly.

There are four clusters of competencies that define fluency:

1. **Finance fundamentals.** AI can detect anomalies or spot trends, but it can't set policies or interpret business logic. Judgment becomes even more crucial as automation handles routine tasks.
2. **Data and tooling literacy.** All employees should have a fundamental understanding of data flows, ERP systems, and reporting tools. Some will develop more technical skills, like basic SQL or

automation setup, but every employee needs to be able to validate data and understand its role in AI outputs.

3. **Model literacy.** Teams don't need to build models, but they have to understand what models do, how assumptions impact results, and why backtesting and monitoring are essential. They should be able to explain model behavior clearly to auditors and executives.
4. **Risk and governance.** Financial reporting standards must still be met, even with AI-driven workflows. Employees record system outputs, log overrides, and retain evidence trails that can withstand audit scrutiny.

Communication influences all four areas. All finance professionals should be able to convey technical results in a way that executives trust. Competence without communication goes unnoticed; communication without competence is unreliable. Together, they build credibility.

An AI-ready finance function emerges when a CFO can confidently answer three questions for any employee:

1. Do they understand how AI affects their work?
2. Can they use it responsibly?
3. Can they explain it to others?

When the team answers yes to all, competency becomes a shared operational asset. Equipping your team with the essential skills and training is a necessary step in the process of becoming AI-ready.

Training, Upskilling, and Culture

Training and upskilling can't be treated as occasional initiatives anymore. For the AI-ready CFO, capability-building needs to be part of regular operations. Skills have to keep pace as processes evolve and tools advance, and this applies across the entire function, not just technical roles.

I noted in my previous book, *Deep Finance*, that training should never be treated as a perk. It's a strategic investment that starts with fundamentals.[3] Employees need solid fluency in their current systems: the ERP, general ledger, reporting tools. That foundation makes analytics, scenario modeling, and GenAI achievable rather than overwhelming.

Clear role definitions help people understand what they need to learn. When employees see how AI connects to their actual responsibilities, they know which skills matter and why. Managers can guide development more deliberately, instead of leaving it to chance.

Development doesn't follow a fixed timeline, but most employees move through similar stages. They build core knowledge, take ownership of AI-enabled workflows, and eventually contribute back by teaching colleagues or creating reusable templates. The sequence varies, but the pattern holds.

Many CFOs structure this journey in three phases: 90 days, six months, and one year.

The first 90 days focus on baseline fluency. Staff revisit ERP mechanics, general ledger fundamentals, and reporting tools. They see practical AI applications in daily work: invoice matching that catches duplicates, anomaly detection that surfaces exceptions, prompts that generate draft commentary. These early experiences build confidence and reduce uncertainty.

At six months, employees should own small AI-enabled workflows end-to-end. An AP clerk monitors vendor anomalies and prepares monthly summaries. A staff accountant documents the rationale for AI-executed standard overrides in ways auditors can trace. The focus shifts from exposure to accountability. AI becomes part of work that others depend on.

By the one-year mark, employees contribute to shared practices. The AP clerk who understands anomaly detection teaches peers how to interpret the signals. The staff accountant who built reconciliation documentation publishes templates others can use. Individual skills become institutional knowledge.

Department culture determines whether any of this takes hold. Employees watch leadership for signals about what AI means for their roles. Messaging that emphasizes role elevation and capacity redeployment toward analysis builds confidence. Messaging that emphasizes automation without context creates anxiety. The CFO has to reinforce the right narrative through visible engagement, recognition of new skills, and consistent communication across managers.

Informal signals matter just as much as formal ones. How teams talk about AI when leadership isn't present reveals whether the culture will support or resist adoption. Managers who notice these subtle cues can work with senior leaders to adjust messaging and address concerns early.

The larger goal is professional identity transformation. Finance professionals who view themselves primarily as processors need to see themselves as analysts, advisors, and control experts. That shift develops through repeated experiences and sustained leadership support.

> [In the future] our profession is going to look like a pentagon shape—a fat middle and a smaller base… and the skill set will be a T-shaped professional with "boundary crossing skills" on top of deep accounting knowledge.[4]
>
> —*Tom Hood, AICPA/CIMA*

Success and Communication

You can't scale AI without first defining success. The AI-ready CFO needs a structured measurement framework that converts pilot wins into broader organizational buy-in. AI in finance works when you can measure its impact, validate the results, and explain them in financial terms that hold up under scrutiny from executives, auditors, and the board.

Defining Success in Finance Terms

With all the questions an organization faces when deploying AI, one stands out: What does success actually look like? Many implementations fail because nobody ever answers this clearly.

Consider a common scenario. A vendor demo promises workflow time savings. You deploy the solution and employees report that the workflow "feels easier." Will those subjective impressions hold up during an audit committee review? Will they justify investment in a broader rollout? Almost certainly not.

The tendency to rely on vague productivity phrases like "the model improves decision-making" or "the tool saves time" is understandable. It's also insufficient. You wouldn't accept a forecast from your analyst labeled "about right." AI should face the same standard.

Success needs to be defined using metrics finance already relies on. If the current close cycle runs six days, success might mean getting it down to four. If three-month revenue forecasts hit within 10% accuracy, success could mean narrowing that band to 5%. If analysts spend 20 hours weekly on reconciliations, success isn't just the hours saved but the hours redeployed to variance analysis, cash forecasting, or board reporting.

Take an AI-enabled fraud-detection system. You should evaluate it based on measurable reductions in investigation hours and testable precision/recall rates from historical data. Linking AI outcomes to familiar KPIs makes adoption more credible to executives and clearer for the team implementing it.

An AI-ready CFO should also distinguish between AI-driven productivity and genuine value creation. A team that saves 100 hours a week on manual reconciliation does little if that time isn't redirected toward higher-value work. The key question is: How were the additional productivity gains reinvested? The strategic benefit of AI-led productivity improvements is most evident when it results in more tangible outcomes like faster cash flow, wider margins, or additional decision support.

> If I'm spending less of my time doing all the number crunching... then I can focus more of my energy on: What story do I actually want to tell?[5]
>
> —*Ranga Bodla, Oracle NetSuite*

The definition of success must also include accuracy, compliance, and auditability. A new AI-led reconciliation process that reduces cycle time but increases the number of unreconciled items does not qualify as a success. The metrics used to evaluate success should accurately reflect the full scope of finance's responsibilities.

Measurement Discipline: Accuracy, Risk, and Evidence. With success defined by a range of quantitative and qualitative criteria, the CFO needs measurement systems that rigorously evaluate results. In the last chapter, we discussed creating a dashboard to monitor AI project performance. Measurement systems ensure the benefits are genuine, consistent, and transferable.

Forecast Accuracy and Error Metrics. Forecast accuracy is a good place to start. Finance teams often rely on percentage error, but there are several ways to calculate it, and the choice matters. Mean absolute percentage error (MAPE) is the most common, but it can overstate errors when volumes are small. Weighted absolute percentage error (WAPE) gives more importance to high-volume items and is often more meaningful for revenue or cost-of-sales forecasts. Symmetric MAPE (sMAPE) adjusts the calculation so that over- and under-forecasting are treated equally. The key step is choosing one method and applying it consistently across cycles. When the board asks whether accuracy is improving, the answer should come from a standardized metric, not one that is adjusted to make results seem favorable.

Detection Metrics: Precision and Recall. Detection metrics require consistent discipline. In fraud monitoring, compliance testing, or anomaly detection, precision and recall are the two key measures. Precision indicates how many flagged items are truly problematic, while recall indicates how many issues are identified. A system might perform well on precision if it flags only obvious cases, but if it has poor recall, it will miss many real, but less severe, problems. Conversely, a system might appear strong if it flags everything unusual but then suffers from too many false alarms. Achieving balance involves considering both metrics. Finance leaders should insist on viewing the full confusion matrix, including true positives, false positives, true negatives, and false negatives, along with the cost implications of each. This approach helps avoid the common pitfall of celebrating fewer false alarms while overlooking more genuine risks.

Cycle-Time Integrity. AI-enabled tools may reduce cycle time, but success metrics must encompass the entire process, not only the segment touched by automation. Trimming a window to exclude upstream or downstream steps distorts results. The metrics need to reflect complete workflow performance.

Minimum Detectable Effect and Kill Criteria. Minimum detectable effect thresholds prevent over-interpreting small changes. For instance, if forecast accuracy usually varies by five percentage points from quarter to quarter, claiming success on a three-point change is premature. Confidence bands can illustrate the range of expected performance, making it easier to identify real improvement against normal variation. Over multiple cycles, these concepts should be explained in simple language, showing to executives that project results are not only positive but also statistically credible.

In line with this minimal effect, projects should also have clear kill criteria. These are the specific conditions under which a pilot should be halted or re-evaluated. Kill criteria prevent projects from continuing indefinitely without any clear benefit. Multiple cycles below the minimum detectable effect could serve as a metric for deciding to end the initiative.

Documentation as Assurance. Every metric used to measure success in an AI implementation needs a short definition sheet: formula, data source, owner, and calculation frequency. Don't see this requirement as bureaucracy. It's the only way to ensure results are consistent and reliable across cycles and teams.

Vendor Accountability and SLAs. Many finance teams rely on external vendors for forecasting, anomaly detection, or AP automation, and many of these vendors are now using AI. Outsourcing technology does not outsource accountability. Vendors must meet the same measurement standards as internal teams.

Contracts should specify the exact metrics, such as WAPE, precision, cycle time, and error rates, and their target ranges, that will be used to measure vendor performance. The SLAs that dictate reporting, drift monitoring, retraining windows, and log access must permit review. Transparency is crucial; without evidence, auditors will not accept outputs. CFOs also need clear exit rights and data-portability provisions to ensure that poor performance results in consequences.

Well-designed SLAs do more than prevent failure. They strengthen the partnership. Vendors that align with clear standards better meet the finance department's goals and become more dependable contributors to enterprise value.

Executive and Board Communication

Even if progress is evident and well-measured, it must be communicated in a way that resonates with other C-suite executives and the board.

Consistent communication is the first requirement. AI performance should be reported in the same rhythm and format as other finance metrics, for example, as a monthly dashboard embedded in close packages or management reports. This signals that AI is part of core operations, not a side experiment.

Numbers alone won't carry the message. A two-day reduction in the close cycle becomes meaningful when it enables earlier discussions on capital allocation. A fraud-detection model with stronger recall becomes compelling when it ties to avoided losses and preserved reputation. A clear narrative moves the conversation from features to financial outcomes.

Transparency is what sustains credibility. Boards respond well when CFOs explain the wins and the boundaries, including where models perform reliably and where they don't. That level of candor builds trust and supports continued investment.

Governance alignment needs to be explicit. When AI outputs tie into ICFR or SOX controls, audit committees get comfort that automation hasn't introduced hidden risk. CFOs should use plain language to describe how the workflow retains evidence, routes exceptions for review, and produces logs that auditors can test.

Finally, communication drives momentum. A clear, consistent reporting format builds confidence and makes it easier to secure future investments. Over time, the board will transition from viewing AI as merely an experiment to recognizing it as a fundamental capability of the finance function. The CFO's leadership is instrumental in making this happen.

Keys to AI Leadership Success

Across industries, AI adoption in finance and accounting will take many forms. As you have seen throughout this book, corporate culture, resources, legacy systems, and risk posture all shape the path your organization takes. There are, however, unmistakable patterns in the success of introducing and deploying AI at scale. These characteristics will show up in leadership. There isn't a specific style or strategy, but rather a clarity about what AI needs to succeed.

The following are shared traits and actions displayed by leaders who have been able to translate their AI ambitions into results:

- **Treat data as infrastructure, not input.** AI reflects reality when the data is structurally clean, accessible, and organized. Truth precedes intelligence.
- **Use pilots to explore and expose.** Early experiments are used to find opportunities and expose what scaling will demand.
- **Build for integration from day one.** Don't isolate AI as a side tool. From the beginning, plan how the model will connect to, influence, and be influenced by other systems.
- **Sequence with discipline.** Resist the allure of the "big bang." Progress is structured, cumulative, and paced. Wins are stacked, not scattered.
- **Foster a culture of ownership.** Accountability is active. Assign ownership before use cases go live.
- **Proactively cultivate trust.** Build trust through transparency, testing, and clarity about what the AI system can and cannot do.
- **Invest in hybrid fluency.** For finance and AI to work together, it requires people who think in both domains and can communicate across them.
- **Redesign work, not just workflows.** When an AI initiative saves time, reallocate it. When roles change, realign them. Evolve the work as the organization evolves.
- **Prioritize value over pure innovation.** Fund that which solves problems, not what draws attention. Impact is the metric.
- **Governance is infrastructure.** Governance isn't an add-on. It's the foundation that accelerates adoption and makes scale sustainable. It comes first, not after a failure.

Anticipating What Comes: The Next Chapter

Even as the now AI-capable CFO works to integrate AI into their current operations, they must also prepare for what's coming next. Technology, regulations, and stakeholder expectations will continue to develop. Finance leaders who see achieving maturity as a fixed goal risk falling behind just as their teams start to feel confident.

We'll explore the future of AI in finance thoroughly in the final chapter. For now, let's set the stage.

Finance will see more automation ahead, but that future only works if it's built on solid guardrails and oversight. Every AI-enabled workflow needs to answer three questions: Can auditors follow the process documentation? Do employees have clear authority to override decisions and record their reasoning? Is the system monitored for accuracy, security, and drift? All three need to be yes for AI adoption to scale with confidence. Otherwise, the CFO is just adding risk.

Several trends deserve attention. Finance-focused foundation models are emerging. These are large-scale enterprise LLMs trained specifically on financial data, designed to understand accounting structures, forecasting methods, and regulatory requirements. They offer faster adoption because their core design already aligns with finance department needs rather than requiring extensive customization. Expect the market to shift from generic platforms toward specialized solutions with better integration and tighter controls.

Integration with other technologies will shape what comes next. Blockchain and distributed ledgers can create immutable records that support AI-driven audit trails. IoT data from supply chains or energy usage can feed directly into forecasting models. Continuous auditing, long discussed as an aspiration, becomes feasible when AI and real-time data streams converge. Finance leaders need to think about how these technologies connect in actual treasury, FP&A, and reporting workflows.

Notes

1. Bayer and Bento, interview, December 17, 2025.
2. Bodla, interview, December 16, 2025.
3. Glenn Hopper, *Deep Finance: Corporate Finance in the Information Age* (Dubai: Leaders Press, 2021), 176.
4. Hood, interview, December 17, 2025.
5. Bodla, interview.

Chapter 12

Conclusion: The Future of Finance and the Impact of AI

Key Takeaways

This final chapter steps back from implementation details and looks at the trajectory of AI in finance. The takeaways below pull together themes from across the book.

- **The technology is already good enough.** Even if AI models stopped improving tomorrow, the current generation of tools can automate reporting narratives, flag exceptions, reconcile data across systems, and compress cycle times. The bottleneck has shifted from capability to adoption. CFOs who wait for the "perfect" tool will find themselves playing catch-up against competitors who started with what's available today.

- **Governance is the multiplier.** Every chapter in this book returns to the same theme: AI without controls creates risk; AI with governance creates leverage. The CFOs who succeed with AI will be the ones who built auditability, logging, and human oversight into the process from the start. Governance doesn't slow things down. It's what makes scaling possible.
- **The CFO's role is evolving from scorekeeper to architect.** AI is shifting finance from backward-looking reporting to forward-looking decision support. That transition requires new skills, new workflows, and a willingness to rethink how the finance function operates. The AI-ready CFO doesn't just approve budgets for AI projects. They set the pace of adoption, define what "good" looks like, and hold the organization accountable for turning investment into measurable outcomes.
- **AI doesn't need a breakthrough to change finance. It needs adoption.** The tools available today can already compress close timelines, surface exceptions earlier, and turn variance analysis from an after-action report into an early-warning system. The limiting factor has never been the technology. It's readiness: clean data, clear ownership, and the discipline to embed AI into real workflows instead of treating it as a side project.
- **Good finance fundamentals are AI fundamentals.** Data governance, process documentation, clear definitions, and auditability make everything work better, with or without AI. Organizations that skip this foundation in a rush to deploy will spend more time fixing outputs than using them. The checklist is simple. Executing it takes commitment.
- **The compounding advantage belongs to the teams that start now.** Every small win—a workflow that saves an hour, a process that eliminates a bottleneck, a report that writes its own first draft—becomes a template for the next improvement. Finance teams that build this muscle early will operate at a fundamentally different speed than those still debating whether to begin.

Finance Was Always Supposed to Work Like This

Making precise predictions about the future is difficult. That's why it's tough to be a futurist. Ask any options trader.

Getting predictions directionally correct, however, isn't hard. You don't need tea leaves. Just try to understand what is delivering your best returns.

AI is firmly in that category. Even if today's AI models never get any "smarter" than they are now, we would still see meaningful change in how finance work gets done. Most of the value doesn't come from a single breakthrough. It comes from boring, relentless improvement in the stuff that makes technology useful inside a real company: context, integration, guardrails, and adoption.

The Tech Will Keep Getting More Useful, Even Without a Miracle

When people picture AI advancements, I think they often imagine a trend line that goes straight up. In reality, it will be more like product gravity. More AI and AI-adjacent tech gets pulled into the systems we already use. We continue to use and incorporate it into our work, until it's hard to remember what work looked like without them.

Two improvements consistently drive real value, regardless of the headline model: the ability to work with more context and the ability to operate inside existing platforms.

More context is the difference between "help me write this memo" and "help me understand what changed in the business." It means reading the whole close package, not just a page. It includes referencing prior periods, customer notes, contract terms, and policy language without forcing a human to assemble the entire puzzle first. Finance runs on context. Without it, you get answers that sound right but can't be used.

Integration into existing systems and workflows makes AI operational. A chatbot that can draft a variance narrative is helpful, but a system that pulls the right reports, reconciles the numbers, flags key exceptions, and attaches evidence in a way that survives audit is how you run a close. When AI becomes part of your workflow, your close checklist, your ticketing, and your document repository, it's infrastructure.

Reliability is equally as important. Finance teams need consistency, control, and traceability. The tools surrounding AI will make it easier to constrain outputs, log actions, preserve lineage, and keep people accountable for what gets approved.

This is how AI becomes a normal part of the finance stack.

AI Technology Winters Happened: That Doesn't Mean AI Is Going Away

It's reasonable to be skeptical. We've seen technology hype cycles before. Big promises and funding, followed by disappointment and pullback. Then the field regroups and comes back under a different label.

The important point to note is that AI has been quietly doing real work for a long time. Long before GenAI and chatbots, we were using ML-based AI models that rank, score, and predict. Think credit risk scores, fraud detection, demand forecasts, and alerts for unusual journal entries. In the early days, it sounded like science fiction because the "algorithm" was invisible: a computer-coded model turning data into a number you trusted enough to act on. Today, these tools are commonplace and used extensively across every industry. Many of those systems were imperfect at the start, but they produced enough value that the underlying direction never reversed.

That's why this moment, with the advancement of AI tech, feels different. Leaders have already seen what it looks like when software can draft, summarize, detect patterns, and answer questions against messy, disparate information. Once an organization has tasted that kind of leverage, that kind of productivity accelerator, it doesn't willingly go back to doing everything by hand.

We've Been Talking About Digital Transformation for 30 Years: Have We Actually Transformed?

If you put modern tools into a legacy decision-making culture, do you get transformation, or do you just get a more expensive version of the same habits?

A lot of companies modernized systems without modernizing their decisions. They implemented ERPs and still ran the business on emailed spreadsheets. They built dashboards and still argued from anecdotes in the meeting. They invested in "single sources of truth" and still spent half the month debating definitions.

This is where finance earns its keep. The job isn't just to report the numbers. It's to make those numbers usable in decision-making.

The best CFOs and controllers have instincts for what looks off, what doesn't reconcile, and what smells like a one-time story pretending to be a trend. That judgment is real. And judgment gets stronger when it's paired with evidence. Data lets you move from hunch to hypothesis.

It lets you say, "I think we're seeing margin erosion," and then test where it's coming from: mix shift, pricing leakage, freight, rework, labor efficiency, vendor terms. Data turns an intuition into a structured investigation. It's the discipline of asking: What would I need to see to change my mind?

New thinking, eventually reflected in new tools, is what transformation looks like in practice.

From Data to Understanding: What Finance Teams Are Really Paid to Do

There's a brilliant quote distilled from the writings of American scientist Clifford Stoll that perfectly describes the evolution of data to understanding: "Data is not information. Information is not knowledge. Knowledge is not understanding. Understanding is not wisdom."[1]

I think of this quote every time I consider what CFOs do as stewards of finance and users of company data. Most businesses are swimming in data. Many can produce information. Far fewer turn that information into knowledge that holds up under scrutiny. The difference between a finance team that's busy and a finance team that's valuable is whether it can reliably turn raw business exhaust into decision-quality understanding.

Data is the transaction trail. Information is the reconciled reporting layer. Knowledge is knowing what changed and why. And understanding is knowing what to do about it, with the constraints and second-order effects in view. Wisdom, then, is the ultimate layer: it's the foresight to consistently apply that understanding, make ethical decisions, and set the long-term strategy of the business, using all available context and judgment to navigate uncertainty.

AI helps at every step, but it doesn't eliminate the steps. When the cost of producing words and charts drops, discernment becomes more valuable, and human understanding and experiences shine.

What This Means for the Office of the CFO

Every major technology shift changes work in two ways: it changes what's possible, but it also changes what's expected.

The Industrial Revolution didn't just introduce new machines. It reorganized work, redefined roles in the workforce, and changed what "competence" looked like. The finance parallel is straightforward. As more of the repetitive and mechanical work of finance becomes automated, the need for finance and accounting professionals doesn't disappear. It evolves. And transforms into something more valuable and better.

Think about the activities that finance professionals spend time on today: chasing down missing information, reconciling systems that should already agree, reformatting reports for different audiences, explaining the same variance three different ways because three different people asked, hunting through email threads to find the last time someone explained a particular accounting treatment, and manually testing whether a forecast assumption still holds.

Most finance and accounting employees didn't get into the business for this kind of work. Instead, it has been the tax they pay for operating in an environment where information moves slowly and context gets lost.

AI collapses that tax. When the opportunity cost of search, retrieval, synthesis, and reformatting drops to near zero, finance professionals get their time back to do what actually matters: understanding the business, challenging assumptions, designing better processes, identifying risks before they become problems, and helping leadership make decisions with incomplete information.

It's already running in thousands of AI-enabled organizations. Teams who have automated their variance commentary are using the time to build better forecasts. Teams who've automated invoice coding are using the time to analyze payment terms and vendor concentration. And teams that already automated data collection are using the time to investigate anomalies that would have previously gone unnoticed.

When you remove friction from the mechanical work, you create capacity for the work that requires judgment.

AGI Timelines Are a Distraction for Finance Leaders

I don't know how many years or decades it might take to reach something like artificial general intelligence (AGI). I'm not sure anyone does.

But CFOs don't need AGI to feel the impact on their business. It's already here: the marginal cost of drafting, summarizing, and analyzing is dropping. The speed of iteration is increasing. The accessibility of institutional knowledge is improving. And the set of workflows that can be partially or wholly automated is expanding every quarter.

This is enough to change how finance operates—and the organizations that move first get a compounding advantage.

Every department feels the same pressure. Sales and marketing see it in outbound messaging and pipeline analysis. HR sees it in recruiting workflows and policy management. Operations sees it in planning and issue detection. Nobody gets to opt out, because the competitive environment won't allow it.

The office of the CFO is simply where these pressures become measurable.

How Finance Teams Are Using AI Today, and How That Evolves

Most finance teams have started with AI as a "new way to Google" (i.e., a better search interface). They use an available model connected to the company's files to search how a particular revenue recognition policy applies to a new contract type, or what happened during last quarter's close when inventory didn't reconcile, or which vendor contracts are up for renewal. The information exists somewhere in a policy document, a close checklist, an email thread, or a contract repository. AI makes it findable without forcing someone to remember where it lives or who to ask.

This sounds mundane. It is mundane. It can also be one of the highest-leverage applications for any organization because it reduces friction and rework.

But the next wave in use cases is now showing up in transactional processes: AP systems that suggest GL codes based on vendor history and invoice descriptions, month-end checklists that flag exceptions automatically, and data quality issues getting routed to the right person before they compound. These are small improvements individually, but they reduce downstream noise in ways that compound across hundreds of transactions.

AI is also being applied in management reporting. Finance teams know what good variance narratives look like. GenAI accelerates the first pass, standardizes tone, and makes it easier to generate variants for different audiences. The humans in the finance department still own accuracy and judgment, but the basic mechanics of drafting the report happen faster thanks to AI.

Over the next few years, the change will be less about new AI features and more about AI becoming increasingly embedded into finance systems as standard plumbing. That's great. It means we don't have to worry about the "how," as software companies will have solved that for us. It just means we see the benefits already baked into the software we use daily. Month-end becomes less of a cliff because more reconciliation and validation happens continuously. Variance analysis becomes less of an after-action report and more of an early-warning system. Forecasting becomes more dynamic because the cost of re-forecasting drops. And the narrative gets better because it can be grounded in more context, with evidence attached.

But the real and most valuable shift happens when finance stops thinking about individual tasks and starts thinking about end-to-end workflows.

Imagine a close process where the system continuously monitors for exceptions, automatically drafts variance explanations with supporting evidence, and surfaces only the items that need human judgment. Imagine FP&A where you can ask your data directly, "why did our gross margin change in the Southwest region last quarter?" and get an answer that traces back through product mix, pricing actions, cost changes, and customer behavior with the underlying data available for inspection. Imagine a treasury where cash forecasting updates in real time as invoices are issued and payments clear, with scenario analysis available on demand.

The building blocks for this future exist today. The capability isn't missing, just our readiness.

Further out, the most interesting shift is from analytics to decision support. Finance has long described a maturity curve that starts with describing what happened, then diagnosing why it happened, then predicting what will happen, and finally prescribing what to do about it. In practice, most organizations stall somewhere between diagnosing and predicting because the work is hard and the data is messy.

Thankfully AI lowers the cost of moving between those layers. It makes it feasible to test more scenarios, model more options, and explore more what-if questions. A finance team that can run 50 forecast scenarios in the time it used to take to run three can better understand the range of possible outcomes. A team that can quickly model the cash impact of different payment terms can negotiate better. A team that can trace margin changes down to individual customers and products can make better pricing decisions.

The limiting factor is whether the inputs are trusted, the logic traceable, and the results usable. That's a finance problem, which means it's also a finance opportunity.

The Point of Becoming AI-Ready

This book has shown in some detail the steps you need to take to prepare for this future. Becoming AI-ready is about improving the way finance work gets done right now.

Good data governance makes everything better—with or without AI. Clear definitions reduce meeting time. Clean processes reduce close pain. Better documentation reduces key-person and audit risk. A disciplined operating model makes automation easier and safer.

This simple, but challenging, checklist is the foundation for everything that comes next.

At the same time, it's important not to lean so hard into AI that you outsource your judgment. This technology is powerful, but like all technology it is a tool that touches and impacts the financial truth. It needs controls, review, and a clear line of responsibility.

As of 2026, we are still in the "trust but verify" phase of GenAI usage. Just like when working with a new analyst or engineer, we respect their knowledge and abilities but still need to ensure it has been applied appropriately to the task at hand.

There is simplicity to the right mindset as well. Routinely ask, "How can I do this with AI?" Not as a gimmick, and not as a mandate, but as a habit. Sometimes, the answer may be "you shouldn't." Sometimes, "use it for the first pass." And sometimes, the answer will be "you can build a workflow that saves the team 10 hours a month and makes the output more consistent." Or something similarly impactful.

Leaders and teams who ask this question consistently will find dozens of opportunities, and each small win compounds across the organization. A workflow that saves an hour can evolve into a workflow that saves a day. A process that eliminates one bottleneck reveals the next one. An improvement that helps one person becomes a template for the whole team.

Automation and efficiency are a big part of the potential, and AI also opens doors to work we rarely tried before because to do so was too expensive or too slow. If you can pull signals across finance and operational data in minutes instead of days, you can ask better questions. You can detect drift earlier. You can test more hypotheses and spend more time on what finance is supposed to do: help the business understand itself well enough to make better decisions.

This future is actually within our grasp. Finance gets faster, more accurate, and more strategic. The team stops spending most of its time assembling information and starts interpreting it. Financial insights show up when they matter, now, not weeks after the fact.

That future doesn't require more new breakthroughs, though those will come too. It requires discipline, investment, and a willingness to change.

The technology is ready. The question today is: Are you ready?

Well, that is the future of finance… at least directionally. It's a reinforcement of the CFO's real job. For the teams that get there first, it will be a sustainable competitive advantage that compounds every quarter.

But remember, I'm not a futurist. Just a tech-savvy CFO who has seen what is happening with AI in companies big and small, and I'm wildly confident it will continue.

Note

1. Clifford Stoll, *High-tech Heretic: Why Computers Don't Belong in the Classroom and Other Reflections by a Computer Contrarian* (New York, NY: Doubleday, 1999).

Index

Note: Page numbers in *italics* and **bold** refers to figures and tables respectively.

B